KEEPIN' IT REAL

TRANSGRESSING
BOUNDARIES
Studies in Black Politics and Black Communities
Cathy Cohen and Fredrick Harris, Series Editors

The Politics of Public Housing:
Black Women's Struggles Against Urban Inequality
Rhonda Y. Williams

Keepin' It Real
School Success Beyond Black and White
Prudence L. Carter

PRUDENCE L. CARTER

KEEPIN' IT REAL

SCHOOL SUCCESS BEYOND BLACK AND WHITE

OXFORD

UNIVERSITY PRESS

2005

OXFORD
UNIVERSITY PRESS

Oxford University Press, Inc., publishes works that further
Oxford University's objective of excellence
in research, scholarship, and education.

Oxford   New York
Auckland   Cape Town   Dar es Salaam   Hong Kong   Karachi
Kuala Lumpur   Madrid   Melbourne   Mexico City   Nairobi
New Delhi   Shanghai   Taipei   Toronto

With offices in
Argentina   Austria   Brazil   Chile   Czech Republic   France   Greece
Guatemala   Hungary   Italy   Japan   Poland   Portugal   Singapore
South Korea   Switzerland   Thailand   Turkey   Ukraine   Vietnam

Published by Oxford University Press, Inc.
198 Madison Avenue, New York, New York 10016

www.oup.com

Oxford is a registered trademark of Oxford University Press.

Library of Congress Cataloging-in-Publication Data
Carter, Prudence L.
Keepin' it real: school success beyond black and white/by Prudence L. Carter.
p. cm.—(Transgressing boundaries)
ISBN-13 978-0-19-532523-2

1. Multicultural education—United States. 2. African American students—Ethnic
identity. 3. Hispanic American students—Ethnic identity. 4. Academic achievement—
Social aspects—United States. I. Title. II. Series.
LC1099.3.C374   2005
371.829—dc22   2004027134

Printed in the United States of America
on acid-free paper

PREFACE

It has become fashionable these days to assert that many African American and second-generation Latino students reject academic excellence because they perceive it as "acting white." The expression is an old one, originating in an era of American history when former slaves and some freed Blacks used "acting white" to characterize those group members who either resisted affiliation with the slave experience or passed as White in exchange for high status and success (Fordham 1996). The idea's currency increased in the mid-1900s as the Black middle class grew and as poor Blacks viewed the middle class and wealthy as "sell-outs" (Frazier 1957). In this contemporary era, the "acting white" moniker still has not lost its resonance. As the argument goes, Black and Latino youth have chosen to define their identities in opposition to whiteness by refusing to speak standard English, do their schoolwork, earn high marks, or fully engage in school because they do not want to be seen as embracing behaviors that they label as "acting white" (Fordham and Ogbu 1986; Lewin 2000; McWhorter 2001; Gates 2004).[1]

And yet, over the years as I have presented talks in numerous forums on the topics about which I write in this book, I always encounter audience members who say, "I wish they would just get it! We don't disown or devalue education. It has never been a white thing for us!" And indeed, historically, Blacks and Latinos have pursued hard-fought legal challenges for quality education and equity in school resources, from the Supreme Court battles of *Brown v. Board of Education* in 1954 to dismantle segregated schooling to *Castañeda v. Pickard* in 1981, a case brought to court by Mexican American families to ensure adequate bilingual education, access to quality school programs, and equal participation for their language-minority children. These efforts indicate that education and socio-economic mobility are valued as precious resources and goals in such communities.

How can we believe that the youths of the post–civil rights, hip-hop generation, however, actually hold the same values for education that their parents and foreparents espoused? How can we comprehend that they do not intentionally collude in academic failure? As I will argue, though Black and Latino youths may describe certain practices as "acting white," or in contrast as "acting black" or "acting Spanish," they employ these expressions primarily for cultural reasons, not academic ones. They use their racial and ethnic identities to facilitate in-group solidarity and to assert various cultural symbols of pride and self-worth, not as signs of opposition to conventional formulas for success. However, once these students are enrolled in schools—those cultural places that transmit evaluative messages about whose ways of life are noteworthy and whose are not—and once they exhibit low academic performances, their practices and proclamations get translated by many educators as a rejection of excellence.

This book gets at the crux of a social tension between students' educational and career aspirations and their confrontations with a hierarchy of cultural meanings within schools. Black and Latino students face this hierarchy of meanings as a contestable source of social control, and publicly and privately, they critique how the middle-class and Whites dominate school organizations and the labor market, two spheres integral to their economic attainment and productivity in U.S. society.

Moreover, this book examines how these minority students deploy culture to gain status, a complex story that is better understood as a continuum of cultural attachments rather than a reflection of their educational values. For many African Americans and Latino youths, their ethnoracial cultures are important sources of strength and are not merely reactive or adaptive by-products of their positions in a stratified opportunity structure. Their cultures provide them with senses of belonging, connection, kinship, and with mechanisms for dealing with experiences in a society where resources and opportunities are not entirely accessible and open. Many appreciate who they are as cultural beings, their differences in speech, interactions, and social tastes; and they intentionally seek distinction, not sameness, to maintain active sociocultural boundaries.

The current mainstream perspective about Black and Latino students' resistance to "acting white" in education backs itself into a conceptual wall through oversimplification. It depicts ethno-racial cultures as primarily responses to exclusion, discrimination, and historical interracial tensions. One consequence of such a perspective, however, is to disregard the substantive contributions of ethno-racial cultures and also to ignore how heterogeneous the members in these ethno-racial groups are. That is, racial and ethnic group members hold multiple intersecting identities shaped by varied forms of socialization and experience, from different class and gender identities to different ideological perspectives on how in-group members should behave and interact with out-group members. Some seek achievement from both a personal and collective perspective, while others individuate and seek primarily personal achievement. Some desire socioeconomic mobility in a nonassimilative way and others adhere to mainstream cultural paths.

The scope of this book is limited, however, and does not focus on all of the multiple identities that members of the same racial or ethnic groups hold. Rather, I focus only on the experiences of groups of *low-income* African American and Latino male and female youths living in particular families and attending specific schools in Yonkers, New York. And these youths are discussed in the contexts of their different racial and ethnic, cultural, and gender identities.

The following pages are filled with stories of students who all profess a strong belief in education but who negotiate both schooling and their communities differently. This book discusses how three groups of students from similar class backgrounds, and in some cases similar ethno-racial backgrounds, all aspire to the American dream of middle classness, to the benefits that an education brings, including jobs that pay high salaries, home and car ownership, and intact families. For some, though, a disjuncture between their aspirations and their performances exist. Some of this split is linked to these youths' limited access to and familiarity with dominant resources and cultural know-how. Other parts of the disjuncture are associated with students' contestation of the schools' cultural environment, especially when they perceive that educators ignore the values of their own cultures.

The gatekeepers of schools and different economic organizations maintain cultural expectations that do not necessarily mesh well with African American and Latino youths' cultural practices. And I argue that both school officials' and minority students' failure to reconcile their differences—dominant cultural expectations for achievement with nondominant students' cultural styles, tastes, and displeasure in what school curricula provide them—facilitates, in part, the students' limited attachment to school and their academic disengagement. In this "No Child Left Behind" and school accountability era, these cultural conflicts and differences can undermine educators' effectiveness and production of high results. By paying careful attention to the effects and dynamics of culture at the institutional, group, and individual levels and by enlisting the aid of those whom I call "multicultural navigators" (sources of what social scientists dub as social capital), principals, teachers, parents, and students could find better ways to communicate, interact, and improve students' attachment and engagement to school.

The study on which I base these arguments began in the summer of 1994 while I was working with a research team to survey low-income mothers and their children about their perceptions of communities, economic opportunities, interracial relations, and various aspects of their lives in several Yonkers, New York, neighborhoods. After a brief period of limited contact between 1996 and 1997, I reconnected with many of the families to conduct my own follow-up study with the youth in these families. As a graduate student, I was on the cusp of that age between the mothers' generation and that of their adolescent children, but I came to know the youths better than I came to know their mothers (fathers were rarely present in the households). Though I moved back and forth between the worlds of adolescents and adults, I spent most of my time hanging out with the students in their homes and in the social spaces they frequented, such as the local community center and a fast-food restaurant a few blocks away. And by the time the study was completed in the late 1990s, it was centered on the sixty-eight students whom I introduce here.

In this setting I interviewed and surveyed second-generation Cuban, Dominican, and Puerto Rican, and Black or African American youths who had ancestral roots that stretch mainly from the southern United States and New York.[2] Three in the latter group mentioned having at least one parent who had emigrated from Africa (Liberia) or the Caribbean (Antigua). The majority of the Latino boys (seven out of twelve) identified themselves as "Black Hispanic," while five identified as only "Hispanic." As for Latinas, two identified as "Black Hispanic," two as "White Hispanic," and eight as only "Hispanic." (Throughout this book, I will refer to females of Hispanic descent as "Latina" and males as "Latino.") Overall, females composed more than half—56 percent—of the sample.

All of these students' families qualified for government-subsidized housing assistance. More than half lived in homes with an annual household income of less than ten thousand dollars, headed primarily by a single female. At least 90 percent of them came from families who had been dependent on Aid to Families with Dependent Children (AFDC) before the implementation of the Personal Responsibility and Work Opportunity Reconciliation Act of 1996 (PRWORA) that established the Temporary Assistance for Needy Families (TANF) program.[3] Some lived in what housing analysts refer to as "scattered-site" public houses (government-subsidized homes with neatly manicured front yards and fenced-in backyards, to which the back door was the only entrance) located in predominantly White, middle-class neighborhoods. Others lived in traditional high-rise buildings located in high-poverty, predominantly minority neighborhoods—what is commonly referred to as the "ghetto." As table A-2 (see appendix) shows, however, there were no significant differences on key demographic and family characteristics by neighborhood type.

The students' home city, Yonkers, is racially diverse and highly segregated, the largest municipality in mostly suburban Westchester County (pop. 188,000 in 1990), and the fourth largest in the state of New York. In many ways, Yonkers resembles many other U.S. cities: it includes both a poor urban center whose residents are mainly people of color, and wealthy suburban-like neighborhoods whose residents are mainly White.

The city can be divided into three areas, each with distinct demographic traits. East Yonkers is predominantly White and middle- to upper-income; several neighborhoods here resemble those of more affluent bedroom communities such as Scarsdale and White Plains. Northwest Yonkers is home to both low-income and middle-income non-Hispanic Whites and to a small neighborhood of African American middle-income households. In southwest Yonkers, which surrounds the older central business district, most of the population is African American and Latino, and 22 percent of households in this area make up the city's oldest and most dilapidated housing stock.

In southwest Yonkers, many low-income Black, Latino, and even a few White families congregate in brick high-rises with dark hallways and steel staircases often strewn with refuse. Occasionally, I lost my way in the maze of hallways where units sometimes went unmarked. Youths from the southwest and I chatted at the tables in their modest kitchens or on the couches of their living rooms, where in the summer we sat near the window in un-air-conditioned spaces; they were not afforded the luxury of central air-conditioning like their peers in east Yonkers who lived in the new townhouses. Younger siblings sometimes regaled me with stories or sang along with a musical celebrity as the latest R&B and hip-hop hits played on the radio.

School was located not far from home for the Yonkers youths. With two exceptions, all of the students in the study either currently attended or had attended one of the eight public magnet middle and high schools in the city. In 1980, the Yonkers Public School System faced a major legal challenge by the U.S. Department of Justice, the federal Office for Civil Rights, and later by the Yonkers chapter of the National Association for the Advancement of Colored People (NAACP). These plaintiffs accused city officials and the board of education of maintaining racially segregated schools, and on May 13, 1986, federal appeals court Judge Leonard Sand ordered the school district to develop a plan that would ameliorate school segregation. The plan submitted by the Yonkers Board of Education sought to bring about voluntary school desegregation through magnet schools. These magnet schools were designed to attract White students from the wealthier east side of town to the minority districts on the west side, and vice versa. In this way, Black, Hispanic, and White students all boarded school buses and crisscrossed the city to attend newly created magnet programs.

While I was conducting this study, the school district comprised thirty-two elementary and secondary magnet schools, some with different focuses and specialty areas. Each year the schools held fairs and open houses to help parents decide which magnet schools to send their children to, and in a designated week, parents listed three school choices. The district held a lottery for students' school placement. According to estimates, the schools became racially balanced with a more equitable distribution of resources after the implementation of the board of education's plan in the late-1980s. Increasingly, however, the school ratio of minority to nonminority students shifted significantly from a ratio of 47 percent minority and 53 percent nonminority in 1985, to 70 percent and 30 percent, respectively, in 1997. As for personnel, of 824 teachers in both the middle and high schools, 82 percent are White, 10 percent Black, 7 percent Hispanic, and 1 percent Asian.[4]

More than a decade after implementing the desegregation plan, the unequal performances between racial and ethnic minorities and White students persisted (Brenner 1998). Census data reveal that in 1990, the enrollment rates in the Yonkers schools were roughly the same for White sixteen- to nineteen-year-olds—92 percent—but lower for Blacks and Hispanics—86 percent and 79 percent, respectively (U.S. Bureau of Census 1991). In spite of significant improvements in school enrollment rates, the unequal performances of minority and White students on standardized tests also persisted. Yonkers Public School System data showed that since 1987, the gap between Black and Latino students and all others (Whites and a small percentage of Asians) actually widened on the Metropolitan Achievement Tests. Black and Latino students score nearly two grade levels behind White students on standardized tests, just as they did in the early days of the desegregation drive (Brenner 1998). While White students in the Yonkers Public School System represent only about 30 percent of the district enrollment, they received 76 percent of high school regents' diplomas in 1997. The statistics also revealed that Black and Latino students have been suspended from school at a disproportionately higher rate. For example, of the 5,641 suspensions in the 1994-95 school year, 82% were given to Black and Latino students.

Graduation, suspension, and test-score profiles constitute and perpetuate a master account of "Black" and "Hispanic" student achievement. Some educators and researchers do the same as they spin these data, and the fallout is the tendency to homogenize the social and academic experiences of students who fall within a particular racial/ethnic or class groups. To fully comprehend what is going on for those students with the lackluster academic profiles, we should make sense of why some Black and Latino students disengage from their schools while others strive for and achieve academic excellence.

Keepin' It Real does not present a fully representative story of the educational and socio-cultural experiences of *all* African American and Latino students living in the United States, nor are these findings generalizable to all of the students in Yonkers, New York. Thus I caution the reader to interpret the survey findings in the context of my study. Nevertheless, the patterns found here are illustrative of social and cultural processes that may occur in wider society, and I would hope that the discussion that follows would inform the practices and views of researchers who conduct large-scale, nationally representative studies. In addition, they should provide some insight to educators examining similar issues that confront students with similar profiles elsewhere.

I have written this book to add another perspective on a matter of importance to many: social scientists conversant with the theoretical concepts and frameworks used to guide educational research; parents and students from disadvantaged groups who seek fuller incorporation in schools; and teachers, principals, and policy makers who desire to produce quality educational results. Collectively, they strive to increase Black and Latino students' school engagement and performance, and I hope that my contributions here will assist in thinking about how school success can indeed move beyond "black" and "white."

ACKNOWLEDGMENTS

I am indebted to a number of people who helped to bring this project to fruition. I dedicate this book to and especially thank the youth and their families who took hours of their time to speak about their experiences. It could not have been written had they not been so generous with their time and thoughts.

I owe much gratitude for the instruction, supervision, and guidance of my Ph. D. dissertation committee at Columbia University—my advisor Kathryn Neckerman, who set the cogs in motion with an assignment to develop a substantive research proposal in my first class with her; Angela Aidala, who taught me much about the design and setup of a research study; and Herbert Gans, Francesca Polletta, and Katherine Newman, gracious and critical committee members and scholars who helped to hone my interpretative skills in many ways. I am also grateful to Robert Crain, Joseph Darden, Joyce Moon Howard, who along with Angela Aidala provided me with formative research experiences with the Yonkers Family and Community Project funded by the Ford Foundation.

Generous financial assistance from the National Science Foundation

(SBR-98-01981), the Spencer Foundation, and the Ford Foundation Program on Poverty, Social Policy and the Underclass at the University of Michigan paid for research expenses and provided opportunities to write. I owe a special thanks to Harvard University for granting me research leave to complete the book. I am also especially grateful to these institutions for introducing me to a network of scholars and researchers who either mentored me or engaged me in some debates and discussions that enriched my ideas—Lawrence Bobo, Cleo Caldwell, Tabbye Chavous-Sellers, Mary Corcoran, Sheldon Danziger, Susan Frazier-Kouassi, Margaret Gibson, James S. Jackson, Laura Kohn-Wood, Catherine Lacey, Annette Lareau, Samuel Lucas, Hugh "Bud" Mehan, Roslyn Mickelson, Marcyliena Morgan, Pedro Noguera, Carla O'Connor, the late John Ogbu, Margo Okazawa-Rey, Robert Sellers, Catherine Squires, Robert Taylor, Karolyn Tyson, Lauren Young and colleagues at Harvard who offered support and feedback on various parts or all of the book, especially Mariko Chang, Ronald Ferguson, Christopher Jencks, Michèle Lamont, Peter Marsden, Orlando Patterson, Joel Podolny, Mary Waters, Marty Whyte, and William Julius Wilson. I am deeply appreciative of Lani Guinier who took much time out of her very busy schedule to guide me through the final stages of revisions. Our intellectual exchanges pushed me for more clarity and precision of thought.

I am also grateful to a community of scholars, friends, and graduate school classmates who either read some drafts, discussed ideas, or made the arduous writing process more bearable by either imparting advice or encouraging perseverance: Jennifer Lee (an amazing friend and colleague who has spent innumerable hours on the phone with me sharing and affirming ideas and experiences!), Lori D. Hill, Mica Pollock, Meira Levinson, John L. Jackson, Amanda Lewis, Tyrone Forman, Glenda Carpio, Kim DaCosta, Marla Frederick, Laura Morgan Roberts, Gwendolyn Dubois Shaw, Sonya Anderson, Eric Coburn, Gilberto Conchas, Xavier de Souza Briggs, Nadia Kim, Helen Lee, Martin McLee, Ainissa Ramirez, Meredith Woods, Darrick Hamilton, Jacqueline Olvera, Catherine Squires, Regina Del-Amen, Spencer Downing, Alix Gitelman, Makeba Jones, Heather Pleasants, AnnDenise Brown, Tami Friedman, Melanie Hildebrandt, Lynette Jackson, Kim Johnson, Martha S. Jones, and Jo Kim. This is only a partial list of those who offered support; I owe thanks to many others from various spheres of my life who have contributed to my intellectual growth.

For their invaluable research assistance, I am indebted to Audrey Alforque, Albert Jennings, Rejoice Nsibande, Joyce Hellew, Cynthia Reed, and Victoria Kent, and to Chauncy Lennon who generously shared the coding and analysis program that he designed. My editor at Oxford University Press, Dedi Felman; the coeditors of the book series, Cathy Cohen and Fred Harris; and the anonymous reviewers offered great advice, assistance, and feedback as I trundled along to get this book done. Thanks too to Nancy Levinson for her incisive copyediting and to Gwendolyn Colvin and the Oxford editorial and production team.

Finally, I acknowledge the love, continuous support, and encouragement of some very special friends and loved ones who have put up with me through all of the writing: Reena Karani who read every draft of this work in its dissertation incarnation and who continues to support me in the most profound way; Laura Wernick for an open heart and ears and shoulders to lean on; my parents Clara Carter and William H. Carter Sr. who paved the way through determination and sacrifice; my siblings Melanie Carter-Ayoub, Camissica Carter, and William H. Carter Jr. for their cheerfulness and continual reminders that life is greatest in its balance of family, friends, and work; and Patricia E. Powell for inspiring me with her gift for writing about the complexities of life and exposing me to its many joys.

CONTENTS

KEEPIN' IT REAL

INTRODUCTION

Minding the Gap: Race, Ethnicity, Achievement, and Cultural Meaning

A few years before I embarked on the study discussed in these pages, I traveled across eight states to recruit academically talented students for admission to Brown University. I visited an array of schools, from those in Detroit's inner city to the upper-middle-class suburban enclaves of Shaker Heights, Ohio, to the de facto segregated schools of Memphis, Tennessee, to the vast campuses of wealthy prep schools along the eastern seaboard in Massachusetts. The students I encountered varied, too, from the top achievers to the students who loitered in the hallways and cut classes. Often those in the latter group pointed me in the direction of either the principal's office or the counselor's office or would even escort me to the door. Most of the students visiting me during my information sessions, however, made up the schools' academic elite, usually Asian and White students who were among the top 1 to 5 percent of SAT scorers and exuded the confidence that they were the right matches for a selective university. There were also those like the Latino boy from Indiana, the son of semiliterate farm workers, and the African American girl from Montclair, New Jersey, the daughter of doctors—both top students in their graduating classes, one the first in his family to attend college, the other a second-generation collegian-to-be.

The farm workers' son and the doctors' daughter, however, were members of a small group of Latino and African American students whom guidance counselors considered the "cream of the crop," and often I wondered why was there such a low representation from these groups. In addition, I was curious about the apparent academic disengagement of my occasional escorts and about what would become of them. They did not jump at the opportunity to visit with a college admission officer, though when I asked them about higher educational plans, they responded, "Yeah, I plan to go to college. Got to get that degree." Teachers and counselors answered cautiously when I inquired about the low proportion of African American and Latino students who applied to places like Brown each year, and usually they said that these pupils did not perform as well as Asians and Whites, nor did they enroll in the advanced placement and honors courses—classes that selective university admission officers look for—to the same degree.

Over a decade after my contact with a multitude of American high schools, I still hear scholars, journalists, and politicians asking the same questions I had raised with those counselors and teachers: Why are so many African American and Latino students performing less well than their Asian and White peers in classes and on exams? Why are fewer African American and Latino students enrolled in advanced placement and honors courses in multiracial schools? And why are they seemingly less attached to school? Nowadays, newspapers headline the significant racial and ethnic achievement differences: "Reason Is Sought for Lag by Blacks in School Effort" (Belluck 1999), one shouts. "Closure Sought for Hispanic Education Gap," cries another (Henry 2000). The test-score gap, meanwhile, has become the focal point of an enterprise of research studies (see Jencks and Phillips 1998; Kao and Thompson 2003). Social scientists provide myriad explanations such as poverty, limited parental education, underfinanced schools, low teacher expectations, bad curricula, low parental involvement and limited access to information, and vestiges of racism in schools.

Culture makes a difference too. One reason that gained prominence and continues to have much currency within research and policy circles is Signithia Fordham and John Ogbu's provocative claim (1986) that many racial and ethnic minority students do not perform well in school because they avoid the "burden of acting white." After the completion of an ethnographic study of a predominantly black high school in a low-income community in Washington, D.C., Fordham and Ogbu argued that Black students equate speaking Standard English and other achievement-oriented behaviors, such as studying hard and excelling in school, with whites. And to avoid being labeled as "white," these students succumb to peer pressure *not* to do well in school. Black students, Fordham and Ogbu suggested, either consciously or unconsciously develop ambivalence toward learning and achievement. The result is a collective resistance to the white, middle-class organization of school, or an oppositional identity that perceives schooling as a "white" domain and high academic achievement as being incongruent with their racial and ethnic identities (Fordham and Ogbu 1986; Ogbu 1974, 1978; Ogbu and Simons 1998; Ogbu and Matute-Bianchi 1986).[1]

Like many American educators, school researchers, and policymakers, I also want to understand the academic achievement gap, and I aimed to understand it first by examining what factors are associated with students' attachment to school. I became dissatisfied with prevailing cultural explanations for low academic success, however, while a part of a team of researchers studying issues of poverty and social attainment and working with scores of low-income African American and Latino adolescents in the late 1990s. I, too, had heard students use expressions like "acting white," and even "acting black" and "acting Spanish" (the ethnolinguistic identity embraced by the Latino youth to describe those of Hispanic descent) when they described each other. Yet I did not find that these students equated studying hard and excelling in school with whiteness. Instead, I heard how minority youth often face social pressures to embrace cultural practices or "acts" associated with their racial and ethnic identities. Expressions like "acting white" also signaled various dynamics about social power and control among students *within* their ethnic, racial, and gendered communities.

It occurred to me that any explanation that links identity and culture to student engagement and achievement required further investigation, and so for a ten-month period from 1997 to 1998, I conducted a study with sixty-eight students, ranging in age from thirteen to twenty and focused on the students' educational, racial, ethnic, and cultural beliefs and practices.[2]

The students lived with their families in Yonkers, a few miles north of New York City, in government-subsidized apartments and town homes. In more than one hundred hours of intense and insightful conversations, these youths revealed their perspectives on race, ethnicity, culture, achievement, and mobility. Just as books and periodicals provide scholars and researchers with platforms to explain their ideas, this book has become a platform for the students to have their say on achievement matters.

Keepin' It Real addresses four main issues that deal with how students handle everything from the institutional, the cultural, and the personal, when it comes to their school attachment. First, in our society, not all groups, but rather a privileged few get to define what knowledge is or to define the images of the intelligent student. Students expressed their awareness of these dynamics, wrestling with their perceived unfairness of it all. If a pupil does not conform to these images, no matter how sharp his native ability, then he is marginalized. Students in this study, as the evidence will show, claim that their school attachment and engagement are often affected by how teachers and principals, the school's cultural gatekeepers, parcel out rewards and sanctions according to who abides by dominant cultural rules (Darder 1991). They call attention to a hierarchy of cultural meanings in schools and in society that further perpetuates social inequality.

Second, I challenge a predominant yet persistent view that a reactive culture among African American and Latino students towards white and middle-class dominance engenders attitudes and values that inhibit their academic achievement. I claim that the ethno-racial cultures serve positive functions, including a sense of belonging, distinction, and support for how to critique and cope with inequality. Their ethno-racial cultures are not mere adaptations and reactions to experiences with closed opportunities. Neither are bad behavior, deviance, and delinquency the principal components of these cultures. Rather, their cultural presentations of self are better understood as practices of distinction based on a critique of an undiscerning mainstream culture in schools rather than a submission to powerless and oppression (Bucholz 2002).

The story of how these youths deploy culture to gain status is complex and varied, however, and their approaches are better understood as a continuum rather than a fixed, singular cultural narrative. Some students comply with the dominant or mainstream cultural rules, while others challenge them and create and maintain their own repertoire of cultural codes and meanings. Thus, the third major argument of *Keepin' It Real* is that students' differences in attachment and engagement to school are connected to their ideologies about how in-group members should respond to social inequalities and about how in-group members should respect the cultural boundaries that they create between themselves and others.

Fourth, the common cultural explanations for Black and Latino student achievement miss another key variation within these groups that comes from the intersections between ethno-specific culture and gender socialization among low-income African American and Latino students. As I explored the functions, values, and meanings of culture for this particular group of youths, I learned that there is also an untold gender story in the race, ethnicity, culture, and achievement literature. Research has hinted at the "feminization" of achievement and schooling in the United States (Mickelson 1989; Jacobs 1996), and within many Black and Latino communities, the ratio between the number of girls and boys completing high school and attending college has doubled (Massey et al. 2003). My examination of the nexus between gender socialization, family relations and culture in these students' lives sheds further light on the relationships among students' multiple identities and social experiences and their engagement in learning and achievement.

Throughout this book I engage with two major cultural paradigms—and by extension other theoretical frameworks that draw on these paradigms—that are used often in research on culture, education and identity among nondominant or subordinated racial and ethnic groups. They are (1) the oppositional culture component of cultural-ecological theory developed by anthropologists of education John Ogbu and his associates; and (2) French sociologist Pierre Bourdieu's cultural capital theory. My intent here is to challenge, refine, and offer a different articulation of the ways in which culture is used to explain low-income African American and Latino students' school engagement and their academic and socioeconomic attainment.

During the last three decades, cultural-ecological theory has claimed that what determines racial and ethnic minorities' folk beliefs about academic and economic success is their mode of incorporation into U.S. society (Fordham 1996; Fordham and Ogbu 1986; Ogbu 1974, 1978;

Ogbu and Simons 1998; Ogbu and Matute-Bianchi 1986). That is, those groups—such as African Americans, Native Americans, and Mexican Americans—brought into U.S. society involuntarily by means of slavery, conquest, or colonization maintain deeply entrenched memories of institutionalized discrimination and subjugation. As a result, these "involuntary minorities" tend to "culturally invert," to establish practices in direct opposition to those of middle-class Whites (Ogbu 1978; Ogbu and Simons 1998). In essence, this theory construes sociohistorical forces (slavery, colonization, and conquest) as determinants of cultural phenomena (an oppositional culture to whiteness) that influence educational outcomes (rejection of schooling and lower academic achievement) for entire racial and ethnic groups.

The inherent danger of social science frameworks like that of cultural-ecological theory is the creation of a master narrative that tries to speak of *all* African Americans, Puerto Ricans, Mexican Americans, Native Americans, and other "involuntary minority groups" as if their members were exactly the same. There are no single explanations for how so-called involuntary minorities respond to the belief that middle- and upper-class Whites control the institutions of opportunity. In addition, such frameworks posit a position about these groups' perspectives on education that is not supported by many nationally representative surveys and other ethnographic studies. Not only has research shown that African Americans, for example, subscribe to the basic values of education as much as Whites do, or in some instances even more so than Whites do, but also there is insufficient evidence that a culture equating academic and socioeconomic mobility with whiteness among Blacks and other so-called "involuntary minorities" exists (Tyson 1998; Ainsworth-Darnell and Downey 1998; Cook and Ludwig 1998).

No doubt there are myriad factors that determine the differences in achievement outcomes for Blacks, Latinos and other marginalized groups, but what I contend with primarily in this book is how the notion of *culture* and its influence on student engagement and achievement gets discussed. What I discovered in this research is that students use culture as a vehicle to signal many things, ranging from the stylistic to the political. The oppositional culture framework, however, ignores the full spectrum of why and how culture becomes a social and political response to schooling by discounting the positive values and functions of these students' culture, instead focusing on their culture as a maladaptive response to social marginalization, and consequently paying no attention to the roles and values of nondominant cultural practices in the lives of many minority youth.

Middle and high school students are often in critical developmental stages of adolescence, dealing with their identities and what it means to be African American and/or Latino, or male, or poor, or gay or a fan of hip hop, for example. Youth tend to develop new (sub)cultures, as they appropriate, borrow, or adapt established practices to create new styles that distinguish their particular social group from others (Hall and Jefferson 1993; Bucholtz 2002). As we listen to these students' voices, we learn that "acting black," "acting Spanish," or "acting white" connotes more about perceived ethno-racial cultural styles and tastes than about an opposition to education and a dejection about unachievable success and socioeconomic opportunities. To ignore roles and values of nondominant cultures engenders a distortion of the goals and aspirations of many African American and Latino students.

The findings will reflect not only individual and group-level influences, but also they implicate the structural forces inherent in academic institutions. Schools are not just places where learning comprises how to read, compute, analyze and synthesize information; they are also key sites of socialization and cultural reproduction. On top of teaching the "three R's"—reading, writing, and 'rithmetic—teachers signal to pupils how they should interact and speak, what cultural tastes and sensibilities to cultivate, and what cultural knowledge is needed to be classified as a smart person in our society. Culture dwells in schools, and as Sharon Hays (1994) has written, culture is "a social structure with an underlying logic of its own." In line with Hays' theory, if the school environment engenders a hierarchy of cultural meanings that privileges a dominant culture over others, then it can limit students ideologically by what are deemed the acceptable practices and behaviors of a serious pupil. Furthermore, if students were to challenge the school's hierarchy of cultural meanings, regardless of whether or not they believed in the aims of education, they would risk reprimands, low evaluations and other sanctions that come with embracing cultural practices contrary to the school's expectations (ibid.).

Many educators assume that to communicate and work together across different social categories, students must possess the cultural codes of dominant and mainstream society, or what Pierre Bourdieu (1986) referred to as "cultural capital." However, school authorities often ignore that students should and can possess different kinds of cultural capital. Let me be clear here, I am not arguing that low-income minority students should not accrue dominant cultural capital. In fact they should and must attain dominant cultural capital for upward mobility and communication in dominant settings. However, what is knowledgeable and valuable in one social setting is not necessarily what signifies cultural competence in another. Educators can overlook this when they dismiss these students' own cultural competences and capitals.

Although most African American and Latino students may understand that the use of Standard English facilitates doing well in school, they may not believe that the maintenance of their own speech styles is incompatible with school success. Students, like the ones with whom I spoke, observe that educators privilege the styles, tastes, and understandings of white, middle-class students, and they feel that their teachers deny the legitimacy of their own cultural repertoires and even their critiques of the information that they are expected to learn. Thus, as others have shown, speech and language make up one terrain where cultural conflict arises in schools (Perry and Delpit 1998; Morgan 2002). Writing specifically about the role of different speech codes among African Americans, linguist Clarence Major (1994) wrote: "Though many of the words and phrases may sound harsh and even obscene to outsiders, [black slang] is essential to the cultural enrichment of African Americans." Such cultural codes and styles promote cultural solidarity among members of a heterogeneous African American population (Pattillo-McCoy 1999); and African American students will bring into the classroom the different linguistic codes and interactional styles that they employ outside of the school (Goodwin 1991).

Furthermore, while the oppositional cultural theory, which was originally based on a very limited number of schools, suggests that African American and Latino students are less engaged with school than other racial and ethnic groups, recent national studies show the contrary. In a study of over 11,000 students from schools around the nation, Johnson, Crosnoe, and Elder (2001) found that on average, while African American high school students are significantly less likely to be attached to school than either Latino or White students, they are significantly more likely to be at least minimally engaged in school. Here, Johnson and colleagues separate the affective component of students' academic experience, their *attachment*—that is, the degree to which students feel embedded in, welcomed or a part of school—from the behavioral component, their *engagement*, whether students put effort in school, are attentive, complete homework and so forth.[3] They also argue that attachment and engagement with school are conceptually distinct, though often confused with, valuing education. In what follows, I maintain the conceptual distinction that Johnson and colleagues make between school attachment and engagement. Both of these factors are moderately correlated with actual school achievement (i.e., grades and test scores).

I survey the students in this study by asking a host of questions about education, including the degree to which they believed that education is linked to jobs, success, and economic mobility. Nearly all of them strongly agree that education is the key to success. Moreover, they aspire to the benefits that an education brings, the American dream that includes good jobs paying high salaries, home and car ownership, and intact families. And they aim high, fantasizing about an economic success that has eluded their parents.

Though nearly all of these African American and Latino students are *believers* in education's benefits, some excel in school and others do not. For those who thrive academically, their class performances and study habits converge with their educational beliefs. A divergence, on the other hand, between beliefs and practices—what Roslyn Mickelson (1990) refers to as an "attitude-achievement paradox"—marks those who perform poorly in school. Those students whose school performances contradict their beliefs in education may act out and talk back to teachers or cut classes or fail to do their homework because they feel less attached to or welcomed in the school. Extrapolating from prior research, I suggest that the degree to which students actually convert their values for education into the high levels of school engagement—and ultimately achievement— is shaped by noncognitive factors such as "fitting into the school" or feelings of inclusiveness. Furthermore, I suggest that the students' perceptions of fitting in are linked to their ideologies of themselves as racial, ethnic, cultural, and gendered beings. That is, how much students perceive the school to be receptive to them—their attachment—can be linked to their actual school engagement and performances.

Nevertheless, since the previously mentioned national studies already show that on average, African American and Latino students share values with and at least minimally engage in school as much as other students, then it is highly conceivable that the attitude-achievement paradox may occur more narrowly among specific subgroups of minority students who have become detached and disengaged from school.

Findings from this study will show that several individual differences such as racial and ethnic ideology, cultural styles, access to resources, and treatment within school and family account for the variation in attachment, engagement, and achievement among African American and Latino students. These individual-level differences also affect how students reconcile their social identities—namely, racial, ethnic, class, and gender—with dominant mainstream culture and its influence in the school environment. For example, on the one hand, groups of students can all maintain racial and ethnic identities that are central to who students think they are. These students can also subscribe to the conventional formula for success: obtain a high-school degree, a college diploma, and then a good job. On the other hand, the students can vary ideologically in terms of how they deploy their social identities to engage in schools. Much of this variation is expressed through culture, through students' styles, tastes, and their reactions to the school's norms, codes, and policies. I noticed that students in this study fell into three groups that characterize how they managed their identities, cultural styles, and educational beliefs. These three types I refer to as the "noncompliant believers," the "cultural mainstreamers," and the "cultural straddlers." Noncompliant believers are the students with the widest gaps among their beliefs, school engagement, and their achievement. They believe in education, but do not always comply with the rules of educational attainment. That is, while they embrace what social scientists refer to as *dominant achievement ideology* (or the belief that education is the main route to socioeconomic mobility), their cultural identities and self-understanding as racial and ethnic beings lead them to challenge the compliance with rules that we use to denote good students. Usually, such students have limited knowledge of dominant cultural rules, or they refuse to accept all of the codes and expectations from what scholar and educator Lisa Delpit (1995) refers to as the "culture of power" because they see value in their own body of cultural know-how, which the school does not necessarily acknowledge.

In contrast to the noncompliant believers, the cultural mainstreamers embrace the dominant cultural repertoire, or body of cultural know-how, and although they express their own racial or ethnic background as a central part of their identity, they portray most cultural behaviors as racially or ethnically neutral (Sellers et al. 1998; Fordham 1988). Even when individuals place similarly high levels of significance on race in defining themselves, they may differ a great deal in what it means to be Black or Latino. One individual may believe that being Black or Latino means congregating among other Blacks or Latinos, while another may believe being Black or Latino means that one should integrate with non-Hispanic Whites (Sellers et al. 1998). A cultural mainstreamer is aware of her racial or ethnic heritage and how it differs from Whites, yet she can view the speech patterns, gestures, music, art, and clothing styles that her peers associate with middle- and upper-class Whites as simply the normative, or the "regular" (as youths in this study were apt to say), and not cultural forms that are the province of these Whites. Cultural mainstreamers comply with the mandates of schooling, even if they risk being rejected by their fellow African American and Latino peers for refusing to embrace their own racial and ethnic speech codes and musical, interactional, and social styles.

A third group, the cultural straddlers, deftly abides by the schools' cultural rules. Yet cultural straddlers do not passively obey school rules and cultural codes; rather, they simultaneously create meanings with their co-ethnic peers. Though critical of the schools' cultural exclusivity, cultural straddlers negotiate schooling in a way that enables them not only to hold on to their native cultural styles but also to embrace dominant cultural codes and resources. The cultural straddlers are more socially successful among their African American and Latino peers than are the cultural mainstreamers because they juggle multiple cultural "tool kits."[4] These students possess the resources to navigate strategically between multiple cultures, including their ethnic and peer groups, communities, and schools. For example, a cultural straddler is the African American or Latino student who is a member of the school's academic elite, enrolled in the advanced placement and honors classes, who is recognized by his teachers and selected to represent the school and speak at a special event held at the local university that brings together future young leaders, and who is popular among his peers at school and back at the housing project where he lives because he "keeps it real" by creating rhymes and poetry that resonate with them about the social and economic conditions of their community and society.

Both the cultural straddlers and the cultural mainstreamers do well in school, and the reader will discover why in the following pages. The cultural mainstreamers sought the affirmation of teachers, parents, and employers as their supports for how to effectively negotiate their social and academic lives. The cultural straddlers sought these same supports, but they also included their peers in their considerations. In contrast, noncompliant believers relied on their peers as the primary means of support for their ethnocultural and academic identities. It is the noncompliant believers, a category in which many of the students in this study fall, who compel us to examine why cultural, racial, and ethnic identities matter so much. They ignite the debates about academic achievement differences among racial and ethnic groups, and their own battles over identity and cultural self-presentations have critical policy implications.

As these three groups of students' stories unfold in the following chapters, it will become clear that many students, especially the noncompliant believers, perceive schools as closed cultural and intellectual environments that do not allow them to link the concrete values of education to deeper understandings of their own economic, political, and social realities. When noncompliant believer DeAndre Croix told me that he needed to move beyond what I call symbolic multiculturalism—where certain prominent and historical figures of color would be mentioned at few times of the year, or ethnic celebrations would be observed with foods, fairs, parades, and school assemblies—he meant that he needed his schooling to engage him in a way that goes beyond a cursory recognition of student differences. And he needed role models who could show him how to bridge culturally his poor neighborhood to the white-collar world to which he aspired. In other words, DeAndre needed interactions with people who are multiculturally adaptive and fluent, facile with helping students from varied backgrounds to attach themselves to school. Unfortunately, his school and the teachers did not help DeAndre to understand how the knowledge they conveyed and the cultural expectations they held mattered. Yet, for him and others, a dilemma existed: to reject the cultural expectations of schools and other mainstream social organizations set them up for negative teacher evaluations and academic failure, with profound consequences for their future success. Yet total conformity to dominant cultural practices meant an invalidation of DeAndre's own cultural repertoire and analyses, something that he could not deny. This dilemma, in itself, can complicate many African American and Latino students' academic journeys.

CHAPTER SNAPSHOTS

Each of the following six chapters builds on a new argument about how race, ethnicity, and culture influence low-income African American and Latino students' approaches to school. Chapter 1 profiles the three types of students whose educational beliefs differ according to racial and ethnic ideology—the "cultural mainstreamers," the "noncompliant believers," and the "cultural straddlers." All of these students comprehended that education is critical to success, yet they approached schooling differently because of the variation in their racial ideologies. This chapter discusses how these students' racial and ethnic identities, specifically their beliefs about assimilation, shape their orientations toward schools.

The three believer groups also highlight important differences in students' handling of their cultures, identities, and achievement. Chapter 2, especially, highlights how and why race, ethnicity, and culture influence students' academic behaviors. In this chapter, I discuss Bourdieu's cultural capital theory, which explains how the cultural codes and symbols of high status or dominant social groups become integral in the practices and sensibilities of schools and other social organizations and consequently how these cultural practices yield advantages disproportionately to members of those particular groups. Although Bourdieu wrote specifically about French middle and upper class society and their relations to the poor and working class, American social scientists appropriate his ideas and apply it to our own systems of social stratification, linking it to the attributes of the primarily white, middle and upper socioeconomic classes in United States (DiMaggio 1982; DiMaggio and Mohr 1985; DiMaggio and Ostrower 1980).[5] In prior research, others have drawn attention to the ethnocentric bias in the conventional use of cultural capital, claiming that it ignores the multiple ways in the cultural resources of other groups also convert into capital (Erikson 1996; Hall 1992; Swartz 1997). Throughout the pages of *Keepin' It Real,* I provide evidence of the variableness of cultural capital and how this group of low-income African American and Latino students negotiates their usage of both "dominant" and "nondominant" cultural capital.[6]

In addition, the discussion in chapter 2 departs from prevalent arguments that Black and Latino students resist "acting white," and thus underperform in school. It explores the meanings that these students give to the notions of acting "black," "Spanish," and "white," finding that "acting white" does not connote doing well in school. Conversely, poor performance in school does not connote resistance to "acting white." Rather, assertions of ethnic and racial identity are challenges to perceived cultural norms in U.S. society—white, middle-class styles of interaction, language, dress, and other cultural tastes. As a result, I suggest that acting "white," "black," or "Spanish" highlights how different cultural capitals operate.

Cultural explanations for the academic achievement gap can miss other key differences and variations within these groups. Chapter 3 examines differences in educational approaches between females and males. Why are males more likely to fall into the noncompliant category, as opposed to in the groups of cultural straddlers or cultural mainstreamers? Here is another perspective from which to view culture, one that also exposes the impact of another form of socialization—how students produce and conceive of what is "male" and "female." In this chapter I also discuss the feminization of "acting white" and other cultural styles associated with the white mainstream. Since some of these "feminine" behaviors become synonymous with dominant cultural capital in the school setting, girls may perform better than boys. Moreover, parental reinforcement of how males and females "do" gender (Fenstermaker and West 2002) through variable child rearing practices, in addition to a host of messages transmitted by the media and other social forces in society, influences these differences in academic approaches.

Chapter 4 takes us into the twenty-first century, primarily addressing how Latinos' racial and ethnic identities yield either similar or dissimilar educational outcomes to African American youth. Recent research suggests that second-generation Latino immigrants will become downwardly mobile if they emulate their Black peers' cultural orientation in the inner cities. Again, gender emerges as a strong influence when I analyze other sources of variation—interethnic differences between African Americans and Latinos in behaviors and attitudes about "acting white." Alejandro Portes and Min Zhou's "segmented assimilation" framework (1992) posits that an oppositional black culture lures immigrant youth in poor urban areas toward downward mobility. In addition to challenging the assertion that low-income urban youth are predisposed to downward mobility, I discuss findings that Latinos are more likely than Latinas to share cultural styles, such as those of hip-hop culture, with African American youths. Latinos, like African American males, perform less well in school than Latinas and African American females. But again, I find that these shared cultural tastes are not necessarily the causes of these urban minority youths' level of achievement. Instead, I discuss how other factors such as gender and family socialization influence these males' behaviors and practices.

Once we know how important schooling is and how sensitive cultural matters are, what assistance do students need to engage fully in their academic careers? What does it take? The stories in this book herald a call for assistance for students who are caught in a rut, in a disjuncture between their beliefs in the American Dream and their realities of insufficient social and economic resources to overcome poverty and racial and ethnic discrimination. Social supports, or even the lack of them, influence students' racial and ethnic ideological orientation, which I argue is associated with their approaches to school. Students can occupy the same ethnic or racial groups, but their access to critical forms of social capital, or resourceful personal connections, can vary (Louie 2001; Stanton-Salazar 2001). Usually, students' access to social capital corresponds to their families' socioeconomic status, and for the most part, limited social capital exists within poor, urban communities (Wilson 1996). This book, however, discusses how this variability in social capital occurs even among the poor.

In chapter 5, I describe the students' primary social networks and borrow from social science research on the critical values of "social capital" by calling for the assistance of "multicultural navigators." Being upwardly mobile and achievement-oriented is a necessary, but not a sufficient, condition for one to be a multicultural navigator. Multicultural navigators are individuals who harvest the cultural resources both from their own ethnic or racial heritages and from the opportunities provided outside of their communities. Multicultural navigators possess the insight and an understanding of the functions and values of both dominant and nondominant ethno-racial cultures. They provide critical social ties for co-ethnic members who are less fluent or less successful in navigating mainstream expectations. As social capital, they provide, for example, advice about how to write a college essay or how to interview for a job or even recommend a student for a summer internship that can assist her social mobility. At the same time they demonstrate for youth how to discern different cultural rules and expectations within myriad environments and how to negotiate these rules strategically.

After presenting the evidence that supports my argument about why culture matters in minority students' academic achievement in chapter 6, I present another articulation of the meanings of "acting white" and further explore the students' claims that success—whether in school or elsewhere—has no color. Here I attempt to synthesize my arguments, concluding with research implications, new study questions, and policy suggestions. A trinity of social forces—race (or ethnicity), class, and gender—dictates much about how "acting black," "acting Spanish," and "acting white" emerge as cultural phenomena and become integrated into the identities of minority students. African American and Latino youths should not reject the tools that would make them literate, self-sufficient, politically active, and economically productive. Still, educators cannot continue to disregard the values of different groups' cultural repertoires and must be sensitive to the powerful cultural dynamics permeating throughout schools. The point here is not to fault educators, especially since the findings present one side of a complex story. However, they do provide insight into these students' understandings of their own school behaviors, and this is crucial if parents, educators, social scientists, and policymakers are to gain a more holistic understanding of African American and Latino/a youths' academic patterns, and if they desire to more effectively help these students succeed.

Any education given by a group tends to socialize its

members, but the quality and value of the socialization

depends upon the habits and aims of the group.

—John Dewey, *Democracy and Education*

BEYOND BELIEF

Mainstreamers, Straddlers, and Noncompliant Believers

Racial and ethnic minority students living in poverty now have an un-
fortunate academic reputation among those who have not uncov-
ered the deeper meanings and explanations for how the forces of social
stratification—race, ethnicity, poverty, and culture—really affect students' lives both inside and outside of school. Observers perceive these
students to be at risk for significantly lower achievement performances,
later to be at risk for having little or no skills to hold jobs that pay decent
wages and salaries, to be at risk for supporting their children and families,
to be at risk for participating in illicit activities that will land them in
prison, or to be at risk for dependence on a host of social services sup-
plied by the government and paid with tax dollars that create resentment
among working peoples who view them as undeserving (Duncan and
Brooks-Gunn 1997; Katz 1990). Many of the young persons whom I interviewed for this study fit the profile of the at-risk youth, although only the
best fortunetellers could tell us what would transpire in their futures.
Contrary to popular belief, what I gathered from these students was that
the ideas of being at-risk had little to no impact on to their aspirations.

Thirty years prior, Patricia Gurin and Edgar Epps (1975) also found that although Black college students from economically disadvantaged backgrounds, who came of age in the politically volatile civil rights era of the 1960s, viewed obstacles to equal access as emerging from the social system (system-blame) as opposed to deficiencies in themselves or the group (self-blame), they were still likely to be highly motivated and have high aspirations. Not unlike the generation before them, the students in this study adhered to the dominant formula for socioeconomic success. With the proper supports, they believed that they could achieve a success that had eluded their parents who had not escaped poverty.

Like other American youths, thirteen-year-old Ngozi Gordon, the daughter of a single mother working long hours as an in-home nursing aide, accepted a utilitarian approach to education.[1] When I asked her what success meant to her, Ngozi replied, "Finish school and college." As I persisted with my questions and asked her what she wanted to do with her life, she reiterated, "Go to college." She considered a college diploma as a means of "getting paid"[2] and wanted to finish college so that she could have a better life. Then she could have a job so she could afford a child-care program or after-school activities, if she, like her mother does currently, had to leave her two children home while she worked. She wanted to maybe also own a house and a car so she would not have to rely on public transit to get to work. Ngozi and her younger sister kept each other company daily while their mother worked, and she longed for the trappings of the middle class, an existence several steps away from her working-poor existence. She felt that if she did not attend college, then "I won't get what I want [which is] a house, a car, and a good job."

Her next-door neighbor, Janora Shaw, aspired to be either a lawyer or a doctor, not because of any deep attraction to the practice of jurisprudence or medicine, but rather as a ticket out of poverty and her family's dependence on government assistance to live. In my face-to-face interview with Janora, I asked her many questions about her aspirations, probing for what compelled her to lean toward either law or medicine:

Prudence: You say you want to be a lawyer or a doctor. I've heard a lot of people say that they want to do that. What's so appealing about law or medicine?

Janora: You get a lot of money.

Prudence: So the number-one reason you choose what you want to do is based on how much money you're going to make?

Janora: Yeah.

Prudence: Do you know how much work it's going to take?

Janora: I know it's a lot.

Prudence: What if I told you that it takes twelve [years of elementary and secondary education] plus four years of college plus three more years of school? It takes nineteen years of school.

Janora: So?

Prudence: It doesn't make a difference to you?

Janora: No, I'll be a lawyer.

Part of me wanted to know how much Janora's aspirations were her true desires versus a fantasy, so I probed deeper in order to ascertain how serious she was. I even told her that it would take more than twenty years of schooling—including twelve years of elementary and secondary school, fours years of college, four years of medical school and then practical training—to become a doctor. The twenty years appeared to intimidate her, and subsequently, she dismissed that aspiration since she "didn't want to get blood all over [her] hands" anyway. What Janora focused on were the large salaries that lawyers and doctors were supposed to earn. She desired a financially rewarding career—an aspiration that would require an academic trajectory she did not clearly understand. When I posed the question of which she would prefer—doctor or lawyer—and indicated that the former required more schooling and training, Janora, making a quick adolescent cost-benefit analysis, asserted her preference for being a lawyer.

Unlike Janora, who appeared intimidated by anatomy, thirteen-year-old Wyla Tucker, a peer who lived in a housing complex about a mile away and who was enrolled in the gifted and talented (G&T) program at her school, intended to study medicine. Wyla had the honor of being the student in the study with the highest self-reported grade point average, and perhaps highest in her G&T classes as well. Her mother proudly exhibited her report cards to me, which showed grades of 98s and 100s in math, science, and language arts. It was an expectation that Wyla would attend college, and her mother had even begun saving money for it. Wyla did not feel that either her low-income background or race would hamper her. "No matter where you come from, just represent yourself . . . not where you came from," she tells me. "Like, if you live on the Westside [a high minority and poverty area] and people are doing crack, don't bring that [with you]. Just have a new start, you know, instead of bringing all of that with you. And it doesn't matter what color you are as long as you present yourself nicely. Say, 'Hi,' and, like, know what you're talking about. That's how I think you can get ahead or whatever."

Even the complicated Sylvestre Cabán, one of the neighborhood's "street pharmacists"—a code phrase for drug dealer—maintained strong beliefs in the value of education. I can see his puzzled face and inquisitive brown eyes as clearly now as on the day I interviewed him. He was eighteen years old, a high school dropout who hauled furniture to help support his family. As a side "job," he sold cocaine and marijuana. I recall his explanation for this: "I figure that I'm getting older, and my mom she ain't gonna be around forever. That money that I give her, I give to her so that she can buy some of the things she always wanted. You know, she could buy a car. See, I'm kind of doing this [selling drugs] for better[ment]. I'm not, like, hurting anyone. I'm just doing this, you know what I'm saying, to help out really."

Sylvestre and I discussed his rationale for drug dealing. In his view, he was doing it to help his family, to survive. I argued that drug dealing was dangerous work that could land him in jail and even kill him. Perhaps our conversation stirred something in him. I sensed that he did not want to deal drugs for long. He admitted as much, as I prepared to leave his house that day. "I want to get my life together," he said. "I just need a mentor, somebody to help me. I don't know where to turn." Sylvestre is a young man who wants a better life. "If I can't be a doctor, that's all right, you know what I'm saying," he said. "But for my mom, I want to make decent money to support my needs," he continued. "If I'm comfortable then that's good for me. But I don't want to do too much physical work. I'd rather just stay clean [that is, to do white-collar work and not manual labor]. I want to try to go to school." "But why go to school if you don't enjoy it?" I asked. Sylvestre responded, "I'm saying I don't [want to go to school], but thing is it's not [necessary], and if you get lucky you can find a job. I think I've been lucky.

I'm eighteen. I have a job. I got money in my pocket. A lot of kids at eighteen really go out to look for a job; they get two dollars a day. But I see this job I have now, I don't want to have all my life. It's physical work, and I don't want to do physical work. I want a job where I can sit back in a chair or whatever. I feel that I got to go to school to learn a little bit about business, to own a little store. I'm going to think. I know that I want to have money in my pocket. I'm gonna work, and if I have to go to school, I'll go to school."

Ironically, Sylvestre knew what would facilitate his upward mobility into legitimate and respectable realms of work, yet something had derailed him from turning his beliefs into actions. He had left his previous school after being suspended for shoving the principal—whom Sylvestre claimed had grabbed him as he was preparing to walk out the door during a confrontation. Sylvestre surmised that he would not pass his grade that year, as a result of conflicts and absences, so he decided not to return to school. It is true that Sylvestre had not been a cooperative student, frequently getting into trouble with school officials who didn't quite "get him," as he would say. At the same time, it is also true that the school had not done its best by Sylvestre, failing to keep him from slipping through the cracks into the dropout world.

Ngozi, Janora, Wyla, and Sylvestre all have something in common. Each of them comes from poor families in which their mothers work hard to make ends meet in low-wage service jobs, usually as nursing aides to the sick and elderly. They each understood that in a society reliant on credentials to signify skills and abilities (Collins 1979), the key to meeting their goals is a college degree. Further, for them, "getting paid" meant fantasizing about and aspiring to high-prestige jobs that are both romanticized and glamorized in the media. It was rational, then, for them to see the professions as channels to economic mobility improving their financial standings. Others did too. Forty-one of the sixty-eight youths in the Yonkers study aspired to hold professional or managerial jobs, with physician, lawyer, and businessperson as the top-three preferences.

All the youths I interviewed during the year were believers in the importance of education—all believed that going to school and obtaining the appropriate credentials were the tickets to success. Sixty-four of the sixty-eight youths professed "getting a good education is a practical road to success for young [Black or Hispanic] persons like [them]" (see figure 1.1). "Take as much advantage as you can from [education]," declared

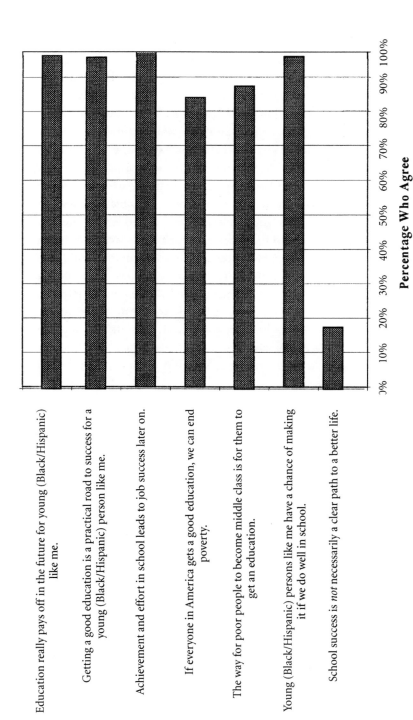

Percentage Who Agree

Education really pays off in the future for young (Black/Hispanic) like me.

Getting a good education is a practical road to success for a young (Black/Hispanic) person like me.

Achievement and effort in school leads to job success later on.

If everyone in America gets a good education, we can end poverty.

The way for poor people to become middle class is for them to get an education.

Young (Black/Hispanic) persons like me have a chance of making it if we do well in school.

School success is *not* necessarily a clear path to a better life.

FIGURE 1.1 Abstract Education Attitudes about the Role and Value of Education (N = 68)

seventeen-year-old Reina Juarez. "It's the only real way you can get ahead," she continued. Similarly, study after study continues to document that racial and ethnic minority students believe in the merits and benefits of education (Solorzano 1992; Cook and Ludwig 1998). In a nationally representative survey study, Douglas Downey and James Ainsworth-Darnell (1998) found that Black students report more optimistic occupational expectations, view education as more important to their future, and maintain more pro-school attitudes than do their White counterparts.

However, while they are *believers*, Black and Latino students are not all *achievers*. If we use standardized test scores as an indicator, then the test score gap is a loud reminder of the comparatively lower levels of achievement for many Black students and some Latino students (Jencks and Phillips 1998). Studies confirm persistent disparities among Asian, African, Latino, and White Americans, with Asian and White Americans scoring better on tests than African and Latino Americans (Kao and Thompson 2003; Jencks and Phillips 1998; Massey et al. 2003). In addition, African Americans' and Latinos' preparation for education beyond high school is not as ample as that of Asians and Whites. Among the Yonkers youth, for example, less than one-third were enrolled in either the college preparatory classes or tracks in their schools, and more than 50 percent reported maintaining lower than a "B" grade point average (see table 1.1).

How do we explain the gap between educational beliefs and school performance among many African American and Latino students? Researchers have considered students' class backgrounds and resources, parents' educational attainment, environmental and familial influences, such as poverty and loss of a parent (see Jencks and Phillips 1998). Still these racial and ethnic-group differences in achievement persist. As discussed earlier, some researchers now have focused on cultural factors, arguing that students and their families have culturally adapted to the legacy of various historical, social, economic, and political forces that have boxed them out of good jobs and schools (Ogbu and Simons 1998; Ogbu 1978; Fordham and Ogbu 1986).

One danger of these prior cultural explanations is the emergence of monolithic narratives about "Asian," "Black," "Latino," and "White" students. While different cultural, contextual, and socioeconomic factors certainly influence educational patterns, it is also true that there exists as much differentiation in educational approaches—both in terms of cul-

TABLE 1.1 School Enrollment, Performance, and Aspirations Data (N = 68)

Percentage	
Enrolled in school	72%
Obtained high school diploma or GED	15%
Had some college experience	8%
Dropped out of high school, no GED	13%
Earned mainly B or higher grades[a]	49%
Enrolled in academic/college prep courses[a]	31%
Enrolled in epecial education classes[a]	16%
Aspired to attend college and/or graduate School	84%
Aspired to hold professional/managerial jobs [b]	60%

[a]Based only on those currently enrolled in middle and high school (N = 49).

[b]Based on the 1980 National Opinion Research Council (NORC) occupational codes.

ture and racial and ethnic ideology—*within* racial and ethnic groups as there is *among* them. First, Black and Latino students, like Asians and Whites (see Lee 1996; Perry 2002), orient themselves in culturally different ways. Some Black and Latino students perceive how those with more privilege "make it" and emulate their actions as much as they can. They acculturate for higher social attainment and for mobility. But in doing so, they risk sanctions from members of their own racial, ethnic, and cultural groups as they fully adopt the ways associated with the dominant class and reject the practices of their own group (cf. Fordham 1988). Others start out with ambitions to do well in school, but then encounter difficulty in it, especially as they find disfavor with the cultural rules of "making it" (cf. MacLeod 1995). And then, there are some who believe in education, strive to do well in school by embracing the required cultural rules, but also recognize the values of their own cultures, and thus learn to navigate effectively between different sociocultural environments, between their primary culture(s) and those of the dominant cultures (cf. Gibson 1988).

Black and Latino students maintain variable racial and ethnic ideologies within their respective groups. That is, they differ in their attitudes, beliefs, and interpretations of how race affects their day-to-day lives. Some Blacks and Latinos may filter most of their interactions with Whites and others outside their group through the lens of their racial and ethnic identities, while other Blacks and Latinos may be less apt to invoke race and ethnicity and to view experiences with others. When questioned about their identities, nevertheless, all of these individuals may regard their race and ethnicity as critical aspects of who they are. Social psychologist Robert Sellers and his colleagues' multidimensional model of racial identity (1997; 1998) is useful here because it allows one to conceive of heterogeneous attitudes, beliefs, and practices within groups and to avoid essentializing the cultural behaviors of Blacks, Latinos, Whites, and other groups. Sellers and his team found four main dimensions to racial identity among Blacks, two of which are relevant here: *centrality* and *ideology*.[3] Racial (and I would also add "ethnic") *centrality*[4] concerns the extent to which people define themselves with regard to race—that is, the degree to which they make their racial identity a principal part of who they are. Racial (or ethnic) *ideology* concerns individuals' beliefs, opinions, and attitudes about how they feel that group members should act. Sellers et al. write: "Members of any racial (or ethnic) group, no doubt, will differ on these multiple dimensions of identity . . . neither of the [dimensions of racial identity] is synonymous with racial identity, just as the individual's arm is not synonymous with his or her whole body. The dimensions simply represent different ways in which racial identity is manifested" (1998, 28).

Most of the students in this study showed a high degree of racial or ethnic centrality. All but two expressed strong pride in their racial and ethnic heritages. Two-thirds also reported that they read about and study their heritages. Nevertheless, the processes by which these students resolved the pull between their collective identities as Blacks and Latinos and their goals for individual achievement and personal fulfillment varied according to the differences in their racial and ethnic ideology. In a systematic analysis of the students' responses to questions about their feelings about their heritage; their expectations of in-group members and the social and cultural behaviors related to their backgrounds; and their general thoughts on their racial and ethnic groups' position in U.S. politics and society, I found significant variation in the *ideological* dimension of the students' racial and ethnic identities. Three types of ideological profiles emerged.[5]

I characterize these student types as the *cultural mainstreamers,* the *noncompliant believers,* and the *cultural straddlers.* These terms parallel some sociocultural and ideological approaches discussed previously by social scientists when they consider the phenomena of assimilation, of opposition and resistance, and of some form of accommodation without assimilation (Dawson 2001; Darder 1991; Mehan, Hubbard, and Villanueva 1994; Gibson 1988).

Cultural mainstreamers emphasize both the similarities between racial and ethnic minority groups and Whites and the incorporation of the former into the opportunity structure. They expect group members to act according to traditional assimilationist values, which call for individuals from minority groups to accommodate to and ultimately be absorbed into American schools, workplaces, and communities (Park 1950; Gordon 1964). Generally, social scientists discuss acculturation under the rubric of "assimilation," as cultural assimilation, defined by Milton Gordon (1964) as the minority group's adoption of the cultural patterns of the host society or dominant social group.

How I use cultural assimilation here requires further explanation since this concept can have many meanings. Residents and citizens of the United States share aspects of American culture. Though in earlier eras of U.S. history Americanization was predicated on the ways of living of White, Anglo-Saxon Protestants, over time the majority of the nation's constituency came to share English as the national language; popular foods contributed by various ethnic groups such french fries, pizza, fried chicken, hot dogs, barbeque, and soda; and the political and civic values imbued in the holidays and festivals of the Fourth of July and Thanksgiving.[6] Thus, one of the critical debates following Gordon's work on acculturation is whether it is either a unidirectional or a two-way process. Is acculturation merely the replacement of minority cultural practices with those of the majority culture?[7] Or rather, do elements of minority cultures fuse with the dominant cultures to create a hybrid American culture? Some argue that the latter process occurs as the food, music, and language of myriad ethnic groups become incorporated in mainstream American culture (Alba and Nee 1997). While I acknowledge that cultural transmission can be a two-way process, and that the metaphorical "melting pot" does indeed characterize much American culture, I would also argue that the balance of two-way cultural exchanges is uneven and fraught with power dynamics. Inequities among social groups create a dynamic whereby less powerful groups feel compelled to adapt to the cultural styles, political ideologies, and ways of life of more powerful groups. Given that socioeconomic mobility is linked to an understanding of the dominant culture (Bourdieu 1986), nondominant ethnic group members may seek to embrace values and behaviors beyond those generally considered to define American culture. Thus, "acculturation" as I refer to it in this book goes beyond the idea of a shared national consciousness and an American identity.

Cultural mainstreamers accept the ideology that nondominant group members should be culturally, socially, economically, and politically assimilated. At the same time, the cultural mainstreamer can be racially and ethnically aware or have high racial and ethnic centrality. He or she is not necessarily "raceless." Though some cultural mainstreamers identify primarily as "human," others may embrace their black or Dominican or Puerto Rican identity. The cultural mainstreamer's approach is to "fit" into the system. Borrowing from Sellers et al., I would claim that the cultural mainstreamer "can be an activist for social change; however, he or she is likely to feel that [racial and ethnic minorities] need to work within the system to change it" (1998, 28).

In contrast, *noncompliant* believers, while understanding what cultural behaviors lead to academic, social, and economic success, favor their own cultural presentations (for example, "black" or "Puerto Rican") and exert little effort to adapt to the cultural prescriptions of the school and White society. The term *noncompliant* does not signify anti-intellectualism or low achievement, which much oppositional culture theory seems to suggest. In his seminal work, *Minority Education and Caste* (1978), John Ogbu argued that minority youths reject the belief that education leads to success because they fail to observe the link between academic achievement and access to jobs. Ogbu asserted that many African American, Chicana/o, and Native American adolescents react to their parents' and other relatives' experiences with the "job ceiling"—the discriminatory practices barring non-Whites from certain jobs—and consequently reject school. As a form of collective resistance, these students develop an oppositional identity. They perceive school as a "white" domain and render high academic achievement as being incongruent with their racial and ethnic identities.

Noncompliance, as I came to understand it from these youths, is a form of challenge of cultural practices that are tacitly understood to be the codes and symbols of intelligence, success, knowledge and good cultural conduct. But as Gurin and Epps (1975) have argued, ideological debate and a heightened cultural consciousness do not necessarily contradict non-dominant students' aspirations and desires for personal achievement. Further, as Gurin and Epps conclude, achievement need not be based on an illusionary belief in equal access and the openness of the American opportunity system.[8] As the following stories show, noncompliant believers often subscribe to the functional aspects of a good education, but they slip through the cracks because they comport themselves differently and do not view cultural assimilation as a prerequisite for achievement.

The *cultural straddlers* bridge the gap between the cultural mainstreamers and the noncompliant believers. Characterized by bicultural perspectives, they are strategic movers across the cultural spheres. The cultural straddlers span the spectrum, ranging in nature from students who "play the game" and embrace the cultural codes of both school and home community, to students who vocally criticize the schools' ideology while still achieving well academically. Some cultural straddlers resemble Margaret Gibson's Punjabi Indian students (1988) who viewed the acquisition of skills in the majority-group language and culture as "additive" and avoided rejecting their own identity and culture and instead embraced a form of biculturalism that led to successful participation in both cultures. Gibson's informants avoided equating certain behaviors and values with assimilation or Americanization or "acting white"—all terms used to describe forgetting one's roots or rejecting one's racial or ethnic identity. Although the cultural straddlers I interviewed sought successful participation in multiple cultural environments, unlike Gibson's students, they did not avoid equating certain behaviors with "acting white."

In comparison to Gibson, A. A. Akom (2003) has proposed a variation of the accommodation-without-assimilation perspective. Drawing on a study of academically successful Nation of Islam students, his "resistance within accommodation without assimilation" framework challenges the idea that acculturation is necessary if marginalized groups are to be incorporated into the U.S. opportunity structure. It allows for minority resistance to dominant cultural and linguistic patterns and for the critique of systemic inequalities, and yet it also embraces an idea of mobility that values education and its rewards. Unlike Gibson's Punjabi students, who did not criticize systemic inequality, Akom's informants stressed the social and political realities of being Black in the United States and of controlling their own destinies. The cultural straddlers resemble Akom's students, though their racial and ethnic ideologies are not determined by a specific political, cultural, and religious organization like the Nation of Islam.

A grasp of the complexity of racial and ethnic identities is crucial to understanding how many youths confront education, work, family, and community, and also to understanding why some low-income African American and Latino students succeed academically and others either disengage or fail. These African American and Latino students' engagement with school corresponded to the type of racial ethnic ideologies and cultural approaches they maintained. In the next section I describe each group—the cultural mainstreamer, the noncompliant believers, and the cultural straddlers—by profiling a representative student.

CULTURAL MAINSTREAMERS

Rosaria

Seventeen-year-old Rosaria Lopez and I sat in her family's cozy living room, which was graced by a figurine of the Virgin Mary. Soft-spoken and thoughtful, Rosaria described the complexity of navigating school, class work, peers, and aspirations. Rosaria had chosen to enroll in advanced placement and honors courses, though she was not officially in the A.P. and honors track. One thing Rosaria disliked about her school was the perception that school officials scheduled classes to favor students in the higher tracks. "Well at Gramson [High School], they have two types of programs," she explained. "They have the tech side and the trade side. The tech students are required to take Regents classes. They have honors and A.P. classes. The trade students have what they call survey classes, and they don't have to take the Regents classes. I think that they have some discrimination against the students and I don't like it."

"Why do you say that it's discrimination?" I asked.

Rosaria continued, "I mean, they schedule all of the honors classes around the schedules of the tech students, so that makes it difficult to schedule my classes. See, the trade students do not have to take these classes; it's an option. Like I wanted to take Century Honors English and an honors history class, but because of a schedule conflict, I had to drop one of them. If I had been a tech student, I wouldn't have had that problem, but they don't care about the trade students' schedules. They schedule around the tech students."

A self-motivated, high achiever, Rosaria had already been accepted at the Fashion Institute of Technology (FIT) in New York City and at five other colleges. Since she aspired to be a fashion designer, Rosaria had settled on FIT. When I asked her how her peers responded to her doing well in school, she smiled and blushed. "They always call me nerd and think that I know everything," she said. "I don't know everything. Sometimes I feel so much pressure, because they are always saying, 'Rosaria, she so smart. Ask Rosaria, she knows the answer.' They like to say that I'm a nerd." Rosario said that it didn't bother her to be called a nerd but that she felt pressured to perform now that she had been marked as one of the smart ones.

Rosaria also struggled with how her tastes and preferences differed from those of her peers. Because she preferred "to dress preppy, with the khakis, the crisp shirt, and a scarf around my neck," her schoolmates teased her about the way she dressed. "Why are you so preppy?" they charged. Rosaria informed me later that her Dominican and Black peers and friends referred to her as "white" because of how she dressed and spoke. Rosaria felt self-conscious about these matters. Her strategy was to argue that clothes, speech, and music styles (Rosaria preferred Michael Bolton and Mariah Carey instead of R & B and hip-hop stars like the Yonkers' natives Mary J. Blige and DMX) were not linked to particular racial or ethnic groups. "It's not 'Spanish,' it's not 'black,' it's not 'white'!" she exclaimed. Rosaria, who was independent-minded and not easily swayed by what her peers thought ("I act like who I am and do what I want to do!"), chose an academic path and comported herself in ways likely to bring her some educational success.

The cultural mainstreamers—the smallest group of my interviewees, only five of sixty-eight—are at the opposite end of the spectrum from the noncompliant believers. They often rejected their co-ethnic peers' cultural codes about how to dress and speak, about musical tastes, about racial composition of friendship networks, and they spoke rarely about the political and social experience of being Black or Latino. With one exception, all of the cultural mainstreamers were enrolled in their grades' advanced classes—usually each was one of the few African American and Latino students in these elite classes. The cultural mainstreamers fit the teachers' student ideal. They walked the walk and talked the talk of schooling, conforming to most norms, rules, and expectations. In addition, they had highly respectable grades.

Cultural mainstreamers frequently found themselves at odds with some co-ethnic peers. Their classmates often failed to see the signs of "coolness" (Danesi 1994). Some were labeled "nerds" or "brainiacs." Some were even perceived as "acting white," since they either refused to conform or avoided conforming to ethnic linguistic, musical, dress, and interactional styles. Provided that they were given sufficient financial support (taking into account their modest and poor backgrounds), the cultural mainstreamers aimed to move into the middle class.

As Rosaria's profile suggests, some racial and ethnic minority students accept the dominant precepts of cultural assimilation for social and academic mobility. Rosaria's response to schooling and education was to work within the system. Scoffing at affirmative action, Rosaria told me that she would never enroll at a university if she believed that her being Latino or Dominican had influenced her acceptance at the school. She did not want affirmative action to undermine her beliefs in herself and in the system that she believed worked fairly and equitably if one exerted enough effort. "If you really push and work hard, you can overcome anything. You have to want to do it," she declared. When she exclaimed, "Education is the only way up! I don't care if you are White, Black, Hispanic, or whatever, if you don't have an education, you're going nowhere," I understood that Rosaria had embraced the educational mantras of contemporary society.

Although Rosaria was not as critical of inequality, racism, and discrimination as some of the cultural straddlers and noncompliant believers, she still saw her Dominican heritage as central to her identity, which became clear to me when she described her discomfort with her White peers and teachers' low expectations of her. When I asked her to elaborate, she told a story: "Once I got a higher grade than my [White] friend who is very smart and who got a lower grade [than I]. She asked me what I got, and I told her, and she was like, 'Oh!' as if I wasn't supposed to get that high of a grade. When we both found out that we had gotten into college, she asked me what I wanted to major in. I told her journalism, and she was, like, 'Journalism?' She acted as if I was supposed to major in architecture or something like her. She kinda looked down on it—that I was studying something easy. That's why I don't like affirmative action."

Rosaria realized that her ethnicity influenced how others perceived her. She could not escape the sting of racial and ethnic prejudice and stereotypes. Moreover, Rosaria had apparently not told her friend that she also aspired to be a fashion designer. She had told me that she was considering two professions: journalism and fashion design. She wanted to earn a master's degree in journalism from Columbia University after graduating from FIT. Did she (mis)calculate that journalism would garner more respect from her friend than fashion design? Was she succumbing to the pressures of status and approval and keeping her other dream, fashion design, a secret from her competitive friend? Rosaria's strategy was to combat misperceptions about her talents and ability through hard work and effort, and she wanted to slip as easily as possible into the mainstream without calling much attention to her ethnic difference.

NONCOMPLIANT BELIEVERS

DeAndre

In the spring of 1998, I met DeAndre Croix, a charismatic teenager of African American and Antiguan heritage, whose slightly tousled afro was reminiscent of Black power hairstyle trends of the 1970s. He greeted me at his new home where his family and he had been placed after his mother won a spot in a lottery of housing placements for low-income families. We met after he had decided to stop selling marijuana on the streets and instead to concentrate on graduating from high school, despite the "$250 to $400 a day" he claimed he earned—much more than any job at McDonald's would pay. DeAndre spoke matter-of-factly about how he was attending his third high school, having been expelled from two others. He struggled with school because he found it "boring" and because he was unable to get into the magnet program of his choice. "If you can't get into the school you want to go to, then you're not really doing what you want to do, because you're going to the school that they [school lottery officials] pick," he explained.

DeAndre's boredom and disengagement was not only about his lack of school choice. This seventeen-year-old ardently expressed his disgust with the "savage inequalities" that educational reformer Jonathan Kozol (1991) has described—the symbolic ways in which officials show disrespect for the education of the underprivileged. "My school is, like, straight up like the sewer. The other schools are, like, nice and painted. My school is like the sewer. The walls are chipped; lockers don't work. They don't do nothing in my school. They don't fix nothing. If a light thing is hanging, it will just be hanging there until it falls. They don't do nothing at my school." Degradation, squalor, disparity, and poverty both inside and outside the walls of school reign in the lives of youth like DeAndre.

DeAndre also criticized the curricular content and the curriculum's failure to create more complex historical narratives about African Americans in U.S. society. "I hate, like, in school a teacher gives you something and you already know how to do it. Like, in social studies a teacher gives you a report to do on Abraham Lincoln. . . . I already know about him. I learned about him back in the sixth grade. Why do I want to learn about him again? I want to learn about somebody I don't know. Like, I know about Malcolm X, Martin Luther King, and that lady Rosa Parks and stuff that they did. But I want to know stuff about what I don't know. I want to know about Black, Black . . . how can I say this . . . Black historical figures besides the main people. I know that there are other people." DeAndre sensed that the curricular representation of African Americans needed to go beyond the figurative and familiar names heard annually in February during Black History Month.

DeAndre was willful and challenging, and struggled with school officials, with their dress codes, and their policing of him and his peers. "Like, in school, a lot of Black people wear their hoods on their head. Then they think we down with a gang or something. It's not really like they a part of a gang or something. People do that because they want to do it. Anybody could put they hood on they head," he said. "I understand why you can't wear a hood in a building or something, but if a sweatshirt came with a hood, why you can't wear it? Why you got to be a part of a gang or something?" Why, he wondered, were he and his Black peers marked as gangsters because they fashioned themselves after the "thuggish" appearance of favored rappers in the hip-hop world?

Explanations for the academic failure of poor African American and Latino students like DeAndre and Sylvestre (introduced earlier) ordinarily run the gamut from the macrostructural (for example, the effects of intergenerational poverty, discrimination, segregated housing, poor quality schools) to the cultural (sociocultural deprivation, bad values, deviance, and family dysfunction) to the individual (limited skills and personality disorders). Some explanations concentrate on how different racial and ethnic groups became incorporated into U.S. society. Though the noncompliant believers, thirty-eight of the sixty-eight respondents, view education as a means to an end, they are both challenged by and disengaged from schooling in ways that lead either to academic failure or to low school performances. These students both attend and cut classes. Some do enough work to pass from one grade or class to another, while others fail. Many frequently come into conflict with teachers because of talking, acting out, or failing to complete assignments. Noncompliant believers range from average to subpar students. Some are popular, athletic, and leadership-oriented. Others spend time with their friends and attend school for its social benefits.

Noncompliant students struggle with school policies and various social and cultural codes. They create and embrace behaviors that signify their collective racial, ethnic, and gender identities. Deemed as "black" or "Spanish"—although these two cultural rubrics are qualitatively different—the tastes and styles of these constructed identities often cause school officials and adults to wrinkle their noses. Implicit in the actions of the noncompliant believers are critiques of the educational system and its cultural structure, its curricula, pedagogy, and codes of achievement. The noncompliant challenge the conventional and traditional dictates of the school system.

In *Streetwise*, sociologist Elijah Anderson writes, "The master status assigned to Black males undermines their ability to be taken for granted as law-abiding and civil participants in public places: young Black males, particularly those who don the urban uniform (sneakers, athletic suits, gold chains, 'gangster caps,' sunglasses, and large portable radios or 'boom boxes'), may be taken as the embodiment of the predator. In this uniform, which suggests to many the 'dangerous underclass,' these young men are presumed to be troublemakers or criminals" (1990, 167). Although Anderson's ethnographic details focus on the neighborhood streets of a city, his analysis can be extended to schools and classrooms as well. DeAndre's and Sylvestre's choices and behaviors had been characterized as "street," a code word for "poor" and "black" behaviors and for resistance to the mainstream, which is coded as "white" and middle class. While DeAndre and Sylvestre viewed education as the conventional key to success, they perceived some of their school experiences as a devaluation of their own cultural codes and a dismissal of their academic concerns, and, in turn, responded to this devaluation with actions not conducive to conventional academic success.

THE CULTURAL STRADDLERS

Valerie

Within days of meeting DeAndre, I met fourteen-year-old Valerie King, a confident and stylish girl who was aware of her popularity in school and of the differences between her and her friends. Of her immediate circle, Valerie was the only one enrolled in the honors program at Townson High School, and she excelled. When I asked what made her different, she replied, "I want something with my life, I want to do something with my life. I want a future. I don't want to be stuck in the projects with a baby daddy, waiting for him to come by and bring me some cigarettes. I want a husband. I want to be married at least two years before I have a child. And I at least want to be called Dr. King before I am Mrs. Anything." Valerie had learned how to navigate between her social circles and the classroom, and she claimed that the reason was self-determination. "I don't pay no mind to the things that [my friends] do," she said. "I hang around with them. I'll talk to them and converse [sic], but I won't pay no mind to the things that they do." In fact, it appeared that the more her friends behaved in ways that stalled their academic progress, the more she ran the other way. Several of Valerie's girlfriends had gotten pregnant, for instance, while Valerie joined the campaign against teenage pregnancy, refusing to risk becoming a mother before she achieved her career goals. Strengthened by the belief that she could succeed as much as anyone else, Valerie proclaimed, "I live in the projects, yeah. I may be African American, but I have the same chances as any Caucasian person. Let me put it this way, I have the same chances as them. I don't think like that [meaning that because she is Black, she does not assume that she cannot excel as much as Whites]. I can't let anyone or anything like that affect me," Valerie continued. "I feel sorry for you that you feel that way, but sorry I can't do that." Despite this, Valerie maintained friendships mainly with kids outside her honors program. She said that she counted only two persons in the program as friends.

Valerie spoke explicitly about racial and ethnic identity and blackness. About black slang, she commented, "Every time I hear a White person talk slang, I wonder is it just at school. I guess they just get it in school. It makes me think, like, before there was slavery and they didn't want us above anything and then all of a sudden, now you want to be like us? That, that kind of makes me wonder. But I don't think of them any different. If you choose to talk like that . . . well, everyone has their own dialect." While distinguishing between her cultural world and that of Whites, Valerie scoffed at anyone who chose to cross those boundaries in an artificial way. "If you don't try to act like what you are not, if this is the way that you naturally are, then there is no problem with it. But if you are just acting, then it is no good," she claimed. Valerie, like many of her peers, made her blackness a central part of her identity. But contrary to the "burden of acting white thesis," this high-achieving girl made it clear that the utterances of phrases like "acting black," "acting Spanish," or "acting white" had little to do with her belief in the value of education but rather how she constructed her racial identity. She had already let me know how critical education was to her dream of becoming an obstetrician and gynecologist.

In contrast to the noncompliant believers, the accommodating believers—twenty-five of the sixty-eight respondents—usually achieve high academic success. Many are socially popular. Accommodating believers successfully negotiate both the social and academic demands of school, balancing the expectations of teachers, parents, and peers. They tend to be bicultural and bilingual, if not multiskilled in these areas. They can move back and forth between their peers' slang and cultural codes and Standard

English and other academic signifiers of intelligence and compliance. Many accommodating believers are college-bound and headed toward the middle class.

EMERGENT PARADOXES: IDEOLOGY, ASPIRATIONS, AND PERFORMANCE

The profiles of DeAndre, Valerie, and Rosaria encourage us to examine how racial and ethnic identities and cultural practices influence approaches to education. A close examination of students' identities, as indicated by their racial and ethnic ideologies and cultural behaviors, both provides clarity about their attitudes and beliefs about achievement and exposes paradoxes—how and why school practices often diverge from educational beliefs. For instance, while the noncompliant believers articulated high aspirations and acceptable educational beliefs, it is probable that their expectations of upward mobility differed markedly from those of the cultural straddlers and the cultural mainstreamers. In their case, an "attitude-achievement paradox" thrives.[9]

Roslyn Mickelson (1990) analyzes the attitude-achievement paradox, calling attention to the multidimensionality of attitudes. In a study of more than eleven hundred Black and White students from diverse socioeconomic backgrounds in California, she differentiated between what she calls "abstract" and "concrete" attitudes. Here, "abstract" corresponds to normative values—to dominant ideas about the functions and values of education. In contrast, "concrete" attitudes correspond to beliefs about actual connections between education and mobility, given their perceptions of their parents and own actual experiences. In the late 1980s, Mickelson compiled a battery of questions and constructed scales of survey questions to measure students' abstract and concrete attitudes. For example, she asked students either to agree or disagree with these abstract statements: "Achievement and effort in school lead to job success later on"; "Young Black [Hispanic] people like me have a chance of making it if we do well in school"; and "Education really pays off in the future for young Black [Hispanic] people like me." And then with the following, students indicated their concrete attitudes: "Based on their experiences, my parents say people like us are not always paid or promoted according to education."[10] Mickelson found that Black and poor students express high regard for education in the abstract. In examining concrete attitudes, however, she found significant differences between Black and White students. "The paradox of poor grades but positive attitudes toward education among Blacks vanishes when concrete, rather than abstract, attitudes are related to high school grades," she concluded, arguing that Black and poor students' low expectations of the benefits of education explained their weaker school achievement when compared to Whites.[11]

Like Mickelson, I found that most of the study participants in Yonkers subscribed to educational ideals. Using Mickelson's seven questions about abstract attitudes, I created a scale ranging in value from a low of one (very strong pessimism) to a high of five (very strong optimism). Agreement with each statement would yield a score between four and five; disagreement, a score between one and two; and mixed feelings, a score between three and four. Table 1.2 shows no significant statistical differences among the three groups. In general, all the students expressed faith that education should ideally operate as a means to social and economic mobility. That is, all three groups are believers in education.

Further, I created a scale using several of Mickelson's concrete educational attitude statements, ranging from a low of one (very strong pessimism) to a high of five (very strong optimism), and I found that each group held mixed views. The statements to which the students responded included: "My parents face barriers to job success, despite their belief in a good education"; "People in my family have not been treated fairly at work, no matter how much education they possess"; "People like me are not paid or promoted based on education"; and "studying in school rarely

TABLE 1.2 Mean Scores on Abstract Educational Attitudes by Believer Groups (1 = very strong pessimism to 5 = very strong optimism)

Group Type N	Mean Abstract Educational Attitude Score	Overall Assessment
Cultural Mainstreamers (5)	4.63	Optimistic
Cultural Straddlers (25)	4.17	Optimistic
Noncompliant Believers (38)	4.33	Optimistic

pays off later with good jobs."[12] On this five-item scale, agreement with each statement would yield a score between one and two; mixed views, a score between three and four; and disagreement, a score between four and five.

The cultural mainstreamers and the cultural straddlers were significantly more optimistic that once they were educated, discrimination would not impede their economic attainment (than were the noncompliant believers). The cultural mainstreamers were the most optimistic, averaging a score of 3.36; the cultural straddlers ranked second, averaging a score of 3.10; and, as I predicted, the noncompliant were the most pessimistic with a score of 2.76. Furthermore, these concrete attitude scores correspond significantly to the mean grade point averages provided by the students who were in middle or high school at the time of their interviews with me. Table 1.3 shows that the cultural mainstreamers had grade point averages of about ninety (out of a possible one hundred), while the accommodative averaged eighty, and the noncompliant seventy-three.

In addition, the majority of the cultural straddlers, the cultural mainstreamers, and the noncompliant believers aspired to attend college: twenty-one out of twenty-five, five of five, and thirty-one of thirty-eight, respectively. Aspirations are not equivalent to expectations, however. Aspirations signify what a student dreams of or envisions given ideal conditions, while expectations take into account the student's reality, and his or her actual material, familial, or academic circumstances, which may or may not support one's aspirations. Thus, it is not unusual for the percentages of students expecting to attend college to decline from that of those aspiring to attend. While all the cultural mainstreamers (five of five) and nearly three-quarters of the cultural straddlers (eighteen of twenty-five) expected to attend college, less than half of the noncompliant believers (seventeen of thirty-eight) did.

In addition, I found that the cultural straddlers had the smallest gap between their views about education's ideals and their views about how education influences access to opportunity, given one's race, ethnicity, and class background. In other words, their concrete and abstract attitudes deviated, on average, by fewer points than did the abstract and concrete attitudes of the cultural mainstreamers and the noncompliant believers.

As in Mickelson's study, I found a positive association between stu-

TABLE 1.3 Mean Concrete Educational Attitudes and Grade Point Averages
by Believer Groups

Group Type N	Mean Concrete Attitude Score (1 = very pessimistic 5 = very optimistic)	Overall Assessment	Mean Grade Point Average[a]	Aspiring to Attend College	Expected to Attend College
Cultural Mainstreamers (5)	3.36	Mixed	90***	100%	100%
Cultural Straddlers (25)	3.10	Mixed	80	84%	89%
Noncompliant Believers (38)	2.76**	Mixed	73	82%	55% *

[a]Grade point averages based only on the number of those in secondary school at time of interview.

*Marginally significant mean group differences between the noncompliant believers and the other two groups (p < .10).

**Significant mean group differences between the noncompliant believers and the other two groups (p = .05)

***Significant mean differences among all three groups (p = .00).

dents' concrete attitudes and their grade point averages. In addition, students' scores on the concrete scale support the finding that racial and ethnic minority students do not fully subscribe to the myth of schooling and education as the great equalizers. Despite their rankings, all three groups had mixed feelings about the benefits of education, especially for people from racial and ethnic minorities. It should come as no surprise that these students doubt that educational systems and job markets work for them. In fact, their responses resonate with researchers' findings that even middle- and upper-middle-class African Americans, in spite of their economic successes, maintain critical political viewpoints of the opportunity structure in U. S. society because of experiences with racial discrimination and prejudice (J. Feagin 1991; Collins 1989; Hochschild 1995). But their critical viewpoints do not deter them from upward mobility (cf. Gurin and Epps, 1975).

Likewise, the mixed concrete views of the cultural mainstreamers and the cultural straddlers students in my study do not deter them from doing well in school or from intending to go to college. Although these students acknowledged the necessity of academic achievement for occupational success, many displayed a healthy disrespect for the romantic tenets of achievement ideology. That is, while the "education-and-effort-lead-to-success" mantra was the acceptable belief, they also understood that this dictum does not hold equally true for all social groups. More than two-thirds of the students believed that despite education's value, they and their families faced or would face many obstacles to job success (see figure 1.2).

So what does all this mean? The current literature on the attitude-achievement paradox suggests that Black students are more likely to maintain significant differences in concrete attitudes and educational practices than Whites. This analysis among low-income Black and Latino students reveals a more specific pattern linked to racial and ethnic ideology, concrete attitudes, and achievement. In addition, it shows that even high-achieving African American and Latino students may maintain somewhat mixed or pessimistic views of education's real effects. In the long run, the cultural mainstreamers and cultural straddlers like Rosaria and Valerie are more inclined to attain academic and social success than are the noncompliant believers like Sylvestre and DeAndre. Thus, the noncompliant believers' grades, aspirations, and expectations indicate that they are the critical academic cases.

Academic performance is only one of the students' considerations. As both a sign of the times and a legacy of the past, African American and Latino youths grapple with issues of race, ethnicity, age, class, gender, sexuality, and culture. Many develop ways to make sense out of an inequitable world. Every day they struggle to balance the principles and practices that schools espouse and the difficult realities they face. Issues of group cohesion and social solidarity emerge as they cohere around their social identities. I found that the cultural straddlers found success academically, socially, and culturally, while the cultural mainstreamers faced disapproval among their peers for their rejection of ethnic or in-group cultural codes.

Previous studies support the claim that cultural straddlers would follow a more balanced social, cultural, and academic trajectory. Gurin and Epps (1975) first challenged the traditional psychological achievement theory that posits that familial and group loyalties can inhibit achievement because they reduce a person's willingness to leave the group or

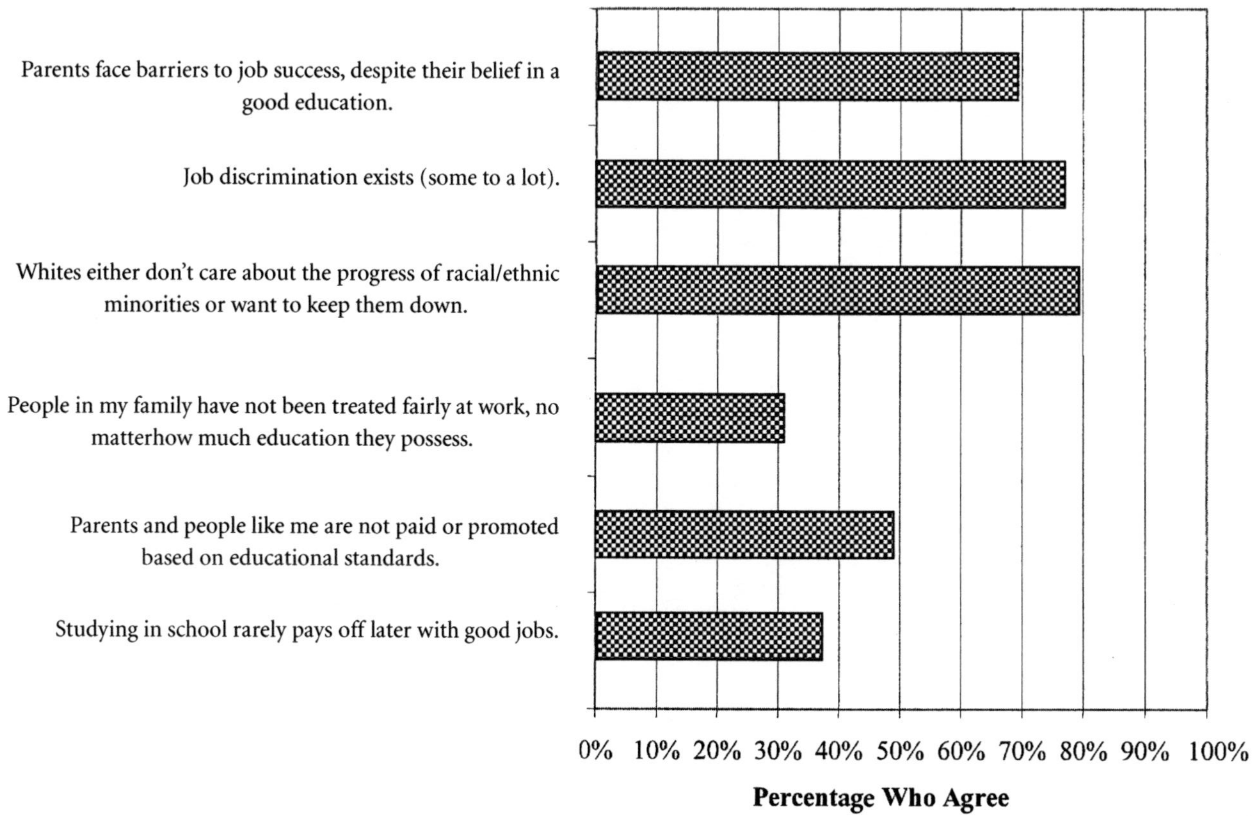
Parents face barriers to job success, despite their belief in a good education.
Job discrimination exists (some to a lot).
Whites either don't care about the progress of racial/ethnic minorities or want to keep them down.
People in my family have not been treated fairly at work, no matterhow much education they possess.
Parents and people like me are not paid or promoted based on educational standards.
Studying in school rarely pays off later with good jobs.
0% 10% 20% 30% 40% 50% 60% 70% 80% 90% 100%
Percentage Who Agree

FIGURE 1.2 Respondents' Concrete Attitudes about Education, Opportunity, and Race Relations (N = 68)

home to pursue advancement. Instead they found that group identification and collective commitment play important roles in minority identity formation, and many students who were politically active, fighting for improved social and economic conditions for African Americans, showed high motivation to achieve. In addition, other social psychologists have shown that a strong ethnic identity is linked to higher academic achievement (Bowman and Howard 1985). More recently, Daphna Oyserman et. al (2003) found that among racially conscious students, those who are bicultural perform better academically than do those with either an acculturative or a nationalist orientation.

Anthropologists and sociologists investigating the role of culture in schools support this finding too. For example, in an ethnographic study of a southwestern school, Donna Deyhle (1995) reveals how the more successful Navajo students were those who were bicultural. Navajo youths who were well integrated into their own culture and somewhat adapted to the mainstream were more successful, regardless of racial, ethnic, cultural, and economic barriers. Hugh Mehan et al (1994) and Antonia Darder (1991) also found that African American and Latino students who navigated between the dominant society and their own ethnic cultures enjoyed successful academic careers. In the last decade, research has emerged about the high achievement of students with both high race centrality *and* a bicultural ideological orientation. In short, these researchers suggest that biculturalism is key to understanding effective approaches to academic mobility.[13] In subsequent chapters I will provide more insight into *why* this is the case, as I explore how students negotiate their racial, ethnic, gender, and academic identities.

An attitude-achievement paradox is most apparent among the noncompliant believers.[14] Their racial and ethnic ideological differences from the cultural mainstreamers and the cultural straddlers raise the question of how they can *effectively* reconcile the gap between the ideals of education and achievement in U.S. society and their own social, material, and political realities. How can these students incisively critique our society's failure to live up to its ideals and not be penalized for having their say? Rather than concluding that the noncompliant students are rejecting pro-achievement ideology and successful school behaviors because they do not fully acculturate, we must understand how and why they have adapted differently than have the cultural mainstreamers and the cultural straddlers. A firm reality that dominant cultural repertoires prevail, coupled with noncompliant believers' desires to use various skills and talents within their own cultural repertoires, derails the high aspirations of noncompliant student believers like DeAndre and Sylvestre.

These students pose intriguing, weighty sociological questions about the links between identity, ideology, culture, and academic achievement. Answers emerged as I explored how the students expressed their identities through cultural practices. Not only did the groups of believers in education set the record straight about how they construct ethno-racial practices and meanings, they also exposed a crack in the system. From their stories, I discovered that students perceived that schools did little to adapt and adjust to how racial, ethnic, and class issues play out in the classroom, in the curricula, and in society at large. They also perceived that teachers and principals expected them to accept the cultural milieu of the school with little to no challenge. As far as the students were concerned, cultural engagement is not one-sided, and it left me wondering, "Well, what are the responsibilities of schools and educators, the cultural gatekeepers?"

When the major institutions in society are constructed

within the culture and interests of one group instead of

another, even when the subordinate group is included

within those institutions, its performances will be, on

average, less proficient than the dominant group.

—Mark Gould (1999)

"Black" Cultural Capital and the Conflicts of Schooling

Schools are more than institutions where teachers impart skills and lessons; they are places where teachers transmit cultural knowledge. As a child growing up in Mississippi and attending de facto segregated schools, I did not realize that education is as much about being inculcated with the ways of the "culture of power" as much as it is about learning to read, count, and think critically. This culture of power, as scholar and educator Lisa Delpit (1997) calls it, encompasses a body of rules, tastes, appreciations, and styles for success that are fashioned by the dominant social classes whose members are mainly White, middle- and upper-class. Not only do the dominant classes determine what is included in the canons of Western literature, music, history, social studies, and the sciences but they also control the norms of cultural preservation and self-presentation.[1]

On the one hand, the "culture of power" can sound like a misnomer, especially when applied to mostly Black elementary, middle, and high schools with a significant percentage of Black teachers. On the other hand, my well-intentioned instructors, also schooled in the culture of power, worked to teach us what they had been taught. Many of us accepted instructions without any questions. As Delpit describes:

> These teachers . . . successfully taught the more subtle aspects of dominant Discourse . . . that students be able to speak and write eloquently, maintain neatness, think carefully, exude character, and conduct themselves with decorum. They even found ways to mediate class difference by attending . . . to hygiene of students who needed such attention—washing faces, cutting fingernails and handing out deodorant. All of these teachers were able to teach in classrooms the rules for dominant Discourse, allowing students to succeed in mainstream America who were not only born outside of the realms of power and status, but who had no access to status institutions. These teachers were not themselves a part of the power elite, not members of dominant Discourses. Yet they were able to provide the keys for their students' entry into the larger world, never knowing if the doors would ever swing open to allow them in. (Delpit as quoted in Perry 2003)

I recall how a sixth-grade teacher firmly schooled me on the importance of looking someone in the eye as I spoke to him or her. Once, she took me aside and stated, "Always remember to look someone in the eye, especially Whites, when you are speaking to them." I understood from her that direct eye contact would signal confidence and assuredness during those times when I would be applying for positions. Now, in some cultures, sustained eye contact is perceived as disrespectful (see Duranti 1992; White 1989), an anthropological fact that I did not learn until later. While on a research trip to several schools in South Africa in 2004, I learned about how student-teacher cultural conflict arises over the issue of interpersonal eye contact. Several White teachers of Anglo and Afrikaans backgrounds described their initial displeasure with many of their Black students of Xhosa, Zulu, and other ethnic backgrounds who refused to look at them while being disciplined. Unbeknown to the teachers, the students' cultures taught them that no eye contact was a sign of deference to elders. Meanwhile, the teachers had been reprimanding their students further for not looking at them, taking the students' actions instead as signs of disrespect and obstinacy. This student-teacher cultural misunderstanding was further compounded by the residual social effects of South Africa's system of apartheid, an era of interracial division and strife. The South African teacher, like my sixth-grade teacher, wanted me to know that in the culture of power eye contact was a sign of confidence and even attentiveness.

The cultural production within schools is, no doubt, quite valuable to students' socialization. It is here that students begin to accrue *dominant* "cultural capital." As theorized by Pierre Bourdieu (1986), cultural capital includes resources that eventually can yield students social and professional success. It exists in three forms: embodied; objectified; and institutionalized. Embodied cultural capital consists of schemes of appreciation and understanding—for example, a taste for certain music, art, literature, or an elite sport. We acquire embodied cultural capital through socialization. Objectified cultural capital, inhered in such things as books, artwork, or music collections, yields specialized cultural knowledge of the ways of life of the middle and upper classes; and finally, institutionalized cultural capital helps one attain professional success by attaining credentials and higher degrees. You display your embodied cultural capital, for example, if you read Bob and Nina Zagat's guides to fine restaurant dining and learn what urban professionals say about the latest epicurean delights of any major metropolitan areas. Cultural capital is in your possession if you are familiar with the names of symphony halls and know who's who in the classical music world, or visit the latest Picasso, Rembrandt, or Monet exhibits at the MOMA or the MFA and know what the acronyms stand for. Students who attend the Head of the Charles in New England in the fall and learn that an oarsman is to regatta as a sprinter is to relay race find cultural capital working for them academically, especially as they prepare for their SAT exams. And in the workplace, familiarity with Tiger Woods's and Ernie Els's handicaps could easily facilitate small talk and build rapport over lunch between a young manager and his supervisor.

While many poor, African American students have little familiarity with the dominant society's body of cultural know-how, they, nonetheless, possess cultural capital. But instead of using it for long-term economic gain, they use cultural capital to maintain group identity and distinctive cultural boundaries. Two types of capital are thus discussed here: *dominant* and *nondominant*.[2] Dominant cultural capital corresponds to Pierre Bourdieu's notion of cultural capital as a resource that can eventually yield some economic and social returns. It constitutes the cultural knowledge and skills of high-status racial, ethnic, and socioeconomic

groups. Nondominant cultural capital consists of a set of tastes, appreciations, and understandings, such as preferences for particular linguistic,
musical, and dress styles, and physical gestures used by lower status
groups members to gain "authentic" cultural status positions in their respective communities. The process that different social groups use to create internal cultural boundaries separating the "real" member from the
"not real" member defines what is authentic for that culture. Group
members construct self-conscious ways in which they use "natural" and
specified characteristics to signify affiliation (see, for example, Tuan 1999).
As groups socially construct what is authentic, their members require facility with myriad in-group cultural codes and signals or nondominant
cultural capital.

Dominant cultural capital provides students with access to certain
attitudes, styles, preferences, and tastes that enable their entry into high-
status social groups, organizations, or institutions (Lamont and Lareau
1988). It armors students with an awareness of how to "walk the walk" and
"talk the talk" of the economic, social, and political power brokers. Being
characterized as a "bright," "brilliant," or "smart" student depends on the
possession of sufficient cultural capital. Moreover, cultural capital has
been shown to positively influence high school grades, college attendance
and completion, and marital selection for both men and women (DiMaggio 1982; DiMaggio and Mohr 1985).

Conventional formulas for academic success prescribe that students
accrue dominant cultural capital—for instance, styles of speaking (Standard English) and interacting; knowledge of certain books, music, art,
and foods; and experience of foreign and nationwide travel. Cultural
capital also means being savvy about how to interact with teachers, apply
to competitive colleges and universities, and participate in extracurricular
activities, such as playing in the school orchestra or doing community
service, to enhance one's chances of getting into college. Not all students
are presumed to possess dominant cultural capital, however. Many researchers have described poor and ethnic minority students' and their
parents' apparent lack of dominant cultural capital (Lamont and Lareau
1988; Lewis 2003; Lareau and Horvat 1999). Such students are at a disadvantage because of limited access to this dominant cultural capital. For
example, many poor parents are unfamiliar with the benefits of advanced
placement and honors courses, possibly because of their own inexpe-

rience with the college admissions process. In contrast, in interracial schools, middle-class, White parents often jockey to get their children into prestigious academic tracks (Wells and Serna 1996). In these instances of social exclusion (often of poor, African American and Latino students), schools reinforce the class hierarchy by privileging and rewarding the cultural attributes of dominant social groups (Lareau and Horvat 1999).

While many social scientists acknowledge that cultural knowledge and its value can vary with social settings or fields, they usually do not apply the capital metaphor to African American and other nondominant social groups' cultural resources because, as David Swartz (1997) argues, the capital metaphor works less well for groups with little or no economic resources to invest. Bourdieu's seminal work on cultural capital was built on Marxist frameworks and focused primarily on the dominant and middle socioeconomic classes. I argue that not only is cultural capital specific to context (Hall 1992; Erikson 1996) but also that its effects extend beyond the sphere of the economic. The cultural styles, tastes, preferences, and symbols associated with the White middle class do not necessarily operate with the same effects in the communities I visited. For example, while the knowledge of fine wines and familiarity with the latest CD produced by either an internationally acclaimed jazz or opera diva might serve an African American person well at a cocktail party attended by professionals and managers, it would carry little weight in settings where soul food and R & B and hip-hop music were what mattered. To be accorded some respect as a culturally competent African American, that person would need to know what were the "flavors" (urban African American slang for "in," "popular," or "fashionable") and to be familiar with either the Delfonics, Chaka Khan, Al Green, India.Arie, DMX, Queen Latifah, Outkast, Lil' Kim, Bow Wow, and other acclaimed R & B and hip-hop singers. Many African American youth in poor, urban areas construct group identities, employ certain cultural markers, and in the process make it apparent that "where you are" (or to use the speech style of my in-formants—"where you at") determines what reigns as a high-status cultural symbol.

For many African American students, nondominant, or more specifically "black," cultural capital matters because it signifies in-group allegiance and preserves a sense of belonging.[3] Before I continue, first let me qualify my usage of "black cultural capital." Conceivably, many ethnic groups of the African Diaspora that are racially identified as Black possess their own ethno-racial cultural capital. Here I use the term black cultural capital to refer specifically to the resources, codes, and symbols of this particular group of low-income African American youth.[4] Strategically, these youth use their capital to signal their own cultural competences by adhering to certain speech codes, dress styles, music preferences, and gestures. Black cultural capital also helps to protect boundaries around racial and ethnic identity. Thus an African American student's cultural status depends upon the degree to which he or she can "do" or "act" blackness appropriately in his or her peers' eyes (Jackson 2001). If he or she either refuses or fails, the student might be perceived as "acting white."

Through their use of the expression "acting white" and through their descriptions of their school experiences, these students exposed ethnocentric biases in the concept of cultural capital. What happens when students attend schools with different taste cultures and preferences for other specialized cultural knowledge, use different linguistic codes, or even employ another cultural "tool kit?" How is the student who wears a hooded sweatshirt and baggy pants big enough to fall below his waist, whose speech is peppered with black vernacular dialect (like many in this study), and who loves to write poetry but has little interest in T. S. Eliot or Sylvia Plath, perceived in comparison to the clean-cut student who dresses in Eddie Bauer and Gap fashions, uses proper English with near flawless subject-verb agreement, and but who has never heard of Paul Laurence Dunbar, Nikki Giovanni or Amiri Baraka? Often we ignore the very real tensions between the symbolic, cultural boundaries established by racial and ethnic minority students—which have little to do with their desire for achievement, mobility, and success—and the cultural markers used by educators to mark intelligence and to categorize students. That poetry-loving student who comes with the baggy pants and the cool demeanor may get pegged as an angry and rebellious student with little interest in academic achievement because he challenges an English teacher's opinion, or because he shows minimal interest in the topics and authors chosen for his English class (Kochman 1981). And because he clings to his "black" styles, observers might say that he's resisting "acting white."

Because many do not fully grasp the functions and values of nondominant cultural capital, they mistake the utterances of "acting white" by Black students as an explicit rejection of school achievement. On the contrary, resistance to "acting white" for many African American students is about maintaining cultural identity, not about embracing or rejecting the dominant standards of achievement. As the students in the study schooled me on "acting white," they provided me with a deeper and more contextual understanding of its impact in their lives. They informed me that "acting white" and its attributes are suffused with cultural power and that resistance to "acting white" refers to their refusal to adhere to the cultural default setting in U.S. society, to what is seen as normative or "natural"—the generic American, white, middle-class patterns of speech and mannerisms, dress and physical appearance, and tastes in music and art forms.

For ten months, as I spoke with these youths, I listened and observed, searching for evidence of any serious anti-academic currents surging through their communities. What I found is that no one devalued high academic achievement, or cared if either they or their friends were smart, but they did care if their peers repudiated in-group cultural codes and knowledge. In what follows, I explain how the students create cultural boundaries to demarcate important differences not only between them and other groups but also among themselves. In the course of my interviews, I discovered that the students had developed sharp critiques of both the conspicuous and hidden cultural messages transmitted by school officials.

The students also revealed how schools collude in the perception of what is "white" through certain practices, especially ability grouping and tracking, both of which are notable for disproportional representation of students from various racial and ethnic groups. Students attached meanings to different types of classes within the school, much as they assigned meanings to different social groups and cultural practices. The underrepresentation of Black and Latino students in higher ability classes and their overrepresentation in low-ability classes (Oakes 1985; Slavin 1979; Mickelson 2001; Tyson, Darrity, and Castellino 2003) inclined students to mark courses by race and ethnicity. College preparatory, honors, and advanced placement classes have become known as classes for Asian and White kids. And just as adults choose neighborhoods because of their demographic and social compositions, students often select courses based on who is likely to be enrolled in them. But because college preparatory courses expose students to dominant cultural capital, the opportunity costs are high for students who do not enroll in them.

MATTERS OF AUTHENTICITY: THE FUNCTIONS OF "BLACK" CULTURAL CAPITAL

One of the instrumental purposes of black cultural capital is to signify ethnic authenticity. Authenticity is no simple matter. It entails deciding who is in or out, which is an especially slippery proposition when it comes to racial and ethnic identities. The process of authenticity requires signifiers or signs that someone is truly part of a group (Peterson 1997), and frequently, these students judged one another's authenticity, or rather, legitimacy as "real" Black persons. In some cases, physical features determined membership in the group. In other cases, these lay social constructionists indicated that group membership involved more than the biological, that it also included the capacity to exhibit and use in-group cultural knowledge.

"There's no difference between anybody. An Indian kid can act like he's Black. A White boy can act like he's Black. A Black boy can act like he's White. You know what I'm saying?" seventeen-year-old DeAndre Croix told me. As we sat discussing everything from teenage romance to interracial relations, this noncompliant believer cut through the conceptual quagmire and reduced the notion of "acting" race or ethnicity to a set of social performances and acts. DeAndre believed that people who differ in phenotype could easily imitate one another. Implying that race and ethnicity are not real and that biology is unimportant ("There's no difference between anybody"), he was certain that only socially marked behaviors set people apart and that cultural practices circumscribe identities, from Black to Indian (South Asian) to White. Yet the boundaries were not impermeable because "an Indian kid can act like he's Black; a White boy can act like he's Black; and a Black kid can act like he's White." Acting is merely a matter of performing, which DeAndre insinuated could include symbolic practices, such as language, gossip, dress, stories, rituals of daily life, and art.

If DeAndre and his peers sometimes said that race and ethnicity are mainly about cultural acts, then at other times their comments belied this belief. Sometimes, in discussing markers of racial identity, they essentialized race, challenging the notion of race as a social construction and declaring that some characteristics were "natural" traits of blackness. For example, Samurai Kitchens, a noncompliant believer, wrestled with seeing certain practices as essentially "black" as he described the situation of his neighbor, Jaime, a light-skinned Puerto Rican boy who lived in Samurai's housing complex where the majority of the teens and children were African American. Jaime loved rap music as much as any urban teenager coming of age in the late 1990s; and he used his taste for the music as a means to fit in with his neighborhood peers. Aware of how Jaime tried to use his knowledge of rap music to gain acceptance, Samurai determined that sharing similar musical tastes was not enough:

> A person that's not Black trying to be somebody they always
> wanted to be or a person that they look up to . . . like you
> might have Jaime, he might try to be like me or Michael.
> Yeah, he want to get everything I get, and I'm Black and he
> might listen to Spanish music. Once I start listening to DMX—
> everybody around the block listens to DMX—then he wants to
> listen to DMX, he don't even know what he's talking about. He
> just want to be Black, but not Black like the color, but the person
> that I am.

I asked Samurai why he thought that Jaime wanted to be like him, and he responded: "'Cause he's in the middle, because Black people are all around him. Like mostly, it's more Black people over there than Spanish . . . so he's in the middle and he's, like, surviving with all these Black people." Samurai not only associated "blackness" with certain cultural practices but he also recognized that its definition included phenotypic factors conventionally used to ascribe racial identity ("but not Black like the color"). He suggested that Jaime wants to "be Black" like his neighborhood peers because he had a taste for DMX, a renowned rap artist (who hails from Yonkers). Rather than accept the possibility that the music of a hometown native would appeal naturally to Jaime, or even recognize the contributions made by Latino musicians to hip-hop culture, Samurai construed DMX's rap music as an important cultural marker of his essential blackness.[5] Although Samurai granted that Jaime could understand and appreciate DMX, his fair skin and Puerto Rican heritage precluded "authentic" membership in the cultural sphere of his African American peers. Thus Samurai questioned Jaime's knowledge of hip-hop music ("he don't even know what he's talking about . . .") because Jaime is not Black. In this case, Jaime's love for DMX and other rap music did not gain him membership and acceptance in a Black peer group. And this example shows that black cultural capital, like dominant cultural capital, can be very ethno-specific. How race links to culture allows the holders of capital (the in-group and Samurai) to limit access to outsiders (Jaime). While Jaime could acquire cultural know-how in any field or social setting, dominant or non-dominant, he could not avoid the power of racial ascription, which limited his opportunity to be perceived as "authentic" by his Black peers. Further, when out-group members like Jaime "try too hard" to be like the in-group, they come across as "acting," as Samurai claimed.

African American youths of modest income are not alone in setting boundaries. Many social groups draw symbolic cultural boundaries between themselves and others (Lamont and Molnár 2002). Such symbolic cultural boundaries not only create groups but they also potentially produce inequality because they enable individuals to acquire status, monopolize resources, or ward off threats. Consider the following example: while a lottery winner can win millions, move into the wealthy class with his "new money," and can afford to purchase many goods and luxuries, he is not guaranteed acceptance into an invitation-only country club or social organization whose membership is determined by pedigree and family background. Setting boundaries allows people to develop a sense of group membership, argues sociologist Michéle Lamont (1992). Samurai revealed how he and his peers mark the boundaries of in-group membership in their schools and neighborhoods by limiting access to "authentic" Black peer groups. They created capital from a set of tastes, understandings, and appreciations for particular cultural styles, and these cultural boundaries were reinforced by ascribed identities, in this case the external classifications of race.

According to Pashan Kemp, one of the high-achieving students in the group and a cultural straddler, this creative process generated territorial feelings about who could legitimately embrace these cultural cues: "Yeah, among my friends, they always say . . . like, the way they like to dress baggy and stuff . . . and if they see . . . like a White person dressing baggy, they get really, really upset . . . like, they say, 'Oh they're trying to be 'black' and stuff.'" Pashan underscores the idea that black cultural capital functions in a market of cultural resources, codes, and differences. Pashan's friends seek to maintain this distinctiveness by guarding the boundaries of their cultural repertoire, and her friends express disfavor, as Samurai does toward Jaime, with any "outsiders" who encroach upon it, becoming territorial in the process. In-group/out-group distinctions are based not only on belonging to a collectivity or relating the self to the group but also on distinctions that allow individuals to categorize, compare, and maintain psychological uniqueness (Tajfel 1974; 1982).

Another function of black cultural capital is to create a coherent, positive self-image (or set of images) in the face of hardship or subjugation. Some cultural processes provide individuals with alternative ways to judge their self-worth and to maintain high self-esteem (Crocker and Major 1989). The latent psychosocial value of black cultural capital became apparent as Rayisha Simmons, a noncompliant believer, described to me how she and her friends negotiate the meanings of race:

> Being Black means to me to be special. We all, all of us is . . . special. As the years go by, we are strong. And each generation has an advantage. Each generation we get stronger, and people look down on us and we know they do. But we look at them and say, "Yeah. We're here." Well, me and my friends sit around and talk about being Black, we always talk about it. Always. We need to do this. This is how we were raised. If you live in Yonkers, you know the Abrams [High School] Steppers. They're Black. All of them. And I think it's twelve . . . yeah, it's twelve of them, it's eleven girls and one boy, and they're all Black. One may be half Spanish. . . . Well, it's a black thing . . . going to a fashion show [at her high school]. Well, I'm not going to say because it's black . . . it's not a black thing. If you want to make it a black thing, you can make it a black thing. And then there's this White kid [who wanted to try out for the group but did not because it was mostly Black]. But if they wanted to step why didn't they try out? Just because it's the color of your skin don't mean we're not going to let you in. We're not racist, because . . . but they're racist to us. We're in a racial school.

Rayisha used "stepping" (a syncopated foot-stomping dance used these days to forge a sense of solidarity in African American fraternities and sororities, especially on college campuses) as another marker of racial group identity ("If you want to make it a black thing, you can make it a black thing"). Her taste for stepping and participation in community events gave Rayisha feelings of strength and cultural solidarity. Her familiarity with the Abrams High School Steppers (a pseudonym) counted as a measure of cultural distinction; it elevated her sense of pride and "specialness." Moreover, Rayisha indicated that her and her peers' embrace of the Abrams Steppers signified in-group cohesion. I gathered, however, that Rayisha and her Black peers risked the perceptions that they were being exclusive. They were not unsusceptible to charges of racism—an irony for a group whose practices emerged in the context of historical racial disadvantage—especially since there was a White student who wanted to try out for the stepping team. Although I sensed that the lack of a warm reception dissuaded this student, Rayisha strongly proclaimed that she and her peers were "not racist" and did not exclude others because of the color of their skin.

Among the students, being Black did not automatically make a peer an "authentic" member in good racial standing (Fordham 1988). A peer whose cultural tastes fell outside the boundaries of constructed blackness was charged with "acting white." Adrienne Ingram, a bright and confident fifteen-year-old cultural mainstreamer, was sanctioned for her refusal to embrace the speech codes of fellow Black peers. She told me boys at school called her "White girl":

> Yep, like, some boys in school expect me to speak Ebonics or whatever, so they call me a "White girl." They like, "Come here, White girl," cause of the way I talk. I tell them I'm not a thug. I go to English class; this is the way I talk. This is my grammar. I'm not going to sit here and make myself look stupid talking about some "What up, yo." That's not English! So you do get picked on if you speak a certain way or you act a certain way. I know some of the boys say "White girl" just because of the way I talk. And I don't see how you can distinguish between a Black person and a White person talking because of the way they talk. They're just talking. A Black person has to speak stupid in order for you to know that they're Black?

Adrienne believed that language is power and that fluency in Standard English was beneficial to her, particularly when she associated it with "being intelligent." Refusing to uphold her peers' cultural prescriptions of blackness, she criticized their speech styles. She had a tougher time, though, among some schoolmates because she rejected styles that they valued and that they used as code for racial authenticity. Adrienne was willing to acculturate, while her peers were not. She subscribed to beliefs that so-called black English (lately referred to as Ebonics, though linguists classify it as a variant of black vernacular dialect) was "stupid." While her acculturative stance made her less likely to be perceived as unintelligent, her peers marked the boundaries between "black" and "white." They claimed that she "talked white" and acted "stuck up." I witnessed this tension once when I invited Adrienne to participate in a group interview with other girls from her neighborhood. She declined because she felt that her relations and standing with them were not good. Later, the other girls told me that they believed Adrienne behaved like an outsider, acting as if she "were different and better than [they]."

Transgressing cultural boundaries could even affect romantic attractions. Sixteen-year-old Wilson Norris, a noncompliant believer who revealed to me his fondness for poetry and girls, frowned as he described a girl very much like Adrienne, whom he perceived as "talking white," and he admitted that he would not be attracted to the girl because he "would think [that] something would be wrong with her." Wilson's views about the girl who "talked white" were consistent with the views of Joyelle, who said that she "would think that something would be wrong" with her Black friends if they came to school listening to Beethoven.

Whereas a taste for Beethoven would function as cultural capital among certain dominant groups, Joyelle, a noncompliant believer, suggested that a different kind of musical taste is necessary for in-group members to possess black cultural capital. She hinted that those Black "young people" who did not share her taste for rap music had something "wrong with them," particularly since they would be emulating the "regular people." I was struck by her use of "regular," and on a few occasions, the students normalized the cultural experiences of White youth and adults, unconsciously equating behaviors that they associated with Whites with normality.

Joyelle's comments also draw attention to the issues of age and generation, which influence what gets counted as embodied (i.e., taste) and objectified (e.g., music, books, arts) forms of cultural capital. For example, when I urged them to tell me about their musical tastes, Joyelle and her friends switched roles on me. In a bold and confident tone, her friend Melanie Smith questioned me: "I bet you like jazz, don't you?" With that assumption, Melanie signaled to me that age, and even class, separated us. Yet at the same time she chose a musical genre that she thought would correspond to my racial background. Similarly, in Joyelle's view, a Beethoven aficionado not only possesses musical tastes outside the cultural boundaries that she and her peers set but also is considerably older. Young Black people, according to Joyelle, distinguished themselves from the "regular" [White] and the older [both Black and White].

"IT'S WHERE YOU AT": CULTURAL CAPITAL AND CONTEXT

Out of high school and working a part-time job to help her mother support her younger brother and sister, Loretta Lincoln at age nineteen strategically negotiated various cultural spheres: her community, family, and peer group. She made use of both dominant and black cultural capital. Like many with experience in the job world, Loretta understood "proper" decorum in the workplace. She was also familiar with the roles of dominant cultural capital and the politics of race in U.S. society. Aware how widespread Anglo-conformity was, she admitted that she spoke both "black" and "white." In other words, she could codeswitch:

> [I]f I'm talking to my friend or father, [I say], like, "Yo, whasup, whatever." And when I call my job, I have a different attitude toward the whole situation, you know. I don't talk with slang. I make sure everything is correct. But I don't know. Me personally, I think . . . for a Black person to "act white," like when he arrives [at home] I think he don't have to do that. But, like, even if he's in school, he can act like that in a school. Maybe it'll get him somewhere. You know? And when he go out or whatever, he don't have . . . I don't know . . . they don't have to act like that. You can just be yourself. But there is, it is going to be times in your life where you are going to have to put on a little act, or a little show to get the extra budge or whatever, you know.

Believing that black slang would compromise her work evaluation, Loretta made sure that "everything [was] correct." But as she moved from work to home, her preferred linguistic style changed. She felt strongly that in personal social spaces a "Black person" does not have to employ the same linguistic codes as those used at work. A different linguistic currency can operate in personal spaces. According to Loretta, if the pressure to use the cultural codes prevalent at work (or to "act white") presented itself either at home or in the community, then it prevented the culturally multifaceted Black person from being fully herself. Loretta was a cultural straddler.

Moesha, who lived about a quarter of a mile away from Loretta, was fresh out of high school with a few community college courses under her belt. She also worked to navigate the worlds of work, school, peers, and family. Having recently entered the workforce, Moesha, like Adrienne, the fifteen-year-old the boys called "White girl," perceived that language is power and that Standard English is used to signal intelligence.[6] "See I know people who can act ignorant as anything, but they are also smart, and they can also talk in an intelligent way. It's just that when you talk with your friends, you talk in a certain way, or when you're at work or wherever you're at, you have to act intelligent," she claimed. But unlike Adrienne, a cultural mainstreamer, Moesha was an a cultural straddler, and she contested any stereotypical associations of black vernacular with ignorance. "We [African Americans] are not ignorant; there are just certain ways that we talk to each other. It might not seem right, but that doesn't mean we're dumb," she said. Moesha had accepted the idea that to be socioeconomically mobile, she needed to speak Standard English. At the same time, she valued the speech codes that she shared with Black friends and family, which for her fostered community and group cohesion. Thus, she chose to draw on her familiarity with black speech codes to signify her authenticity—currency that allowed her to comfortably invoke the collective "we" in her characterization of the African American community.

Moesha and other cultural straddlers were aware of tensions between their dominant and black cultural capital. Many of these tensions stemmed from questions about their blackness when they employed dominant speech codes within social spaces regulated by their peers. Occasionally, they did not display their black cultural currency and, consequently, peers teased them for "acting white" or "acting other." For example, Bettina Shanks, pregnant and just a few weeks from delivery, proudly affirmed the value of "good English" and understood it as a form of dominant cultural capital that could be exchanged for mobility. Intending to become a nurse, Bettina had completed a few semesters at a local college in New York before getting pregnant at age nineteen. Provided that the lack of financial resources to both take care of her baby and to attend college did not derail her academic plans, Bettina had every intention of moving up the proverbial economic ladder. Bettina's academic trajectory was an unconventional one, however. By all indicators, she underachieved in high school. In and out of juvenile detention, she made it to the tenth grade but dropped out after repeating it a few times. "I didn't have a lot of support," she explained. "I didn't have my mother to love me the way I wanted her to, and I [had so much resentment]. So, I would go back and forth into the system [juvenile detention] until I was sixteen. I didn't realize how much my mother was there for me, though." Attributing her poor school performance to parent-child conflicts and problems, Bettina left school and eventually got her GED. Then she got back on track and enrolled in college. Now, aware of what socioeconomic mobility would require, Bettina clung to the promise of her grandmother, who said that she would baby-sit in the fall so that her granddaughter could return to college. Bettina's formula for success included speaking Standard English, though she recognized the value of having dual linguistic capital. She seldom used her "black" speech codes, however, and as a result, her friends teased her and said that she talked "white." When I asked her to tell me why her friends teased her, she said: "Because I'm different. I mean there are times when I know how to have fun. I know how to relax. I know how to have fun. But there's also times when if I know I'm going to the doctors, or if I have to go to a preliminary meeting about this or that, I know how to talk. I know how to dress, and I know how to act."

Knowing "how to have fun" and to "talk black," Bettina revealed that she could codeswitch and decipher which "act" was appropriate, based on context. Both Bettina and Moesha represented the cultural straddlers who willingly moved back and forth between their uses of "black" and dominant linguistic capital. But Bettina was more likely to privilege Standard English over the linguistic codes of her peers, making her "different," and causing her friends to tease her. Bettina believed that the benefits of dominant cultural capital outweighed the rewards of her peers' full acceptance of her as an authentic Black person.

Bettina and Moesha, both high school graduates and now college students, demonstrated that cultural straddling works for them just as it works for many upwardly mobile African Americans who work daily in professional, white-collar spaces. Inside the school or at the office, youths like Loretta, Moesha, and Bettina read the different cultural codes and exchanged their own "black" capital for dominant forms to signal "intelligence" and similarity to the people in charge who might have devalued their black cultural capital. Once they returned home, however, many exchanged their dominant capital for their black capital and their communities' acceptance of them as culturally competent and authentically black.

The cultural straddlers differ from those characterized by Orlando Patterson (1998) as "cultural appropriators"—acculturative and upwardly mobile racial and ethnic minorities who share cultural tastes with their White, middle-class counterparts and choose acculturation over ethnic distinction. Patterson argues that cultural appropriation is the highest form of rebellion for oppressed and marginalized groups. In this sense, cultural appropriation functions like the old dictum: "learn the master's tools to undo his house." Oppressed and marginalized peoples can acculturate and embrace the ideological practices of dominant groups, while "backstage" they develop forms of protest and rebellion (Scott 1985). Citing great Black national and international leaders and thinkers such as Frederick Douglass, W. E. B. Du Bois, and Frantz Fanon, Patterson asks, "What better role model of an autonomous group is there than that of a ruling elite? And what better way to acquire an elite's sense of purpose and moral responsibility, its aristocratic belief that the world is manipulable, than simply to enculturate its style" (1998, 103)?

Cultural straddlers, like Patterson's cultural appropriators, subscribe to formulas of success determined by dominant or elite groups. Hence, they use dominant cultural capital to gain them mobility and better life chances, or academic or economic opportunities. Presumably their dominant cultural capital could "get them somewhere" (although given these students' poverty and extremely limited resources, the odds are lower). But cultural straddlers also show that the acquisition of black cultural capital is not equivalent to a rejection of commonly shared values about social, economic, or educational attainment. Their black cultural capital has both instrumental and expressive purposes. They lean on it to procure legitimacy among their racial peers, to signal their own allegiance to their cultural backgrounds and heritages, and to maintain a double consciousness (Du Bois 1903), an awareness of their varied social positions and their senses of purpose in the world.

Many students possessed some modicum of dominant cultural capital. Others had more nondominant cultural capital. Much of my understanding of how the African American students in this study constructed their identities and created capital from diverse social resources came from the cultural straddlers and the noncompliant believers. The cultural straddlers gave credence to their own black capital while also participating in the dominant game of cultural production. Though not immune to being teased for "acting white," cultural straddlers balanced their cultural practices, displaying knowledge and facility with "white" styles and with the styles they shared with their peers. They showed great ability to calculate which cultural capital provided them with the greatest returns in various contexts. In contrast, the cultural mainstreamers invested primarily in dominant cultural capital. They were the most susceptible to the charges of "acting white," especially since they often repudiated their peers' cultural ways and chose to emulate perceived "white" styles.

The noncompliant believers' negotiation of cultural currencies differed significantly from those of the cultural straddlers and the cultural mainstreamers. Noncompliant believers had the least social worries about sanctions for "acting white," especially since they framed their racial and ethnic selves as "keepin' it real" and asserting the distinctiveness of their own practices. Yet these students, not surprisingly, who either did not possess much dominant cultural capital or who were aware of its buying power but stressed the worthiness of black cultural symbols, experienced the most conflict. By resisting and rebelling, they did not conform to their teachers' expectations about cultural presentations, which as I will discuss in the next section placed them at risk for negative evaluations and less engagement in school. Consequently, they experienced school as a sorting and selecting machine, penalizing those with different cultural attributes.

THE HIERARCHY OF CULTURAL MEANINGS WITHIN SCHOOLS AND ITS OUTCOMES

I opened this chapter with an epigraph from the work of sociologist Mark Gould (1999). Its relevance becomes apparent as we come to understand the connections between social factors like racial and ethnic identity and processes like assimilation and mobility. According to Gould, most deficiencies in performance among racial minorities stem not from their cultural attributes but from the ways in which these attributes are processed in dominant organizations. And these organizations include our nation's schools. Although racial and ethnic minority students comprise the majority in most large urban school districts, we still expect them to comport themselves according to the cultural mandates of white, mainstream society. "One can hardly pursue success in a world where the accepted skills, style and informal know-how are unfamiliar," writes Ann Swidler (1986). Moreover, one can hardly succeed fully in a place where one's cultural tastes are not welcomed or appreciated.

Noncompliant believers in education disrupt mainstream ideas about what is proper and what is not. Their stories, profiles, and commentaries compel us to reconsider how we distribute cultural power and to note who chooses and who loses in a democratic society that espouses pluralism. The persistence of their various ethno-specific cultural codes and meanings highlights the tensions between the desire for inclusion in dominant social institutions, or structural assimilation, and the desire for cultural distinction, or nonacculturation. And contemporary social scientists and educators must wrestle with these tensions in their analyses of the incorporation of contemporary minority youth within schools and contemporary U.S. society. Cultural assimilation is not necessarily the youths' ultimate goal or their means to the ends of success. Rather, because of their ethno-racial ideologies, noncompliant believers valorize their backgrounds and cultures, particularly as they develop an awareness of how racial difference works in U.S. society.

Consider the following example, which is a composite of real events that I have either witnessed or heard about over the years: Lawrence is a twenty-four-year-old Black male from a poor neighborhood in south central Los Angeles whose parents are strong advocates of quality education and who, with the help of some financial aid, sent him to private schools. Lawrence earned a bachelor's degree from a highly selective university and ultimately enrolled in graduate school at a competitive university. While he achieved academically, he encountered a fair share of prejudice due to his cultural presentation of self. Much to the chagrin of some of his middle- and upper-class professors, Lawrence, though quiet, studious, and respectful, has brought to his elite, predominately white graduate school a style of baggy jeans and oversized sweatshirts, popular among urban Black youth, as well as a tough or "hard" demeanor that includes limited eye contact with his professors. His style of dress and mannerisms are akin to what ethnographer Elijah Anderson (1994) has described as poor and working-class Black youths' "codes of the street." While his professors approve of his academic ability, Lawrence's performance evaluations have been influenced by their opinions of his self-presentation. His style contrasts with that of other Black students in the graduate program, who consciously acculturate and display dominant cultural capital in their dress, their choice of cultural events to attend and discuss, and the confident, deferential ways in which they approach and work with faculty. Unlike them, Lawrence is "keepin' it real"—being true to his tastes with no "acts" in his mind (though the other Black students in the program also view their behaviors as being "real").

Lawrence has already demonstrated his belief that education and strong academic effort matter to his upward mobility, thus revealing his allegiance to dominant achievement ideology. But he is not a young man who carries himself in a way that makes his professors comfortable. He does not exude approachability; he possesses an aura of formidability. And Lawrence's evaluators are likely to judge him not only on his intellectual acumen but also on how well he conforms to their cultural expectations. Their impressions of him will probably influence how they write about or referee for him as he contends for competitive fellowships and jobs. There are many Lawrences in the schools of urban America, and many are destined to failure because they get evaluated as problems, deviants, threats, and miscreants. Black and dominant cultural capitals are not mutually exclusive, and certainly some dominant capital originated in black cultures.[7] But black cultural capital does not yield students high academic marks, get them into college, or even acquire them jobs.

Many of the students I interviewed shared Lawrence's cultural frame of reference, and many aimed high like him, though their limited economic and social capital (see chapter 5) would preclude them from entering the hallowed halls of some of the nation's most elite schools. Rather than dismiss their reasons for their lack of school engagement, I listened carefully to these students' testimonies. Many reported that life in school is not supportive and affirmative. They shared stories of problematic relationships with teachers who seemed to have low expectations of them and their classmates. Even one cultural straddler who had graduated from high school characterized educator-student interactions as less than satisfactory. Nina Lisandro, trying to determine how to pay for college, described the cultural milieu in her high school classrooms:

> Like, I say, . . . the way you present yourself to someone, that's the approach that they take upon you. And some Black kids, you know, when they go to school, the first thing the teacher looks at is how you present yourself. So you come to school with the baggy pants and hat to the back, with the radio, they look at you and be like, "I'm not going to waste my time." But they see the other, like, you know, not the whole [person] White or Black, but when they see another fellow, or male or female, you know, quiet, and then that's the one they'll spend more time with. But not knowing that person came with the baggy pants, could be more intelligent, you know, have more intellectuals [sic] than a quiet person.

Nina refers to two relevant cues that she felt teachers notice: dress and demeanor. Through the lens of race and culture, Nina perceived that teachers evaluated students as deficient based on their own personal standards of cultural decorum, as well as those of the school's administration.

Confirming Nina's take on teachers' expectations, Moesha, a cultural straddler I introduced earlier, talked at length about the difficulties that noncompliant believers had with teachers:

> There were, like, certain teachers, they would give you attitude for no reason. And you're, like, I didn't do anything. But for me, it was only, like, for certain friends that I had because certain of my friends were outspoken, and me, I was very passive. I'd let whoever say whatever. And they [her friends] weren't like that. I guess . . . for my friends, I didn't like the way that the teacher would talk to them. I had friends that . . . were very smart. They were very, very smart, and the teachers think that because they are a certain way, and they act a certain way, that they are not smart. And that's not true. They are. They are very smart. It's important that you learn about people. Even if you don't know, you know, like, certain football players, you think that they're dumb, but when you start talking to people, you realize, "Oh, they're bright."

Moesha discussed the problems of her friends and not herself because she had learned how to circumvent certain problems by conforming and by understanding what practices warranted teachers' high regard. Yet she was aware that the interactional styles valued by teachers often led them to ignore very intelligent students, if those students either critiqued or resisted the intellectual and political positions of schooling (Fine 1991; Fordham 1993). Invoking the "dumb jock" stereotype as an example of unfairness, Moesha called attention to how race and culture can function similarly and cause teachers to underestimate the intelligence and academic potential of assertive or nonpassive Black students.

Other behaviors subject to sanctions by teachers and officials included loud verbal play, a communicative style that might easily be misunderstood by an outsider unfamiliar with it.[8] Frequently, students volleyed quick-witted quips in verbal duels with each other, and these duels would carry over into the classroom—a point that several of my female informants shared with me. Rayisha, a seventeen-year-old high school junior and a self-reported big talker in class, discussed how her grades suffered because her teachers sanctioned her for talkativeness in class. In addition to "three [unexcused] absences," Rayisha admitted that her garrulous nature created both academic and disciplinary problems. She was unafraid of telling a teacher what she felt and told me how she tried to convince one classmate "to stand up for herself" and challenge a teacher about a grade. Without a doubt, Rayisha needed guidance about how to effectively engage with teachers and not compromise her educational performance by using a mode of communication that the teacher might interpret as inappropriate. At the same time, she needed more teachers like her favorite, Mrs. Thompson, whom Rayisha described as an authoritative teacher who demonstrated her "care" for her students with faith in their abilities and a large dose of "tough love." Rayisha believed that Mrs. Thompson, unlike several of her other teachers, did not dismiss her as an intransigent student with limited academic potential. Mrs. Thompson was one of the teachers whom Gloria Ladsen-Billings (1994) refers to as the "dream keepers" because they have an understanding of both the students' cultural orientations and their abilities and because they keep these students on a steady path of achievement.

Ironically, in the upper echelon of academic classes in American elementary and secondary schools, students are encouraged to be assertive and critical, though Samuel Bowles and Herbert Gintis (1976) have argued that the marginalized student, particularly if from a low-income and working-class background, is more likely to be placed in either vocational or low-track classes where conformity, passiveness, and deference to authority are strictly enforced. In fact, data from the National Center of Educational Statistics confirms that Black and Latino students are disproportionately underrepresented in advanced academic classes and overrepresented in vocational and general education tracks (National Center on Education Statistics 2003a; 2003b).[9] Rayisha was enrolled in a general education track, and as she revealed, her assertiveness was more likely to earn her reprimands than positive evaluations from teachers.

Earlier Nina and Moesha offered firsthand observations of social processes that other research corroborates. As gatekeepers, teachers enforce a stratified system, rewarding those students who embrace the "right" cultural signals, habits, and styles (Farkas et al. 1990; Lamont and Lareau 1988; Swidler 1986). While they reward many students for conformity and obedience (Bowles and Gintis 1976), these traits are insufficient for the attainment of better grades. Indeed, Karen Gallas (1998) found that silence can dampen the achievement of some students, particularly female students. One of the few power resources that youths possess is their voice. Often marginalized persons living in a democracy find that their only sources of power and rebellion, challenge and critique, reside within their mouths and bodies (Scott 1985). Similarly, students nested in layers of subordination—namely, race, class, and age—find liberation in speech. By speaking out, they avoid invisibility from peers, teachers, and other adults. These behaviors, however, often get cast in a narrative of badness (Ferguson 2000). Talkativeness and sassiness (often identified as problem behavior among Black students) do not preclude a mastery of the cognitive skills required to perform satisfactorily in modern schools.[10] However, if these students do not conform to cultural expectations, they are likely to be punished, and perhaps even expelled. Or they may drop out after continual conflicts with school authorities (Fine 1991).

A year after I had completed my interviews, *The New York Times* reported that the Yonkers School District had recognized the cultural gaps between its students and teachers (Brenner 1998). There was a large racial and ethnic mismatch between students and teachers in the district; 82

percent of the teachers were White, while 70 percent of the students were classified as racial and ethnic minorities, mainly Black and Latino.[11] To ameliorate the problem, the district had ordered its teachers to take part in a summer program designed to help them recognize the different learning styles and backgrounds of multicultural student bodies.

Citing cultural mismatches of this sort does not imply that racial and ethnic matching between students and teachers would rectify social and academic problems. Many African American and Latino teachers also do not know enough about how culture influences achievement and evaluation to effectively teach the children whom I came to know. As Paula, a young Black teacher enrolled in a program to help teachers understand, manage, and teach difficult students, noted in an interview with researchers: "Black teachers who have been in different programs . . . haven't got this cultural awareness and I know this because they're so negative. . . . A lot of them aren't culturally sensitive to their own culture" (as quoted in Ferguson 1998). Most likely, Paula fails to differentiate between the teachers' racial or ethnic background and their social class. Teachers' own social origins exercise a strong influence on how they respond to students. And their class position might matter, in addition to their professional competence. In a survey of 825 Black and White elementary school teachers from varied socioeconomic classes, Karl Alexander, Doris Entwisle, and Maxine Thompson (1987) found that both Black and White teachers from high socioeconomic classes or advantaged social origins evaluated Black students significantly more negatively than White students on both noncognitive and cognitive factors. Among teachers from low socioeconomic origins, race did not matter in their evaluations. In other words, class, though inextricably linked to race, also matters in spaces of instruction.

The hierarchy of cultural meanings within schools, both implicit and explicit, has serious consequences. Students' discernment of the dissonance between their home and school cultures astonished me. Sharply aware of the structural and cultural imbalances in their schools, students in this study perceived that teachers did not expect much of them, and some met those low expectations, further widening the gap between themselves and other groups of students. "Some teachers . . . you show up, you get a pass," claimed noncompliant believer Rayisha. Continuing, she said:, "[T]hey don't encourage you. Come to their class, come to their class. Don't do no work all the time. Give a test. Pass the test with a grade of sixty-five. Get, like, let's just say you have four tests during the year, pass them with a sixty-five. Then you get that sixty-five already. How come you pass with a seventy or a seventy-five? That makes it easy, you know, for certain kids." "But is that what most people do? That's all you have to do?" I asked. "Yeah," Rayisha responded, "and you know . . . the most people that does that is the predominantly Blacks, the Black kids." I asked Rayisha why weren't Black kids engaged in school, and what made it so hard. "You can't be comfortable in school," she said, "can't do . . . okay, school is supposed to be for education. You're supposed to learn. You can't learn if you're in an environment that's not fun. If you're going to school and it's boring to you and the teachers is just, 'Aaaahh, 1867 . . . and this and that.' That makes it boring. You got to have a teacher that inspires you, that lifts your spirit up, makes you want to get up and go to school. And you got to have parents that have that discipline for the kids. Get up and go to school. You don't get up, you don't go to school, your punishment is you don't get no money. You don't get no Jordans [Nike brand shoes]. You don't get no haircut. You don't get no clothes. You got to have parents like that."

Rayisha exposes something that I became aware of while attending public high school in the 1980s. Teachers are among the lowest paid of professionals—despite their influence on millions of lives—and are often as uninspired as their students. To make it easy on themselves, some teachers merely "child-sit," handing out passing grades if a student simply shows up for class—although current federal and state mandates for testing and accountability may possibly effect change and deter teacher apathy (Richey and Petretti 2002). Many burn out, especially if they are not accustomed to the challenges of teaching in urban public schools where students come to school afflicted by poverty, racism, family crises, unemployment, and often homelessness (Freeman, Brookhart, and Loadman 1999). Some might argue that politicians, administrators, parents, and students have placed too much responsibility on teachers, expanding the notion of a "teacher" or "educator." Not only are these underpaid civil servants expected to produce literate populations but they are also asked to serve as entertainers, child psychologists, surrogate parents, and confidants.

Meanwhile, Rayisha, like many students, operates on the margins, the cusp between success and failure. These students do just enough to proceed from class to class and to progress from grade to grade. The critical commentary provided here elucidates how these teenagers perceive their teachers—those individuals who have been charged with the massive task of shaping minds and lives. Rayisha claimed that teachers need to discern how to "inspire" students, how to teach them in creative ways, and how not to bog themselves down in ineffective pedagogy and repetitious facts and classroom exercises. Finally, not only does Rayisha target teachers and their roles in student engagement but she also criticizes parents who are disengaged from their children's schooling. Parental discipline, she said, was a key factor in keeping Black students like her engaged in school.

Rayisha's comments suggests that teachers, schools, and parents have some distance to travel before schools become effective educators of students from a wide variety of cultures. Students of all backgrounds should be required to master the primary body of knowledge, though they may arrive in the classroom with different styles of learning (see also Delpit 1995). For this reason, it is incumbent for schools to have teaching staff skilled in negotiating multiple styles while simultaneously imparting the skills, codes, and knowledge that students need to be successful. Meanwhile, students are telling us why they feel detached from the educational material that can connect them to credentials and to some form of higher social attainment. In the campaign to widen standard education's appeal and to diminish the widely documented achievement gap, educators, researchers, and policymakers must consider the interplay between multiple forms of knowledge and cultural repertoires. Quite possibly, until educators grasp the value and functions of black and other nondominant forms of cultural capital, they will continue to have difficulty in engaging many African American students. The failure to acknowledge black cultural capital signifies to many of these students a disavowal of their cultural backgrounds, their collective identities, and the value of their cultural practices. They link their own self-importance to this capital and expect to find some place for it within the social spaces they inhabit, whether at home, in their neighborhoods, or in their schools.

WHAT'S SCHOOL GOT TO DO WITH IT? TRACKING, IDENTITY, AND "ACTING WHITE"

This business of cultural capital leads to the subject of tracking—an institutional practice that stratifies students by ability and by race and ethnicity, whether unintentionally or not (Oakes 1985; Mickelson 2001). Students find much meaning in the way classrooms are structured, especially in multiracial schools. These schools send implicit messages to many poor Black and Latino students when the ability grouping is highly correlated to racial and ethnic background. In multiracial and multiethnic schools, certain courses can become known as classes for Black kids, White kids, or Asian kids. If in integrated schools, White students occupy the top of the achievement hierarchy, then many African American and Latino students may tend to perceive that top as the "white" niche and perhaps even avoid it as it makes them feel isolated and invisible.

Thirteen-year-old Jeremy dreaded attending a new high school and entering the International Baccalaureate (IB) Program, which includes classes given for college credit, because his mostly Black friends would be attending the "regular" high school. Though he protested, his mother insisted that he attend the school with the IB program. Yet Jeremy did not want to be isolated in a classroom where very few students, if any, looked like him. The students enrolled in higher tracks were likely to be different from him. He was probably correct in his assessment. Statistics from the *Digest of Education Statistics* in 1997, the year before Jeremy enrolled in the IB program, revealed that 51 percent of Asian, 36 percent of Black, 31 percent of Latino, 23 percent of Native American, and 46 percent of White high school seniors were enrolled in college preparatory classes. These statistics show that, on average, at least half of Asian and White students in a particular school were likely to be in the high tracked classes, while Black, Latino, and Native American students were more likely to be in the general tracks.

Furthermore, according to this study, those few Black and Latino students enrolled in either advanced placement, gifted, or honors courses were isolated from their co-ethnic peers. Two such students include fourteen-year-old Michael Jones and high school senior Rosaria Lopez (introduced in chapter 1) who were the exceptions in their classes, each being either the only student or one of few students of color. "Like in my English class, there is only one African American kid and a few more Hispanics," Rosaria told me. When I asked Michael if he was teased for being smart and doing well in school, he told me, "No," and that the White kids were most likely to be called "brainiacs" because "they're mostly the people who are in honors [classes]."

Research shows that when racial and ethnic minority students are enrolled in college preparatory classes and do well, they are more likely to speak and be literate in Standard American English and to cultivate an appreciation for classic Western (Anglo) literature, music, and art associated with middle-class groups and professionals (Hemmings 1996). These college preparatory classes expose students to forms of dominant cultural capital and teacher expectations. Compared to her brother Alberto's high-school experience, Alma Martinez, a college sophomore at Manhattan College, described her time in high school very differently: "Most of my classes in high school were honors classes, and there was a different crowd there than with those kids who were in more comprehensive classes [noncollege prep]." Her brother Alberto, though college-bound—according to Alma because of both of his sisters' influences and his mother's expectation—said he had trouble with teachers believing that he was a drug dealer because of how he dressed.

The cultural isolation of those few Black and Latino students enrolled in advanced classes, whose primary social interactions at school are with their White classmates, predisposes them to being viewed as "acting white." Not only would Black and Latino students be "acting white" if they socialized with Whites *only* but also White students would be branded as "acting black" or "acting "Spanish"" if their primary peer associations were Black or Latino. Maxwell, a noncompliant believer, stated dryly, "There are some 'White' boys. They don't want to be with no Black kids. They rather hang with some Indians or White boys or Puerto Ricans, kids like that." For Maxwell, when peers only socialized with kids from other racial and ethnic groups and not their own, it signified a rejection of their backgrounds, of their folks. He called them "White boys," much as some once used epithets such as "white-washed" to express disapproval of those who appeared to have rejected their racial or ethnic communities (Cose 1993; Landry 1987; Benjamin 1991).

Other accounts support the connection between tracking and the phenomenon of "acting white." In a study of eleven elementary, middle, and high schools in North Carolina, Tyson, Darity, and Castellino (2003) found that notions of "acting white" emerged only in schools with a disproportionate representation of minority *and* low-income students in rigorous courses and programs. Moreover, a few years after I completed my fieldwork in Yonkers, I read with great interest a statement by Sierre

Monk, granddaughter of the jazz musician Thelonious Monk, to *New York Times* reporter Tamar Lewin (2000): "A lot of people think of the Black kids in the top classes, the ones who don't hang out with a lot of African Americans, as the 'white' Black kids." Sierre was on to something: ability grouping in multiracial and multiethnic schools stratifies not only by academic performance but also by race and ethnicity. Those likely to face social consequences are the token African American and Latino students in the advanced classes who seek friendships and share cultural tastes primarily with White classmates.

Thus, the consequences of tracking are both academic and social. As an institutional practice, it not only perpetuates school inequality (Hallinan and Sorensen 1983; Oakes 1985; Lucas 1999) but it also reinforces racial and ethnic boundaries and discourages students like Jeremy from enrolling in upper-echelon classes where he might be the only Black kid in his class. Yet the IB program would expose Jeremy to material that would only benefit his educational career, while generally, lower-tracked students do worse in school, have higher rates of misconduct and truancy, and are less likely to complete college (Hallinan 1988). Lower-tracked students are also more likely to become disengaged from learning processes. Hence an unintended consequence of tracking is likely to be the discouragement of Black and Latino students from wanting to be placed in those courses that would prepare them to realize their aspirations for college and professional careers. Such classes are perceived as de facto ethnically and racially segregated, and certain groups of students feel compelled "to stay on their side of the track," an expression that summons memories of the days before school integration.

Both educators and students have a responsibility to address how culture affects academic achievement. When dominant social groups define and circumscribe what is appropriate for success and achievement, the choices made by low-income African American and Latino youths can have negative academic consequences. It should be a matter of personal choice whether individuals listen to hip-hop music or soft rock, dress in FUBU or L.L. Bean, or maintain mixed- or same-group peer associations. Certain ethno-specific cultural resources can function as nondominant capital and serve a social and cultural function. These sorts of cultural codes do not intrinsically determine achievement and mobility. Yet many of these students, especially the noncompliant believers, need help in negotiating and expanding their ideas and presentations of self, and ultimately in balancing different social "acts." Both students and schools could benefit from an opening up of society's understanding of culture and capital. Noncompliant believers require some guidance in how to maintain multiple cultural competencies in order to facilitate cross-cultural interactions. Even cultural mainstreamers and cultural straddlers require support, though the latter group might do it relatively better already. If educators recognized the values of different students' cultural repertoires and the impressions that students get from the appearances of racialized forms of tracking, and they managed to diminish student disengagement through improved practices, then the cultural mainstreamers and cultural straddlers would not have to worry about being the only or one of the few brown faces in their classes, if not the only one, and they could avoid being teased for "acting white." And schools would avoid reproducing the dynamics that the stratified, unequal tracking structures create. If we can figure out how to acknowledge and affirm the multiple capitals that exist while avoiding the structuring of achievement by race and ethnicity, then we could be one step closer increasing these students' attachment and engagement in school.

Girls' just smarter than boys. Girls are smarter in class

work, but not streetwise. They fight over stupid stuff. Boys

are, like, smarter than that. Only thing you ain't gon' do is

let somebody play you, or, like, put their hands on you.

—seventeen-year-old Maxwell Tucker

BETWEEN A "SOFT" AND A "HARD" PLACE

Gender, Ethnicity, and Culture in the School and at Home

Soon-to-be high-school graduate Maxwell Tucker, speaking rather point-edly and anecdotally as he reflected on his school experiences with me one evening at his home, presented a picture of his high-school world that was consistent with reports from scholars, researchers, and journalists. Girls are outperforming boys in the classroom (Jacobs 1996; Lewin 1998; Mickelson 1989). Whether they are actually smarter remains to be seen; there are no proven differences in intelligence between the sexes. Still, re-search shows that throughout their scholastic careers, girls perform better in subjects that require verbal competence. Although studies show that boys do better than girls in math and science (Catsambis 1994; Maccoby and Jacklin 1974; Nowell and Hedges 1998; Stevenson and Newman 1986), overall, girls have higher grade point averages and college attainment rates (Jacobs 1996; Mickelson 1989).

Among Blacks and Latinos, however, the gender gap is starker. A *Newsweek* cover story announces that Black women have outpaced Black men in professional and managerial careers, with almost a quarter of Black women holding such jobs, compared to 17 percent of Black men (Cose and

Samuels 2003). Weekly e-zines zines from the *Journal of Blacks in Higher Education* reveal that women outnumber men in professional schools by significant ratios. Twice as many African American females as African American males earned college degrees in the 1990s (Special Report, *Journal of Blacks in Higher Education* 1999). Black female students at many elite colleges and universities personify this statistic (Massey et al. 2003) as they lament the fact that they outnumber Black males almost two to one, which signifies a shallow dating pool, especially if in-group, heterosexual dating is preferred. Although various studies show that the gender gap is not as wide for Latinos as it is for African Americans (Community College Week 2000), Latinas also exhibit stronger relationships to schooling and outnumber Latinos in high school graduation and college enrollment rates (Valenzuela 1999; Lopez 2003). Even among the students in this study, as table 3.1 shows, females outpaced males, earning significantly higher mean and median grade point averages—80.12 and 82.25, respectively, compared to 74.61 and 75 for males. Furthermore, females were more than twice as likely to report being B students, while males were more likely to earn Cs.

TABLE 3.1 Schooling Patterns by Gender

	Females N	Males N
Dropped out of school	18% (38)	10% (30)
Cut class often/sometimes an entire day of school	9% (26)[a]	35%** (23)
Mainly "B" students	61% (26)[a]	23%* (23)
Mainly "C" students	22% (26)[a]	58%* (23)
Mean grade point average	80.12 (23)[a]	74.61** (23)
Median grade point average	82.25 (23)[a]	75** (23)

*p < .10; **p < .05

[a]These total Ns are based only on those who were enrolled in school at the time of interview.

What is happening in urban minority communities in the United States to create such gender differences in achievement and attainment? And why are Black and Latino males now more predisposed to seek "smarts" on the streets of Atlanta, Chicago, Los Angeles, New York, Philadelphia, and other urban centers than in the lecture halls of Howard, Hampton, Brown, and New York universities, to name a few? Trapped in the "codes of the streets," many ultimately head toward the university of the pen[itentiary] instead of the University of Penn[sylvania]. Since there are no innate or essential intelligence differences in our society, the explanations must be social and cultural. More specifically, they must be tied to how gender, as a social process, is lived, experienced, prescribed, and enforced in our society (Lopez 2003; Collins 1991; Frankenberg 1993; Crenshaw 1992). As the following discussion reveals, these differences can occur even within a family, where the boys of the house might not perform as well as their sisters. Maxwell acknowledged the gender divide in education, family, and community, seeing it in at least two dimensions. As he perceived it, girls were more "book" smart than boys but less "street" smart. "Book smarts" entailed reading, going to class daily, finishing homework, and earning decent grades. According to Maxwell, "book smarts" comprise the feminine realm. Having "street smarts," on the other hand, means knowing how to handle oneself in public spaces. As Dance (2002) described from her ethnographic research on "street-savvy" Black boys in Boston and Cambridge, Massachusetts, "the streets could be a park, or an alley, or a street, or a street corner, or a playground, or another publicly accessible outdoors area" (p. 38). Street smarts include knowing how to look someone in the eye, to avert one's gaze at the right moment, to avoid life-threatening fights and encounters, to defend oneself by fighting, and to navigate through dangerous gang territories (Anderson 1999, 1990). Street smarts, says Maxwell, are a male domain where men stand up for themselves and avoid submitting to the control of others ("You ain't gon' let somebody play you, play you and put their hands on you"). Girls, according to Maxwell, did not possess the same interpersonal negotiation skills that boys possessed. Instead, he believed that girls fought over petty matters. "They fight over stupid stuff," he claimed. "'She got my sneakers on!'" Maxwell said mockingly, imitating what he thought girls did.

Sylvestre agreed with Maxwell's assessment of the differences between males and females. "Girls and women are a little bit smarter than us," he declared. "It's true. I'm serious. I see it. They think smarter than guys." When I asked why he believed that girls were smarter, he said, "I know that they got a little more push, a little more drive." I asked Sylvestre whether he felt pressure to conform or to hang out with his friends, and he replied, "I think we [are] bored. I think, like, between the teens and the early twenties, there's, like, a phase that guys go through. Like, guys just got to be guys, like, just hang out, just be on the corner, chill. Some guys stay on the corner, and girls just say 'let me think, let me get my life together.'"

Girls believed that they were "book" smarter, too. Though fifteen-year-old Tiara Mitchell's reasons differed from Sylvestre's, her conclusions were similar: "Well, boys, I know, are not into books. Most girls I know love to read, Whites, Black, all, in the library. Boys just love gym. Boys that I know just love to go to gym. But girls are not. I'm not interested in gym, but I play gym." Tiara further explained her beliefs as I probed: "Most boys just come to school to play. Boys always are in gym; that's one class that boys do not miss. I always think about that. But I'm saying, most girls, I mean, they're just in class. Most boys are always cutting. Like when I'm going to the bathroom or something, the boys in the hallway playing, rolling dice or something." "But girls want to have fun too, don't they? And why do you think that girls stick to the rules more easily than boys?" I asked. "I don't know," she said initially, "but for me, some of my classes I do like to be in and those that I don't like to be in, I still go to. I like to hang out, do what I have to do, but my mother has a rule. If I don't go to school, then I can't go outside. Sick or playing like you're sick, can't go outside. So that's why I go to school, 'cause otherwise I can't do the things that I want to do. When I'm ready to do 'em, I can't. So, that's why I do my thing at school, cause when I get home I want to hang out with my friends, call my friends up, you know, go outside. But if I don't [go to school], then I can't."

Both Sylvestre and Tiara outlined a script that many boys appear in this study to follow. They gambled and risked reprimands and suspensions by being truant or by hanging out with the guys. As figure 3.1 reveals, 57 percent of the males reported getting a kick out of engaging in risky and dangerous behaviors compared to only 37 percent of the females. Also, nearly four times as many boys (more than one out of three) as girls (fewer than one out of ten) reported cutting school. What are the reasons for these differences? Sylvestre believed that males and females have different developmental trajectories, that girls mature faster than

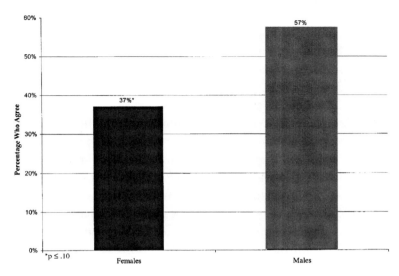

FIGURE 3.1 Respondents Who Enjoy Engaging in Dangerous Activities by Gender

boys, and girls figure out earlier the importance of school. Tiara stayed away from the psychological and instead offered a sociological explanation. She said that the threat of her mother's sanctions motivated her to attend classes and to complete her schoolwork. Results are mixed on Sylvestre's claim about gender and development between boys and girls, though some research shows that females experience several stages of social development more quickly than males (Streitmatter 1993). Although my data would not allow me to explore Sylvestre's claims about social psychological and developmental differences, I did follow up on Tiara's explanation. I found that males' and females' parental monitoring were significantly different. Mothers often gave sons more social latitude than daughters. Further, while conveying messages of masculinity and femininity, parents often reproduced the differential levels of social control that males and females experience in our society.

Gender comprises a set of constructed acts and performances that are both individually and socially meaningful, and sociohistorical scripts about maleness and femaleness are observed, watched, guarded, protected, and reinforced. If men and women cross gender boundaries, their identities can be questioned, and they can face social sanctions (Butler 1993; Guy-Sheftall 1996; Fenstermaker and West 2002). These acts, like ethno-specific acts, are neither biological nor intrinsic traits; rather, identification as male or female is best understood as yet another classification with political, economic, and social effects.

Gender roles enforced by parents, community, and society influence students' personal identities and their approaches to school (Adler, Kless, and Adler 1992); and these roles create disparate schooling patterns for males and females (Epstein, Hey, and Maw 1998). As I investigated how the Yonkers youths' ideas about masculinity and femininity shape how they approached school and how their gender ideology influenced their perspectives on socioeconomic mobility, three striking patterns emerged. First, all of the youths participated in our system of gender relations and reproduced common ideas about what it means to be male and female. These ideas determined how they moved through the world. Metaphors of hardness and softness emerged to characterize male and female ways of interacting in school and among their peers. Males experienced social pressure to be hard. Hardness is akin to the behaviors that urban sociologists have discovered for decades in poor communities of color where males develop "codes of the street," putting on tough coats of armor to protect themselves against bleak social and economic conditions (Anderson 1999; Liebow 1967; Hannerz 1969). During one group discussion, thirteen-year-old Marcus Smith accused thirteen-year-old Michael Jones of being "soft" (like a girl) because he refused to fight. Marcus's actions matched Maxwell's beliefs. Maxwell had exclaimed when we talked one-on-one, "What kind of man would not stand up and fight for himself?" And he believed that guys weren't supposed to let anyone "push up" (physically challenge) on them.

The constructions of masculinity among the males in the study raised an interesting paradox: most aspired to white-collar professions, yet what challenged their aspirations were the conflicts and tensions between their ideas about masculinity and many of the tenets of mobility, especially behaviors in which acculturation is required. I found that ethno-specific cultural behaviors embraced by these youths intersected with their gender-specific cultural behaviors to create different educational, social, and economic experiences for males and females. One noticeable outcome of their blending gender role expectations with ethnic and cultural expectations was the construction of many of the behaviors associated with "acting white" as feminine. As we sat and chatted at his kitchen table, Samurai made an explicit connection between "girl talk" and "acting white." "There's some Black people that 'act white,'" Samurai said. "Who are they?" I asked. He responded, "[They] change their tone of voice when they get around certain people. Like maybe a Black girl talks like, 'Oh yeah, like, where are you going?' And then when you leave and they get around a certain type of person, they're like, 'Come on, oh let's go to the mall, let's go shopping, come on [raising the pitch of his voice, he imitates what he perceives as talking "white"]. I have to be in the house by, like, eight o'clock.' And they know they have to be in the house by 10 o'-clock but they do that to impress the White people." I asked Samurai why he had chosen a girl in the example he gave me about "acting white." "I don't know a Black male that tries to act white. I don't know none. None," he said. "So it's mostly girls?" I asked. "They wear miniskirts to schools and it's mostly girls. It's mostly girls," he responded.

In speaking, Samurai alludes to a number of overlapping social dynamics linking whiteness and femaleness to respectability and decorum. Samurai suggests that "acting white" is just what it sounds like—acting, a social performance in which (Black) girls use affected speech to impress or to be like "certain people," to move up to a more respectable status. He also implicitly associates whiteness with respectability when he describes how girls would tell a peer that they have to be home by 8 PM as opposed to 10 PM and, therefore, suggests that White parents maintain tighter social control over their children. Then he emasculates whiteness by suggesting that tight, social control is what females face, and thus, emphatically he declared that he knew no Black males who "act white," only girls.

Samurai also conflated the ideas of Standard English, slang, and the dialects of white youth subcultures. As he compared "white talk" to "black talk," he made slippery distinctions between English as a language system and slang as an informal language practice. White youth slang, like Black youth urban vernacular, is not Standard English. But Samurai deemed "white talk" to be proper talk and he claimed his (female) peers "talked white," even if it were a slang or dialect. Often, the students in the study characterized speech styles according to their principal practitioners, along racial, ethnic, and gender lines. One type of "white" youth slang is valley girl talk, which some of the youths mimicked for me frequently when I asked them to use "white" talk. And in these instances, "white talk" emerged as a form of "girl talk" (Carter, forthcoming).

In Adrienne Ingrams' case, however, "white talk" was equated with Standard English. "I don't see a lot of boys who talk like me," Samurai's peer and neighbor told me. After some musing, she continued, "Yeah, my friend Daniel . . . he says I 'act white,' too. But his friends pick on him because he talks soft and stuff . . . like they call him gay or something or they say he 'acts white,' too." With the exception of two references to allegedly gay males, all of the principal characters in the fifty-one references to acting white that I heard were female.[1] Sociologist Mary Waters (1996) discovered a similar finding in her study of second-generation West Indian youth in New York; accusations of "acting white" for boys were often associated with challenges to masculinity. Girls like Adrienne would be accused of "acting white" if they employed certain speech styles and voice inflections, while boys like Adrienne's classmate Daniel faced the possibility of not only being sanctioned for "acting white" but also emasculated or perceived as gay.

In a society where masculinity has long been associated with heterosexuality, a person with both X and Y chromosomes who does not conform to constructed norms and cultural expectations is liable to be considered a gender and sexual deviant (Connell 1995). According to Adrienne, Daniel's sexuality was questioned because he talked too "soft," not forcefully or sufficiently deep-voiced. Anthropologist Signithia Fordham, whose early work heightened the debate about the impact of "burden of acting white," argues that African American and Latino females may not reject schooling to the same extent as their male co-ethnics because they do not experience the same level of estrangement from the normalized American female roles as males do from the normalized male roles. On the one hand, as we saw earlier, low-income African American and Latino youth can share sentiments about race and ethnic relations and their social, economic, cultural, and political positions in the world. With varying racial and ethnic ideologies, some males and females assimilate to dominant cultural expectations, others straddle both ethno-racial and dominant cultures, and still others embrace only ethnic culture. On the other hand, who is likely to assimilate and accommodate becomes another question, especially when gender power relations are put into the mix. Historically and conventionally, masculinity has been equated with rebellion and defensiveness, while femininity has been equated with conformity, docility, and acceptance (Hochschild 1973; de Beauvoir 1989). Therefore, when considering these macrosocial dynamics, it is more likely that African American and Latino males will associate whiteness with different meanings than will African American and Latina females.

The idea of assimilation, in itself, threatens the already tenuous power that a racial and ethnic minority male holds in the larger society (Connell 1995). In other words, aspects of cultural assimilation—or closeness to whiteness by means of body norms, language, clothing styles, and interactions—directly challenge many of these males' perceptions of masculinity. As Ann Ferguson writes: "Transgressive behavior is that which constitutes masculinity. Consequently, African American males (like the ones whom I interviewed) in the very act of identification, of signifying masculinity, are likely to be breaking rules," even rules that White men follow (Ferguson 2001, 170). Therefore, it should not be surprising that more males than females in my study fell into the noncompliant believer group or that girls significantly outnumbered males among the cultural straddlers and cultural mainstreamers. Specifically, two-thirds of the males, or rather twenty out of thirty, fell into the noncompliant believer group, compared to less than half of the females, eighteen out of thirty-eight (table 3.2). Moreover, twenty of the thirty students deemed as either cultural straddlers or cultural mainstreamers believers were female. As we discovered in chapter 1, noncompliant believers are significantly less likely to perform as well in school as cultural straddlers and cultural mainstreamers. Without sufficient social and economic resources, the consequences are that poor African American and Latino males, in their quests to assert manhood in a patriarchal and male-dominant society, are likely to collaborate in their own academic and socioeconomic marginalization (Noguera 1996).

"HARD" AND "SOFT": CONSTRUCTIONS OF MASCULINITY

The soft/hard and feminine/masculine dichotomies continue to reproduce the boundaries between boys and girls that maintain differing results between the two groups. Although male and female students in the study shared cultural meanings of blackness and "Spanishness," girls could not be too "hard," a masculine form, and boys could not be too

Table 3.2. Gender Breakdown by Believer Group

	Female (N)	Male (N)	Total (N)
Cultural Straddlers	42%	30%	37%
	(16)	(9)	(25)
Cultural Mainstreamers	11%	3%	7%
	(4)	(1)	(5)
Noncompliant Believers	47%	67%	56%
	(18)	(20)	(38)
Total	100%	100%	100%
	(38)	(30)	(68)

"soft," a feminine expression. Hardness surfaced as a coat of armor developed by males in the low-income communities where the Yonkers youths live. Though many of the boys bemoaned the negative stereotypes of Black and Latino men, often the men in their neighborhoods conformed to those stereotypes, to images of street corner men (Liebow 1967; Hannerz 1969). In my afternoon visits to their housing complexes, I observed men hanging out in the parking lots and street corners. And the Yonkers youths would describe them either as unemployed or as "street pharmacists." The rate to which of these men have had experiences with the U.S. criminal justice system, its courts and prisons, is disproportionate to their overall demographic representation in the nation (Noguera, 2003).

As I moved through the students' neighborhoods, I came to understand how hardness provided marginalized men protection against severe social and economic oppressions, from racial insubordination to the fines of deindustrialization and the loss of jobs in the central cities. The contemporary meanings of hardness stemmed from lives of inner-city poverty where an underground economy "thrives," where turf wars of gang members endanger the lives of its residents, where individuals must generate creative and often illicit plans to survive, and where a different communicative system and styles of interaction materialize (Liebow 1967; Anderson 1999; Kelley 1999; Wilson 1987; Massey and Denton 1993; Dance 2002). In contrast to hardness, softness connotes the feminine forms perceived as compliant and nurturing. Sitting still and paying attention in class are imbued with feminine meanings and therefore might be avoided by students with more masculine identities. Yet the more "feminine" the gender identity of boys and girls, the better their performance when measured by classroom grade point averages (Burke 1989). Meanwhile, hard boys might excel on the "masculine" turfs, especially on the athletic fields and courts, often the channels through which many poor, racial and ethnic minority males become engaged in school (Solomon 1991; Davis 2001).

Differences in gender cultures have led to conspicuous divergences in school performance between boys and girls (Epstein, Hey, and Maw 1998; Mac An Ghaill 1994; Gibson 1991; Gorard, Rees, and Salisbury 1999). "It's easier for a girl to be smart because if a boy is smart, he gets stuff from his crew or whatever like, 'Ah man you're soft, you're soft! I can't believe you know that poetry stuff,'" declared Adrienne, a female cultural mainstreamer who did well in school. "So [boys] try to hide that they're smart, that they know stuff like that, [and] I think that it's easier for a girl," she declared.[2] Adrienne informed me that her male classmates had come to define the classroom and certain aspects of their education as feminine, as "soft." She claimed that facets of school life threatened the already tenuous hold that her male peers had on their masculinity. And she sensed that for boys to excel in English literature classes and know poetry could lead their male peers to question their masculinity. As a result, they either masked their taste for poetry or other "feminine" school-oriented behaviors, like speaking Standard English regularly (also described as "acting white"), or else they subjected themselves to ridicule.

All boys are not lower achievers than girls, however, and some of them disagreed with the beliefs that girls do better in school than boys. For example, John Jamison, a thirteen-year-old cultural straddler and a high achiever, argued that the idea that girls are smarter is a cliché. "It's the stereotype right now that girls gotta do this and that . . . meaning do better in school. But it's not true. But that's the stereotype right now." Yet John was only one of five males in the study who could be categorized as a high achiever, and who was enrolled in advanced courses and maintained more than a B+ average. Others included fourteen-year-old Ramon Diaz who had his sights on earning a degree at the Massachusetts Institute of Technology in a field like computer engineering. There was also Jeremy James (introduced in chapter 2), a ninth grader perceived by his teachers to have the ability to enter the International Baccalaureate program, but who was squabbling with his mother about whether or not to enroll in it.

For most of these boys and their male peers, team sports and rap music were major preoccupations. One out of two of them participated in a team sport, compared to a little more than one in five of the girls. Some thinkers have suggested that a fixation with excelling in sports has become an alternative to classroom success for minority—particularly Black males (Solomon 1991; Hoberman 1997). The love of sports does not mean that these young men did not acknowledge the value of a high-school diploma. But it does suggest that these young men, influenced by normative cultural values about work and manhood, sought a high-school credential as a path to financial success. Unfortunately, most desired to obtain this success through one of the few avenues that an exclusionary limited opportunity structure opens to many men of color—professional sports and the hip-hop entertainment industry—even though less than one percent of college athletes make the cut into professional sports, and few break into fame in the music world. Yet, Black professional athletes and rappers, in particular, have become exemplars of manhood in America's poor, urban communities (Collins 2004), although their fame and wealth have not given much social and political authority to men of color as a group. Still, African American and Latino boys gravitate toward those niches occupied by men whose backgrounds and experiences resemble theirs. These career niches do not require high academic achievement. And the fierce competition for jobs in professional sports and in the recording industry prevents most athletically and musically inclined boys from realizing their aspirations to become professional athletes and entertainers. At the same time, the extremely low representation of Black and Latino men in professional fields, such as medicine, corporate management, engineering, and computer science lends itself to a limited consideration of these career paths by boys like the Yonkers males.

Balancing gender roles and identity are not easy. The social expectations of males and females are inscribed throughout U.S. society; they are inescapable. Figure 3.2 shows that the African American and Latino males in this study subscribed to conventional beliefs about the connection between manhood and job success. Sixty percent believed that respect for men came with the acquisition of a good job. Almost an equal percentage

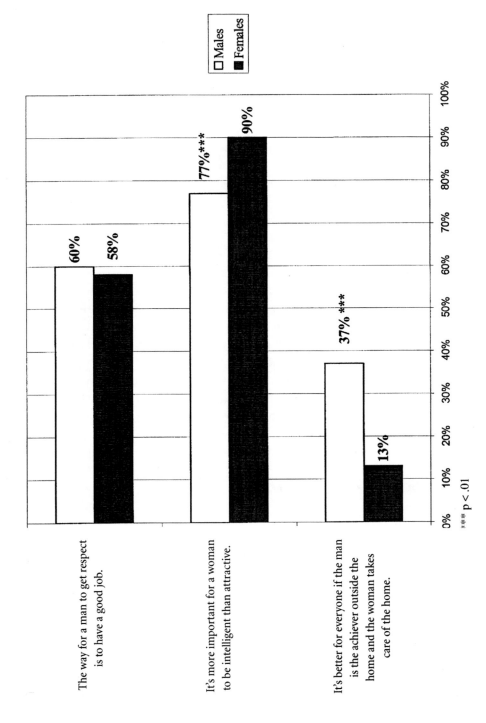

The way for a man to get respect is to have a good job.

60%

58%

It's more important for a woman to be intelligent than attractive.

77%***

90%

It's better for everyone if the man is the achiever outside the home and the woman takes care of the home.

37% ***

13%

☐ Males
■ Females

0% 10% 20% 30% 40% 50% 60% 70% 80% 90% 100%

*** p < .01

FIGURE 3.2 Responses to Sex Role Questions by Gender

of females maintained a similar belief. However, the males were more likely than the females to cling to traditional beliefs about a "man's role" and a "woman's place." More than one out of three of them believed that it was better that a man be the provider and a woman the homemaker, compared to about one out of ten females. The Latino males adhered to these beliefs more so than did the African American males, which accounts for much of the significant difference between males and females.[3]

More than three decades ago scholar and activist Frances Beale argued: "America has defined the roles to which each individual should subscribe. It has defined 'manhood' in terms of its own interests . . . therefore, an individual who has a good job, makes a lot of money, and drives a Cadillac is a real 'man,' and conversely, an individual who is lacking in these 'qualities' is less of a man. The advertising media in this country continuously inform the American male of his need for indispensable signs of his virility" (Beale [1979] 1995). R. W. Connell refers to this notion of manliness as the hegemonic conceptualization of masculinity. Hegemony captures the idea of how we consent to meanings, power relations, and ways of life even when they may not serve our best interests (Gramsci 1994). These boys understood what it means conventionally to be a "man" in U.S. society. Yet a strong contradiction exists in their lives. Massive unemployment and urban poverty, along with institutional racism, have powerfully interacted to reshape the notions of masculinity among Black and Latino men (Liebow 1967; Mirande 1997; Staples 1982).

SOFT WORK FOR THE HARD MAN

The African American and Latino males whom I interviewed desired the comforts and security of middle-class America; they wanted white-collar jobs and big houses and cars with lots of money in the bank. "I just want to make a decent amount of money, support my family, buy a house, and be able to pay my mortgage, and I want to be able to have a little money in my pocket," Sylvestre stated earlier. He also hauled furniture part-time, but blue-collar work reeked heavily of toil and subordination, and Jermaine, one of Sylvestre's neighbors who had taken a different path from Sylvestre and enrolled in college agreed:

My mother was fifteen when her mother, my grandmother, died. She was going through some troubles in school in the tenth grade; she made it through. Then, she started college, dropped out of college, started working in childcare. She built her way up. She got laid off from a couple of jobs. She didn't have the special things that the job needed, like educational qualifications, college degrees that the jobs required. She tried to go back to school, had some trouble, dropped out again around four or five years ago. She just works long shifts, hard shifts, double shifts. Her average shift is, like, double shifts. She works too much. I don't think I'll have to work that much. I won't allow myself to work that much, because I don't like too much labor. Can't stand it. I'd rather [make] decisions, solve financial problems. I don't like doing hands-on [manual] work.

In a study of White working-class boys who rejected dominant achievement ideology and who Paul Willis (1977) identifies as the "lads," manual labor is found to be associated with the social superiority of masculinity and mental labor with the social inferiority of femininity. These low-income Black males from Yonkers viewed labor and gender identity differently. And perhaps, the impact of historic racial and economic conditions determined how they responded to certain types of manual and service labor. Contrary to Willis's lads, these African American males, faced with a legacy of slave/master or "boy/Mr." inequitable relations, high unemployment, and menial labor, did not appear to want to subordinate themselves to anyone. Unlike their grandfathers, who had at most a high-school education but still earned decent wages in factories and automobile plants scattered throughout the Midwest and Northeast in the 1950s and 1960s, urban minority men with little education and few skills increasingly face low-skilled, low-wage jobs in an economy in which industry and manufacturing have waned (Wilson 1987; Bluestone and Harrison 1982). But rather than hold low-paying, menial jobs, the males in the study preferred to give orders themselves and to be accorded the respect that came with white-collar jobs and financial capital. Sociologist Elijah Anderson (1980) attributes some of the desire of the white-collar and professional jobs to the militancy of the 1960s Black power movement. "With the increased emphasis on self, young Blacks are tending to be more selective about the jobs they will perform, and often will not accept employment and work conditions they consider to be demeaning. This attitude appears in striking contrast to that of an earlier generation of Blacks, many of whom accepted almost any available work" (1980, 64).

While they aspire to the white-collar job world, the dilemma is that these jobs require that these young men embrace "soft" skills, in addition to acquiring a certain level of academic training. Employers look for "soft" or noncognitive skills such as a certain type of interactional and communicative style and demeanor (Kirschenman and Neckerman 1991); and according to Philip Moss and Chris Tilly (1996), soft skills are, in part, culturally defined. Studying employers' behaviors toward potential employees, Moss and Tilly found that employers rated African American men poorly on various subjective, noncognitive measures of evaluation. Employers often interpreted the "hard" persona as aggressive and threatening, consequently denying these young, urban, low-income males job opportunities.[4]

Many of the male youths were potentially susceptible to similar treatment by employers. As they constructed their masculine selves through language and dress styles, they risked losing the opportunities they desired. Both males and females in this study had come to believe that employers preferred to hire African American females and Latinas because they were more likely than their male counterparts to possess soft skills. When I asked these youths which gender was more likely to succeed, the consensus was that African American women and Latinas were more likely because they are perceived as less threatening and as more capable of conforming to the "right" (as opposed to "ghetto") dress styles and codes. "To tell you the truth, ladies . . . they're not characterized in that racial group as much as it would be [for] a Dominican man—as they stereotype us to be. Because most Dominicans are characterized as drug dealers," stated Alberto, the younger brother of two sisters who had graduated from high school and gone on to college. His older sister, Nelia, was studying to practice law; and Alma, whom I also interviewed, was a sophomore in college. DeAndre concurred with his neighbor Alberto's assessment, referring to African Americans: "I think for Black women . . . it's easy for them to get a job, but in a lot of jobs only men would do, like construction. Most of the job managers, when you go to apply for a job, might be Black men, and they prefer to hire a female. Most girls carry themselves in a different way from boys. Girls are more well mannered than boys."

Seventeen-year-old Sylvia Escuela, another of Alberto's neighbors, explained why she believed managers prefer females. "I think that it's easier for a woman to get a job now because of the way they dress, the way they present themselves. You look good, you have a job if it's a guy boss. But men, they don't really get hired. I don't know why. That's how I see it because they don't really present themselves. They are very slow." "How do they tend to present themselves?" I asked. Sylvia replied, "Ghetto! There's a lot of ghetto people out here now. A lot of teenagers . . . they ghetto. They like to dress with their pants down to here. They like to have their hair wild, with the braids. You can't really get a job like that."

As young adults eager for money of their own, Alberto, DeAndre, and Sylvia had all looked for work in the service industry, an economic sector sought after by low-skilled young workers. Their encounters with potential employers shaped their perceptions that the soft skills of females make them more employable. To put it simply, they perceived that employers preferred the self-presentations of girls of color to those of their male counterparts, especially when boys appeared "ghetto"—a pejorative, class-based term suggesting intimidation and a certain amount of unseemliness of the inner-city poor. Their adolescent perceptions were not unwarranted. Economist Harry Holzer (1996) found that among Blacks, the hiring of females instead of males increased with the number of tasks performed and credentials required, although both groups' hiring percentages were significantly and strikingly lower than their White counterparts. In addition, the probability of being hired was greater for Black females than Black males when the job required customer contact. Some of these differences might result from the actual feminization of certain job sectors; there are more females than males in clerical and sales jobs. These patterns might also occur because of the differences in occupational choices by gender (ibid.).

Do employers prefer to hire females because of stereotypical beliefs about racial minorities, for example, about "angry" or "aggressive" Black males or the "Dominican drug dealers," as Alberto suggested? Certainly the implications are enormous. "From the employer's point of view, the young (minority) male's perceived subcultural differences may be an important part of the reason he does not deserve trust on the job. Often his language is not understood or appreciated. His presentation of self, particularly his dress, often is not suitable to the employer, and if something is said about it, the young male will probably feel he is being treated unfairly," argued Elijah Anderson (1980). Gender norms influence the presentation of self that Anderson described from his ethnographic research almost two decades ago and that characterize the behaviors of the young men whom I interviewed recently. These young males do not wholeheartedly embrace various social behaviors because they perceive these behaviors as soft. Yet given that minority men who do not conform to the dominant cultural behaviors often fail to obtain jobs because of innate organizational and cultural biases (Gould 1999), these males' chances for academic, social, and economic mobility remain in jeopardy.

GIRLS CAN'T BE TOO SOFT

Although girls approach schooling and mobility in ways more in accordance with school authorities' expectations, they, nonetheless, struggle and often do not perform up to par. Using their noncompliant status as an indicator, I found that at least half of the girls in this study underperformed in school (compared to two-thirds of the boys). Low achievement was a problem for some, and as I explored why, I discovered that males do not hold exclusive rights to a demeanor of "hardness." Frequently, girls projected "tough" images so that they could avoid being picked on by others.[5] Protecting their egos and self-images, they fought much among themselves, a fact that I heard about during a gathering with six young women over pepperoni pizza, chocolate chip cookies, and orange and grape soda in the social room of their housing complex. Beforehand, in one-on-one interviews, the topic of fighting among girls had arisen, so I inquired about the reasons for this antagonism:

> *Prudence:* You know that I've interviewed a lot of teenagers, and I want to know why are girls fighting so much. What would cause you to fight someone?
>
> *Female Respondent 1:* Boys!
>
> *Female Respondent 2:* Boys!
>
> *Female Respondent 3:* Boys!

Female Respondent 4: That's stupid.

Female Respondent 5: If I ain't married to him, I ain't fighting over him.

Prudence: Have any of you ever been in a fight?

Female Respondent: Not over boys! [*Several of them say this.*]

Prudence: Have you ever been in a fight at all?

[*They all say, "Yeah!"*]

Prudence: Over what?

Female Respondent 1: Over trash talking.

Female Respondent 2: Over gossip.

Female Respondent 3: She said, he said.

Female Respondent 4: Trash talk.

Prudence: What about just trying to talk your way out of things instead of fighting?

Female Respondent 1: I'm sick and tired of talking. It don't work! It don't work!

Female Respondent 2: If you try to talk it out, they say, "Oh come home, pussy, you all chicken and that kind of stuff."

All six of the girls had been in fights with other girls (and occasionally with boys) at school. Bickering continually over limited resources and social goods—for example, respect and boys' attention—girls were often described as "fighters" by girls and boys alike. Respect was inextricably linked to a "tough" persona, meaning that the more a girl's demeanor and behavior announced that she could not be reckoned with, the greater her formidability. When pushed further to explain why they fought, these girls often ridiculed and criticized their reasons for fighting. Yet they still fought, and one essential motive was to avoid being considered too soft.

"Soft" has several meanings. It connotes not only the feminine but also the weak. Often, the girls verbalized their understandings of prevalent beliefs about "female" roles. Yet to be female in poor urban America does not mean one is weak. If a girl cannot defend herself, then she's considered weak, which is synonymous with "soft." Still conventional feminine values held in their communities. "Your parents is on you, 'Be a lady. Cross your legs. Don't curse,'" Rayisha told me. "[They say], 'Don't use certain language. Don't scream too loud. Be a lady. Put on skirts and . . . [don't go] punching [others] in the face and fight. My mother's like, 'Don't fight. Be a lady.'" Recognizing the double standard, nineteen-year-old Hannah Cummings, agreeing with Rayisha, also criticized the expectations held for females. "Yeah because a Black woman is supposed to . . . is expected to be nice and conservative. But then the guys, there are no expectations for guys, because guys are going to be guys regardless. And if a girl doesn't, if she doesn't act the way that they feel a woman should act, then they call her all kinds of names and stuff like that."

Hannah was exasperated about the double standards, and she expressed her frustration that female agency is limited compared to that of males, since women are penalized by society for asserting sexual freedom. Although Hannah and other female informants understood that their femininity was linked to how "nice," "conservative," or "ladylike" they could be, they also engaged in behaviors that defied these feminine ideals. Competition, conflict, and tension surfaced in many of their relationships. Tension among these girls, often flamed through hearsay, would escalate to a breaking point, eventually resulting in fights. Consequently, several were suspended from school. At one point during that same group discussion, several commented, "Girls around here will turn they back on you. They tell your business. You don't want to beat them up, but you have to." Their comments confirmed psychologist Niobe Way's argument that as adolescent girls mature and become involved in romantic relationships, trust among same-sex peers diminishes and their sense of betrayal augments as they experience others "stealing" their romantic partners. "These heightened feelings of self-protection and vulnerability may cause adolescents to become increasingly cautious about whom they trust among their peers, who are also physically and sexually maturing and, perhaps, becoming more wary and self-protected" (Way 1996, 187).

Much of the literature on gender stresses different cultures between males and females, but these generalizations about girls' and boys' cultures come primarily from research done on those who are class-privileged and White. Some researchers argue that boys stress position and hierarchy, whereas girls emphasize intimacy and connection (Gilligan 1982). In contrast, studies of racial and ethnic minority and working-class girls have shown that these patterns do not necessarily hold in these communities (Browne 1999). To some extent, physical aggression and verbal assertiveness are common modes of expression among both African American males and females (Stevens 1997; Goodwin 1991). "Playing the dozens"—a colloquial term for brassy exchanges and name-calling defined as ritualized forms of insult to express power and aggression (Gates 1988; Major 1994)—characterizes some social interactions among African American females (Goodwin 1991). The girls channeled a great deal of energy into not being manipulated, not coming across as too soft, and not being made fun of or taken advantage of. Instead, they distinguished themselves through boisterous and assertive language.

Juggling femininity while not appearing too soft also means being able to take care of oneself. Frequently, social science research ignores the interactions of race, ethnicity, gender, and class, and it misses those patterns that do not conform to career choices and career development patterns of White, middle-class youth. In environments where men have difficulties securing jobs, the prospects of both marriage and a dual-income family have dimmed (Wilson 1987). Unlike their White counterparts, many females of color are socialized to view marriage separately from economic security, since, historically, it has not been expected that marriage will remove them from the labor market (Furstenburg, Herschberg, and Modell 1975; Jones 1985; Fuller 1980; Holland and Eisenhart 1990; Fernández Kelly 1995). Thus, some African American and Latino mothers appeared to be raising their daughters to be not too "soft" but rather to be self-sufficient and financially independent of male partners. To understand the family and community context in which these young women were being raised is important. Their family realities resembled those in many poor, urban areas: daily in-home parental contact came from their mothers, who as unmarried heads of households were raising their children alone with whatever financial means they could muster. Only about 15 percent of my research informants lived in a two-parent household, yet almost three-quarters (71 percent) of the youths' mothers worked outside the home.

The high incidence of mother-headed families among these youth raises questions about how children who live in these contexts form expectations about their economic futures and family life courses. As table

TABLE 3.3 Parents' Expectation for Life Chances and School
Aspirations by Gender

	Females	Males
Parents believe that son/daughter has a high chance of a better life than parent	89%	59%**
Parents believe that son/daughter has a high chance of attending college	83%	56%**
Parents believe that son/daughter has a high chance for a well-paying job in future	80%	59%
Parents aspire that son/daughter attend college	91%	89%
Total N	35	27

**p <. 05 (two-sided chi square)

3.3 reveals, a significantly high percentage of the females' mothers expected both that their daughters had a good chance of having a better life
than they did and a high probability of attending college. These data,
based on parents' responses to questions about their children in the previous year, show that 89 percent of the females' mothers expected their
daughters to have a high chance of a better life than they, compared with
only 59 percent of the males' mothers. Eighty-three percent of the females' mothers believed that their daughters had a high chance of attending college, compared with only 56 percent of the males' mothers. Eighty
percent of the females' mothers, versus 59 percent of the males' mothers,
believed that their daughters would some day have a well-paying job. Still,
roughly equal percentages of females' mothers and males' mothers maintained high educational aspirations for their children; 91 percent and 89
percent, respectively, of mothers desired that their children attend at least
junior college or part of a four-year college program.

Unlike studies that show girls tending to avoid high-prestige occupations, and boys trained toward high achievement (Taylor, Gilligan, and
Sullivan 1995), I found that these girls aspired to more high-status jobs
than did the boys (table 3.4). Eighty-four percent of the African American
girls aspired to professional, specialty jobs; their modal job preference was
lawyer.[6] Seventy-five percent of the Latina girls aspired to similar profes-

TABLE 3.4 Comparison of Job Aspirations and Their Prestige Scores by Gender

	Male	Female	Total
Aspire to professional, specialty occupations[a]	38%	76%***	59%
Mean prestige score for job aspired to[b]	55.18	62.54*	59.50
Total N	26	37	63

*p < .10; ***p <.01.

[a]Excludes professional athlete. If professional sports careers were included, this percentage would increase to 63% for males.

[b]The National Opinion Research Council (NORC) developed these prestige scores for the 1980 Census occupational classifications.

sional, specialty occupations; their modal job preferences were physician and fashion designer. In contrast, only 40 percent of Latino males aspired to professional, specialty occupations (excluding professional sports); auto mechanic was the modal job preference. Overall, the Latino males had blue-collar, entry-level aspirations; this may be linked to the overarching social processes of their families' immigrant status, social position, and labor conditions (Waldinger 1996). Excluding professional sports—the modal job preference for African American males—the analysis shows that only 44 percent of the Black males aspired to professional, specialty jobs. When professional sports are included, the percentage of males aspiring to professional, specialty occupations increases to 50 percent and 75 percent for Latino and African American males, respectively. These findings are striking, considering the current body of literature on gender role socialization and career development, and they mirror labor statistics, which reveal that higher percentages of women of color are represented in professional occupations than are their male counterparts (Jaynes and Williams 1989).[7]

Several of the respondents speculated that different socialization patterns and parental expectations help explain gender differences in schooling behaviors and career aspirations. Daughters asserted that they were raised and encouraged by their mothers differently from their brothers and male friends. And certainly these girls valued intelligence for themselves much more than males valued it for themselves. For example, a significantly higher percentage of girls than boys felt that it was more important for women to be intelligent than attractive—90 percent versus 77 percent, respectively (see figure 3.2). Several girls felt that their mothers and fathers pushed girls harder to do better and not to be dependent on males for income and resources. Consequently, parental monitoring of schooling behaviors appeared to be different for sons and daughters. Fourteen-year-old Rakeisha Shaw, like Tiara (introduced earlier), shared the almost unanimous belief among my informants that girls did better in school because they feared their parents' retribution more than the boys did. I asked why she believed this.

> *Rakeisha:* 'Cause mainly when you walk down the halls at my school, you usually see nothing but boys hanging out.

> *Prudence:* What's the deal with them [boys]?

> *Rakeisha:* I don't know. They bring radios to school. They are not allowed, but they bring them anyway.

> *Prudence:* Don't the girls want to hang out in the hallways and listen to music, too?

> *Rakeisha:* Yeah, but if they get caught, then the deans call their mothers and they get in trouble.

> *Prudence:* Don't they call the boys' mothers?

> *Rakeisha:* Yeah, they do, but they don't really care.

> *Prudence:* The mothers?

> *Rakeisha:* No, the boys.

During another gathering with a mixed-ethnic group of young women, again over cheesy pizza, chocolate chip cookies, and orange soda, Teresa Anton, a twenty-year-old who lived on her own with her young children, led the chorus of "amens" about how boys are raised differently. "Men don't do things right. A girl will never get caught selling drugs; men always get caught. It's the way they mamas raised them," she said.

> *Prudence:* Are boys raised differently from girls?

> *Everyone:* "Yeah! Boys can stay out night."

> *Tameka Anton* (age sixteen): They can bring girls over who can

stay out all night, while girls can't have a boyfriend. They spoil the boys. That's why they get more money. That's why they say, "I got you and my mother."

Rayisha: Mothers do it to where girls can wear Reeboks, but they sons got to wear Jordans.

Prudence: How does that make you feel as daughters?

Teresa: That's why we're smarter. We [are] smarter because we get less attention. 'Cause boys they get treated better than us, so we have to think of ways to occupy our minds. So we end of thinking for ourselves.

Everyone: "Yeah."

Teresa, Tameka, Rayisha, and the others affirm that even within impoverished communities with limited access to good jobs—places where the underground drug economy thrives—pervasive gender dynamics hold: males maintain a higher level of status and privilege within society. Referring to status symbols like shoes and to romantic relationships—matters of primacy in adolescent minds—the girls noted three social spaces where conspicuous gender differences exist: the school, the bedroom, and the home. More minority boys than girls spend time in trouble and in detention for school disruption and delinquency (Ferguson 2000); and parental controls do little to deter the boys from getting in trouble. Meanwhile, their sisters and girlfriends perceive that the boys have more personal and sexual freedom (boys don't get called "bitches and hos," Hannah had told me earlier), in addition to more solicitude from mothers who buy sons the more costly Nike shoes that basketball great Michael Jordan made popular, unlike the Reebok, which has developed a strong marketing campaign targeting females. Boys get more attention, they exclaimed, while girls fear their parents' reprisals. However, rather than allow this imbalance to immobilize them, the girls claimed that it made them better prepare themselves for self-sufficiency.

Parents' reports about their treatment of their children may also support claims made by Teresa and the other young women that they "get less attention." When comparing across ethnicity, I found that African American mothers, rather than the Latina mothers, were more likely to report that they "baby and protect" their sons than their daughters (see table

3.5). The African American males' mothers were more than five times more likely to report pampering their sons than their daughters. In comparison, 67 percent of Latinos' mothers reported pampering their sons, compared to 45 percent of the Latinas' mothers. In response to questions about understanding their children's concerns and worries, being emotionally cold, or allowing their children freedom, the youths' mothers reported that they were likely to treat sons and daughters similarly. Still, while mothers gave more emotional protection or support to their sons, their expectations for success in life were greater for their daughters. These findings resonate with an adage that African American mothers raise their daughters and love their sons (Collins 1991; Guy-Sheftall 1996).

Because they were aware of the expectations and trajectories that women of color face, some of the respondents recognized the need to get as much education as possible. After Moesha repeated what I had already heard, that parents raise sons and daughters differently, I asked her for more scoop on why.

TABLE 3.5 Parents' Self-Reports on Differential Treatment of Daughters and Sons by Ethnicity and Gender

Percentage of mothers who report that:	African Americans		Latinos	
	Female	Male	Female	Male
I usually "baby and protect" my child.	8%	43%**	45%	67%
I usually "control everything my child does."	4%	14%	36%	33%
I usually understand my child's problems and worries.	52%	67%	60%	64%
I usually help my child as she or he needs.	24%	20%	70%	27%*
I usually am emotionally cold to my child.	0%	4%	10%	9%
I usually give my child as much freedom as she or he wants.	16%	20%	20%	0%
Total N	25	15	11	10

*p < .10; **p <. 05 (two-sided chi square)

Prudence: Who were the ones who tended to go to class, do their lessons, graduate on time, and those things?

Moesha: All girls [laughs]. Mostly, like my class had girls. There was a little lesser guys than there were girls. There was like sixteen to twenty rows [of the whole graduating class]. It was full of girls.

Prudence: What do you think that's about? Why is it harder for them [boys]?

Moesha: I don't think that it's harder. I think that certain boys are not determined enough.

Prudence: What makes the girls determined and not the boys?

Moesha: See, the girls have to get where they want to go. So, for them to do the things that they want to do, it's kind of easier for them to stay in school. Plus, they have fathers and mothers that push you more. Certain mothers and fathers don't put so much into it [for] the guys. It's like, if you graduate, that's good. If you don't graduate, you got the next year to graduate. Sometimes, it's not good to do that. To encourage your child is good. To *always* encourage your child is better.

Prudence: Why do you think that parents encourage their sons and daughters differently?

Moesha: Because I guess they feel that men can always get a job, and [for] women, it's real hard to get a job. But I don't feel it's harder for a woman to get a job. I feel that it's hard for anyone to get a job. It just depends on the type of job you're going out for probably. I mean, anybody can get a McDonald's job, but if you want to get an educated job, like in the business world, it's kind of hard. It's full of men. For women to get their foot into there, it's hard. They need to know what they are doing, so they push the women further or push them harder so they can do better, so that they can get better for themselves and not to depend on the male.

Moesha made several critical points during this exchange. First, she supported what I showed earlier, that girls attend classes more regularly, earn better grades, and even graduate at higher rates than boys do. Second, she mentioned the different parental expectations for male and female children that have been noted by social scientists over the years and in different cultural contexts (Gibson 1991; Zhou and Bankston 1998). Researchers have suggested that African American mothers do not socialize their daughters to be "passive," but rather teach them how to survive, cope, and succeed in hostile and sexist environments, while maintaining respect for and allegiance to their families and communities (Collins 1991; Cauce et al. 1996). Finally, Moesha makes a distinction between the low-wage service jobs that "anybody can get" and the upper echelon of business and professional jobs. Women's abilities to obtain these jobs, particularly when men control the corporate boards and chairmanships, are impeded by sexism. To get these jobs, females have to be armored with the pertinent credentials that education brings.

The processes that determine the different parental expectations for these minority youth are complex. Minority women who seemed less expectant of future economic support from men might embrace such a strategy. These data highlight the importance of examining career choices and interventions from a sociocultural perspective that stresses the crucial role of structural influences on the behaviors of ethnic minorities (Cauce et al. 1996). I would speculate that the boys' mothers had become more pessimistic about their sons' economic futures based on labor market outcomes for minority men. Both my personal observations and interviews indicated that within their neighborhoods, there were numerous unemployed men hanging out in the parking lots, rejected by an increasingly technology-based service economy that has little use for the unskilled, manual laborer. Thus, if their daughters become self-sufficient heads of households in the future, they would need to be prepared, perhaps better prepared than their mothers.

Another explanation for differing expectations might be that parents themselves were complicit in the reproduction of the gender hierarchy and encouraged distinctions between "hardness" (masculinity) and "softness" (femininity) that might influence school performance and behavior. The fact remains that differential schooling patterns, career aspirations, and parental expectations existed for the males and females in this study.

The analyses in this chapter suggest that gender, race, ethnicity, and economic conditions intersect and likely influence the different achievement patterns in schools and in the labor market. Although their academic performances would not be described as remarkable, the relatively better performance of minority girls in schools could place them at a modest advantage in a limited opportunity structure. In addition, because of the association of "softness" with girls (and, by extension, their higher proclivity for "soft" skills), minority females would likely fare better in the labor market. These patterns have critical educational, social, and economic implications for many African American and Latino youths, particularly since their class and racial statuses already preclude the attainment of certain social and political resources in U.S. society.

Next-Door Neighbors

The Intersection of Gender and Pan-Minority Identity

4

Various racial and ethnic groups experience economic, political and social marginalization. As a result, members of these groups sometimes cohere around a pan-minority identity at whose basis lie the experiences of subordination and inequality. At the same time, members of these groups can also maintain ethno-specific identities that signify their very different social and cultural histories and relationships to U.S. society. I apply this line of thought to the analyses of identity formation and cultural boundary maintenance (Lamont 2000) between the African American and Latino youths in this study. So far I have discussed them as ethno-racial groups vis-à-vis American Whites. But how do their identities either shift or remain stable vis-à-vis each other? More than one-third of the youths self-identified as either Hispanic or Latino, the offspring of immigrants from the Spanish Caribbean—Puerto Rico, the Dominican Republic, and Cuba (see table 4.1).[1] Hispanics or Latinos, counted as 12.5 percent of the U.S. population by the 2000 Census, have become the new majority-minority—a group with the largest representation among racial and ethnic minorities but with limited political or economic power in U.S. society.[2]

TABLE 4.1 Number of Latinos in Study by Ethnic
Origin

Ethnicity	Total (%)
Cuban	4 (16)
Dominican	10 (42)
Puerto Rican	10 (42)
Total N	24 (100)

The Latino population emerged as an ethnic group historically through international migration, and in the Mexican case, initially through conquest. Other ethnic groups, such as Cubans, have integrated more successfully and have enjoyed a relatively more welcoming reception into U.S. society (Bean and Tienda 1999).

"Latino" and "Hispanic" as pan-ethnic identities can mask myriad specific ethnic identities. Cubans, Dominicans, Mexicans, and Puerto Ricans, the four most widely represented Latino groups in the nation and in New York, all have vastly different social histories and migration stories. As the number of Latino U.S. residents grows exponentially, many social scientists have become curious about how this pan-ethnic group fits not only into the U.S. racial and ethnic taxonomy but also into its opportunity structure. Their various hues and mixed racial heritages, for example, tend to complicate the black-white divide that is pervasive in our conceptualizations of race matters. For many Latinos, racial identity is outright complex, even within a family, as one sibling might be a darker hue than another. The troublesome reaches of racism and colorism both outside and within the Latino community can reinforce the perceptions of privilege for fair skin and the higher valuation of white and fair skin over brown and black skin (Oboler 1995). As nineteen-year-old Alma says, "It's a shame that even us as a culture divide ourselves. The darker Dominicans always want to get with the lighter ones so that they can, like, fix up the family or something; but the lighter ones usually want to stay with the lighter ones, too." Alma understands that race and phenotype issues reach deeply into the core of identity among peoples who are described, as well, in terms of language, culture, and immigration history.

Some Latinos partly construct their social identities by putting themselves on the "right" side of the American racial divide—by embracing a "not black" identity (Smith 1997; Gans 1999). Yet given the nature of our racial and ethnic taxonomy, they are often classified as "of color" or "minority." Hence Latinos are likely to share an identity—a pan-minority identity—with their low-income African American brethren, who are often their neighbors and classmates. But while these groups share similar socioeconomic statuses, neighborhoods, and classrooms, their social histories and racial, ethnic, and cultural heritages differ tremendously.

Caught in an "in-between" status in the racial and ethnic hierarchy, the Latino students in this study engaged in identity work, thinking about their cultural standing in comparison to other ethnic Latino groups, in comparison to Blacks and other racial and ethnic minorities, and in comparison to Whites. Toward school, achievement, and socioeconomic mobility, the Latino students expressed three types of identities: (1) ethno-specific, identification with their specific national or cultural heritages such as Dominican or Puerto Rican; (2) pan-ethnic identification with Spanish-speaking people with backgrounds from Mexico, Central and Latin America, and the Spanish Caribbean (Latino); and (3) pan-minority, a collective identity that they shared with African Americans and other groups accorded a subordinate social status in U.S. society. In a matter of moments, a student might shift among all three identities, depending on the context and reference.

The Yonkers African American and Latino students lived as friends, neighbors, and classmates and shared many cultural codes and meanings, which I have already discussed. They frequently invoked a pan-minority identity, especially vis-à-vis Whites, which signified their similar socioeconomic statuses in the racial, ethnic, and class systems of the United States (Lopez and Espiritu 1990). Research shows that two factors—residential and occupational concentration—are crucial to the formation of ethnic-group solidarity because they produce common interests, lifestyles, and social networks. Furthermore, isolation within minority occupational and residential enclaves and systematic discrimination have led to the salience of an ethnic identity that has become synonymous with a minority status (Bean and Tienda 1999).

Although interethnic contact between Black and Latino students was frequent, both groups were still more likely to fraternize with co-ethnics. Students were asked to think of the first five neighbors and friends who came to mind, indicating those with whom they had close contact. As I analyzed responses to questions about more than 680 neighbors and close friends—each teen was asked to name ten persons (five close friends and five neighbors)—the Latino youths revealed that they had more Blacks in their social networks than the African American youths had Latinos. Half of Latino youths' close friends were other Latinos, and almost a third, 31 percent, were African Americans (refer to table 4.2). Similarly, among neighbors, the Latino youth identified nearly half as African Americans and 29 percent as Latinos. (This should not be surprising since they lived among more Blacks than Latinos.) In comparison, the African American youths reported that over three-quarters of their close friends were other African Americans; and only 12 percent were Latinos. Overall, the Latino youths had significantly more contact with African Americans than African Americans reported having with Latinos in both friendship circles and neighborhoods.

Because of the proximity of native Black and immigrant Latino youths in urban and low-income centers, social scientists have begun to wonder about the latter group's paths to assimilation. Would they follow the four-stage race relations cycle posited by one of the pioneers in assimilation theory, Robert Park (1950). Parks's cycle details how White ethnic immigrants in the late-nineteenth and early-twentieth centuries who arrived en masse from Europe over a forty-year period would (a) come into contact with Anglo Whites; (b) compete with them for jobs and other resources; (c) accommodate themselves by learning English and acquiring cultural practices to compete more effectively for economic and political resources;

TABLE 4.2 Racial, Ethnic Traits of Friendship and Neighbor Ties, African Americans vs. Latinos

	African Americans	Latinos
Percentage whose close friends are:		
African American	78%	12%
Latino	31%***	49%***
Percentage whose neighbors are:		
African American	83%	9%
Latino	46%***	29%***

F-test results: ***$p < .01$

and (d) get incorporated into Anglo society through intermarriage and acceptance into their social organizations. Or rather, because of their mixed racial heritages and due to contemporary "racial formations" (Omi and Winant 1994), would Latinos' patterns of assimilation look as jagged as those of African Americans and Native Americans, groups who still have not quite acquired their proportionate shares of America's opportunities?

Echoing an old maxim that "association brings on assimilation," some suspect that Latinos who emulate the cultural styles of their African American peers are susceptible to academic failure (Portes and Zhou 1992). Much of this argument stems from researchers' application of oppositional culture theory to groups of Latino students who live in poor black neighborhoods. Notably, sociologists Alejandro Portes and Min Zhou (1992; 1993), Rubén Rumbaut (1995), and Mary Waters (1999) have generated different models of the acculturative patterns of the post-1965 immigrant groups whose browner faces accord them different racial experiences and statuses than European immigrants knew in previous eras. Blending assimilationist frameworks with Ogbu's cultural ecological theory, Portes and Zhou (1993) explain how both native and immigrant students of color can resist acculturation into the white mainstream. They posit that a "segmented assimilation" process occurs in which Latinos concentrated in poor, predominantly Black areas are subject to economic vulnerability. Not only does this contact lead Whites to perceive the condition of both immigrants and native Blacks as the same, they argue, but also it exposes second-generation children to the adversarial subculture developed by marginalized native youth to cope with their own difficult situation. Thus, many second-generation Latino students can spiral downward into low academic achievement, permanent poverty, and assimilation into the so-called underclass because of the cultural influences of their Black peers in cities, from Miami to New York to Chicago to Los Angeles.[3]

Such perspectives not only cast many native minority students as atrisk, delinquent, and downwardly mobile, but also they frequently disregard the myriad ways in which students often fail to get incorporated fully into school. Indeed, that Latinos and African Americans lag behind other groups academically should cause concern. However, as I have argued throughout, the attribution of poor Latino and African American students' academic performances to their cultural practices and to incompatible beliefs about the values of education is debatable. All three groups of students profiled here viewed schooling as the vehicle of mobility from poverty to success. In addition, such attribution overlooks the intersections among identities, family, society, and school. Most of us possess racial, ethnic, gender, class, sexual, religious, and political identities, among many others, all at the same time. Yet even those who share an identity—perhaps an ethnic identity—show much variation in beliefs, behaviors, practices, and attitudes precisely because of all the other identities that may influence us. This phenomenon became apparent as I came across more evidence among the Latinos than among the Latinas of a pan-minority identity with African Americans. The finding compelled me to return to the issue of how gender is associated with academic and cultural behaviors and to focus on how ideas about masculinity, femininity, and family socialization lead to different cultural, social, and academic patterns for Latinos and Latinas. In what follows, I choose not to ignore the complexity of students' multiple cultural identities and instead choose to highlight the dynamic intersections and tensions of their racial, ethnic, class, and gender identities.

INTERETHNIC DIFFERENCES, MOBILITY, AND EDUCATION

Overall, Latino students, like African American students, lag behind Whites and even other immigrant minority groups, such as Koreans, Chinese, and South Asian Indians. With lower grade point averages and test scores, higher dropout rates, and less college attainment than Asian and White peers, they are often labeled "at-risk." Observers perceive them to be at risk for having few skills to hold jobs that pay decent wages and salaries, for being unable to support their children and families, for participating in illicit activities that will land them in prison, and for dependence on government social services paid with tax dollars that create resentment in others (Duncan and Brooks-Gunn 1997; Katz 1990). What I gathered from these students was that the idea of being at risk had little to no relevance to their cultural constructions and their aspirations for economic mobility. With the proper supports, they believed that they could achieve a socioeconomic success that had eluded their parents.

The distribution of Latinos falling within group of students I profile the cultural mainstreamers, the cultural straddlers, and the noncompliant believers—mirrors that of the African American students (table 4.3).

TABLE 4. 3 Educational Believer Groups by Race and Ethnicity

	Latino	African American	Total
Cultural Mainstreamer	2 (8%)	3 (7%)	5 (7%)
Cultural Straddler	9 (38%)	16 (36%)	25 (37%)
Noncompliant Believer	13 (54%)	25 (57%)	38 (56%)
Total N	24 (100%)	44 (100%)	68 (100%)

While more than half of the Latino students (54 percent), like their
African American peers, fall into the noncompliant category, neither
group rejected dominant ideology about economic mobility and education. Survey evidence suggests that they viewed education as the vehicle of
upward mobility. Again using Roslyn Mickelson's educational attitudes
measures again (introduced in chapter 1), 100 percent of Latino and 91
percent of African American youths agreed that getting a good education
was the practical way to achieve (see table 4.4).

TABLE 4.4 Comparison of Attitudes about Education by Ethnicity

Percentage who agree:	African American	Latino
If everyone in America gets a good education, we can end poverty.	93%	68%**
Achievement and effort in school lead to job success later on.	100%	92%
School success is NOT necessarily a clear path to a better life.	19%	15%
Getting a good education is a practical road to success for a young (Black/Hispanic) person like me.	91%	100%
Young (Black/Hispanic) persons like me have a chance of making it if we do well in school.	98%	92%
Education really pays off in the future for young (Black/Hispanic) people like me.	95%	100%
Total N	43	25

**p < .05 (two-sided chi square)

Interestingly, significantly fewer Latinos believed that poverty could be ameliorated by a more highly educated populace—showing less idealism about that than did their African American peers (see table 4.4). Although both groups share high rates of poverty, their relationships to poverty have come about in different ways (Massey 1993). Blacks and Latinos have distinct social and economic experiences and histories in the American context, which might influence how they perceive opportunities and even themselves. When the doors of immigration opened in the mid-1960s, migrants from territories and immigrants from nations hurt by colonization and imperialist economic policies—Puerto Rico, the Dominican Republic, and Cuba—arrived en masse in the United States. Many came seeking the American dream, but with little education and limited skills, many found only exploitative, low-wage jobs (LeDuff 2000; Bean and Tienda 1999). The poverty that parents and grandparents left behind in their home countries and the low wages of many Latinos across the nation in the United States may help explain the doubt among the Latino students in this study about ending poverty in this nation. Furthermore, the comparatively limited educational backgrounds in the Latino families who participated in this research may have some association with their beliefs. Among these students, 75 percent of the Latino youths' parents had not finished high school, compared to 35 percent of the African American youths' parents.

A random study of California residents has shown that Latinos are more likely than Blacks and Whites to attribute poverty to individual (e.g., the belief that if I do not get an education then I will be poor) instead of structural causes (e.g., the belief that the outsourcing of jobs abroad or outside cities leads to higher unemployment) (Hunt 1996). Both Blacks and Latinos were more likely to attribute poverty to *both* societal and individual forces than were Whites, however. The Yonkers students' responses are consistent with this latter finding, especially when we observe that all of the Latinos in the study agreed that acquiring an education was a practical means to *personal* success, while they tended to agree less that education for all would eradicate poverty. In short, the Latino students viewed success in more individualistic terms than as a result of greater societal conditions.

Characterizing the lives of toil and poverty their parents had endured in their native lands, they suggested that once armed with a high school or college diploma, they would escape low wages and impoverished existences like that of their parents and therefore have an economic well-being that is qualitatively better that of their parents. On several occasions, I heard youth scorn welfare—not an atypical response from those who might have suffered humiliation at the hands of social-service bureaucrats. Alma, a Dominican American college student, described how she hoped her life would be different from her mother's life. "I think [it will be] different, a better job," she said. "I wouldn't have to allow people to treat me like they treat her, 'cause you know she's on public assistance. They talk to you any kind of way, like humiliate you and stuff. I won't have to endure that." Monica, a Dominican student who had dropped out of high school before eventually obtaining her GED and enrolling in the community college, echoed that sentiment too:

> I don't want to be on welfare. I don't want to have a lot of kids. The most I'll have is two kids; and I don't want to have kids when I'm not able to have them, when I'm not able to support them. I don't want to be working . . . like my mother used to work, like, six in the morning to six in the afternoon and she would get paid, like, $120 a week, 'cause she didn't have no education, nothing. I don't want to be struggling.

Monica expressed a common concern of this group of youngsters. They yearned for a better life, free of economic struggle. Monica's comments suggested that she understood the direct correlation between education and job status: a lack of education could mean a life of economic struggle. She also presented an intriguing case to this researcher—a student who had once epitomized the type of school dropouts that Michelle Fine (1991) discussed in her book on academically vulnerable students. Recognizing the dissonance between her comprehension of subjects taught in school and her teachers' abilities to impart knowledge in an understandable manner, Monica characterized her initial view of schooling:

> The teachers really [didn't] care if you [came] to class. They just didn't care. I would be sitting there, and I wouldn't learn anything. They would just give me a book and tell me, "Here, read this." And if I don't understand it, then I don't like to do something. I am not going to do it at all. So, I didn't like going to school *there* (Monica's emphasis).

Already a few years away from that unpleasant high-school experience, having obtained her GED and presumably possessing more maturity, Monica sat in her family's modest kitchen holding her toddler nephew. She told me that her older sister Marta, a college graduate, influenced her decision to enroll in the community college:

> At first I didn't think that school was for me either, but I think that if you put your mind to it, you can do it and finish with it quick . . . but some people, they don't like school. And some are just lazy; they don't want to do anything with their lives. But I feel that school is not for everybody. There are certain things that other people have to do with their lives. It's one of those things that you just have to bite the bullet and get it done and go on and move on in life. I don't want to raise [my nephew] or my [potential] child here either. That's why I decided to go back to school. So I can move out of here and, like, put them in an environment so that they can grow up and have chances to do things that they like.

Only time will tell if Monica will have the assistance of sufficient resources (financial, social, or otherwise) to be able to obtain more academic training to move out of "there." I introduce Monica here for several reasons. First, she is a Dominican brought up in a poor, mainly African American and welfare-dependent neighborhood who eventually sought higher education, despite a rocky start in high school. Before dropping out of high school, she cut class frequently, hanging out in the cafeteria or hallways and playing cards with friends, too embarrassed to continue in classes where teachers seemed impatient with students who did not appear to catch on quickly. In high school, Monica was the type of student I encountered often—the noncompliant believer—who was well represented in social science research that has pathologized the urban, minority poor and characterized them as "downwardly mobile." Yet, in terms of aspirations, Monica was upwardly mobile. At the time of our interview, she appeared to be getting her life together, having already obtained her GED and preparing to enroll in the community college. But Monica indicated that she would do this without acculturating fully into white, middle-class society, particularly if acculturation would mean surrendering her own cultural distinctiveness.

I love to be Spanish. I don't care what anybody says, I love to be Dominican. That's my heritage, and if you ask me, I'll say "'Yes, I'm Dominican.'" I was born here but I say that I'm Dominican, and I feel that I can do whatever I want, as long as I put my mind to it. So, I don't feel like a minority. I feel like I'm just me, and nobody's going to stop me, no White people, no Black people, nobody. It's whatever I want to do.

Similar to the students in sociologist Rubén Rumbaut's (1995) longitudinal study of more than two thousand immigrant youths in Southern California, these Yonkers teenagers did not identify with assimilative mainstream identities (with or without a hyphen). Rather, they valorized either an immigrant identity or a pan-Latino identity. These patterns of identification developed particularly as the youths became increasingly aware of the ethnic and racial categories in which mainstream society classified them.[4]

Idealistic though the "nobody's going to stop me" proclamation might seem to a reader who understands cultural and structural barriers to mobility, Monica asserts that her aspirations for full incorporation into the American socioeconomic and political fabric should and could be fulfilled with her Dominican identity intact, even if she was "born here." Monica emphatically asserts her ethnic identity as a second-generation Dominican American youth, as a member of a group with an identity different from the racialized and binary black and white identities that prevail in the United States. If a student like Monica lives in a poor black area and drops out of school and asserts a strong minority identity, then the post hoc explanation for her "failure" to complete high school is that she succumbed to the influences of her native minority (or those not of immigrant descent) peers in the neighborhood. Contrary to segmented assimilation theory's contention that life among native minorities is associated with downward mobility, Monica did not equate achievement with whiteness and as incompatible with her Dominican identity. If ambition and aspiration—value commitments congruent with the mainstream ideology about success—are any indication of an individual's orientation, then these responses suggest that the Latino youth in my study, as well as their native minority counterparts, are pro-mobility. Yet as they engaged in the constructive processes of establishing their "Latino" identities in contemporary society, narratives emerged to sug-gest that these students did mimic their native minority, mainly low-income African American peers, and resisted "acting white," although they primarily invoked this term for cultural, social, and other nonacademic reasons.

GENDER, ETHNICITY, AND PAN-MINORITY IDENTITY

Specific ethnic (e.g., Puerto Rican) and pan-ethnic identities (i.e., Latino) are only two of the salient identity formations that students whose parents were born in either the Spanish-speaking Caribbean or Central and Latin America maintain. When persons of subordinated groups cohere around certain historical, social, political and economic experiences in society, they can view themselves as members of the same or a similar status group and maintain a "pan-minority identity" (Lee, Carter, and Neckerman 1998). That is, they consider themselves a "minority" or socially and politically marginalized persons vis-à-vis White Americans.

In response to one of my questions about the meaning of "acting white," Monica alluded to a pan-minority identity. Not more than ten minutes after she asserted a Dominican identity, she said:

> Like, if a Black man has more money and they hang out with the White guys, they act just like the White guy. Don't treat me the same way as a White guy would treat me. Like, "'Oh, she's Spanish.'" We're [Blacks and Hispanics] the same. Don't treat me like that. If I don't like it when White people do it, why would I like it with you? Like, you know, we're supposed to be together [united], and you're acting just like the White man.

In this instance, Monica shifted from her ethno-specific Dominican identity to a pan-minority identity—the perception of herself as a member of a group that unites Blacks and Hispanics—since she believed that they were the "same" when it came to treatment from Whites.

Pan-minority identity also emerges when students begin to share cultural tastes, due to a host of factors including their proximity and contact, the influences of media such as MTV, VH1, BET, and Univision, and the wide reach of hip-hop culture, in which the provocative lyrics of rap music highlight the social ills and inequality afflicting their communities

(George 1998). "Most of the Spanish and Black kids hang together, and the White kids hang with the White kids," eighteen-year-old Neal Lisandro tells me, because "it's like the White people listen to that alternative rock and roll, heavy metal stuff, whatever they listen to. And the Black and Spanish probably listen to R & B and rap, you know." Perhaps, it is this cross-cultural sharing of hip-hop culture that concerns oppositional culture and segmented assimilationist theorists who express concern about Latino youths' exposure to "downwardly mobile" native minority culture. Hip-hop culture, commonly expressed through rap music, dance, graffiti art, street fashion, street language, and street knowledge, embodies an overt rejection of many mainstream cultural practices (George 1998; Dyson 1993; Rose 1994), enough to bother some of the nation's main cultural gatekeepers (Harrington 1996).

We know that gender shapes the meaning of different types of ethnic self-identity (Portes and Rumbaut 2001; Waters 1996), and this may include a pan-minority identity. I found several indicators and heard many suggestions that Latinos related culturally with their Black peers more than Latinas. While Latinas and Latinos reported no statistically significant differences in their percentages of close Black friends—26 percent and 35 percent, respectively—Latinos mentioned more Blacks in their overall social networks than did Latinas, 45 percent and 29 percent, which is some indication that the Latinos in this study had more contact with Blacks than Latinas. These findings are consistent with Valenzuela's observation (1999) in an ethnographic study of a predominantly Latino high school in Texas that males tend to be more involved in these hip-hop styles than females are. It is likely that males follow hip-hop culture more than do females because hip-hop embodies a dominant model of masculinity in urban Black and Latino communities (Morgan 2002; Dyson 1993; George 1998).

Prior research shows that Latinos do emulate black forms of masculinity. In an ethnographic study of low-income Puerto Rican males in East Harlem, Philippe Bourgois (1995) describes Caesar, one of the book's main protagonists who says, "I used to want to be Black when I was younger. I wanted to be with that black style cause they're badder. Like malos [bad] . . . ," declared Caesar. "Plus Black people like to dress hard-like, rugged. You know what I'm saying? Look wild, like *black*. Black, just being *black* [author's italics]. Cool. Cause the Spanish people I used to hang with, their style was kind of wimpy, you know . . . that be the moyos [racist Puerto Rican term for Blacks] with the fly clothes" (Bourgois 1995, 46). Caesar emphasized that he associates hardness with black maleness; it is not "wimpy" but rather formidable, as expressed through dress, body language, and demeanor. It is the paradigm of masculinity that predominates in urban Black and Latino communities.

In this study, the Latinos more readily displayed how they shared similar tastes in hip-hop culture with African American males, while the Latinas were more explicit about racial and ethnic distinctions between Blacks and Latinos. For example, soft-spoken, light-skinned Luis Escobar, a nineteen-year-old Puerto Rican male, told me that he talked "black," his speech dripping with the sort of street slang that I had heard African American boys living nearby use. Eighteen-year-old Hector Perez, who was living in the Bronx with his grandmother after leaving Yonkers, wore thick gold chains around his neck and a blue baseball cap twisted to the right side of his head. When I complimented him on his chains, he responded, "Yeah, the chains. There's a couple of kids I know . . . they into rapping, into Heavy D and everybody," thus admitting his penchant for hip-hop culture. Hector also told me that the way he dressed, the cologne he wore, and his ability to rap made him popular at his high school.

While many nondominant racial and ethnic identities cohere around their experiences with racism and discrimination in white society, in a matter of moments, many Latinos and other non-White immigrant youth can distance themselves socially from other racial and ethnic minorities, especially American Blacks, a highly stigmatized group (Rumbaut 1995). Racial ideology over the course of U.S. history has cast Black Americans in the most negative light, deeming them genetically and culturally inferior (Murray and Herrnstein 1994), and describing these factors as the cause of their economic and political marginalization. The reach of this ideology is global, affecting many people's views about a group of persons whom they have never met. Thus, it is no wonder that people come into the United States predisposed to believe that "the Blacks" are the ones to avoid. In a 1999 article in *The New York Times*'s series on "How Race Is Lived in America," writer Charles LeDuff described the contentious relationships between recent Mexican immigrants and African American workers in a North Carolina pork plant, which had an ethnically stratified labor structure fraught with tension. The Mexican workers were segregated in one part of the plant, responsible for select tasks, while the African American workers carried out other tasks elsewhere. LeDuff described how the Mexican workers subscribed to stereotypical images of loud, lazy Blacks, while the African American workers lashed out in anger about the Mexicans' willingness to toil for the pork plant owners at sub-union wages. Moreover, in several school studies, researchers document how in a multiethnic and diverse high school in northern California, African American and Latino students socialize separately within their respective ethnic groups (Pollock 2004; Perry 2002).

In comparison to the Latinos, the Latinas created more social distance between African American urban youth culture and Latino cultures. I witnessed Monica criticize her brother Alex in absentia for identifying as Black during a vociferous exchange with Toni, the mother of Alex's son, who self-identified as African American and "Spanish."[5] Monica described herself as Hispanic and Dominican, though later she would speak in terms of collective solidarity with Blacks.

> *Monica:* Yeah, like people come in here (she demonstrates) and are like [*Monica changes her voice inflection*] "Yeah, what's up man?" . . . acting like you black or something. I'm, like, you're Spanish. What is your problem? Why are you trying to act black? Like, my brothers act like they [are] Black. They don't say that they're Dominican. They say that they are Black. And I'm, like, why do you say that you Black? You're Dominican.

> *Toni* [*interjects*]: Me personally . . . I don't feel that they "act black!"

> *Monica:* They "act black."

> (*Toni and Monica then begin to disagree about whether Alex "acts black."*)

> *Toni:* I don't feel that they "act black!" To me, personally, I don't think there's such a thing as acting black or acting white. There's Spanish rappers, just like there's Black rappers. There are White rappers, too.

Monica: Of course . . . but if you come through the door and you're swearing that you're Black and acting (she mimics). You're Dominican . . . I'm, like, "Why are y'all acting so stupid? Y'all do something with your life. And show that Black and Hispanic people can do something."

Prudence: So it's the mannerisms that you have problems with?

Monica: Yeah, it's the mannerisms, and, like, you go out there and you see, like, Black people saying "All yeah" (she mimics and gesticulates with her hands). I'm, like, why are you acting so stupid?

Prudence: Is it also an age thing? Is it mostly young people who say these things?

Monica: It's young kids that think, like, in order to "act black," you got to stand in a corner and sell drugs or just listen to rap music. It's not that, you know what I'm saying. You act the way you want to act. You act like who you are. I'm just saying that what my brothers, when they were young, used to think they were. They would swear that they were Black. If you were to ask them what is their culture, I would say that I'm Dominican and they would say "Oh, I'm Black. Yeah, that's right, I was born here, and I don't care what anybody says, I'm Black." And they listening to their black music. I be like just because you listen to rap music don't mean that you Black. Don't hide your heritage. You're Dominican.

Toni: [*interjects*] I heard that conversation and I asked both of them, "Why do you say you're Black?"' To me, they just think that Spanish and Black are the same thing.

Monica [*interrupts*]: No, they thought they were Black. [*Toni and Monica disagree again.*] No they thought they were Black . . . all three of them thought they were Black.

Monica and Toni raised intriguing social and cultural issues that are worth unpacking. Illuminating the complexity of identity, Monica described how even within the same family, a brother and a sister could differ in how strongly they embraced either an ethnic or racial identity.

Honey-brown-skinned Monica proudly asserted that she is Dominican; whereas Alex, according to her, identified as "Black." Both identities are possible; these youth can be Black Dominicans, Dominican, and even White Dominican. For some, it's a matter of choice, if their skin is light enough. For those of darker phenotypes, the racial options may be more limited (Waters 1990). The debate between Monica and Toni confirms what Joanne Nagel (1994) has argued, "Ethnic identity is the result of a dialectical process involving internal and external opinions and processes, as well as the individual's self-identification and outsiders' ethnic designations—i.e., what you think your ethnicity is, versus what they think your ethnicity is." Furthermore, even if phenotype limits how others perceive and ascribe another a racial classification, Monica shows that both ethnic and racial identity may be situational, volitional, dynamic, and fluid, as in her case when she shifts between a "Dominican" and "we're the same" (pan-minority) identity, as well as in her brother Alex's case when he chooses to identity as "Black" and while she identifies as non-Black.

Disagreement ensued between Monica and Toni over about what these different self-identifications meant. Using interactional and linguistic styles to signify group differences, Monica distinguished between "acting black" and being Dominican, and she exposed her beliefs about the social undesirability of "acting black." But Toni contested Monica's use of Alex's taste for hip-hop music and styles as the primary indicator of "acting black," acknowledging that a global cross-fertilization of hip-hop music has occurred, since there are Black, White, and Spanish rappers (George 1998; Kleinfield 2000). Though Toni later recognized the influence that African Americans have had on the development of hip-hop culture, she resisted confining this cultural sphere to only a "black" space.

Despite its global reach and the billions of dollars in revenue that hip-hop music generates, many people, especially those active before and during the civil rights era, as well as mainstream cultural advocates, struggle with its social and cultural significances (Kitwana 2002; George 1998). Hip-hop culture has a reputation for rebelliousness and the glorification of sex, violence, drugs, and conspicuous consumption; and despite its emergence as the most popular youth cultural phenomenon of the late-twentieth and early-twenty-first centuries, its stigmatization by the mainstream has not escaped even those born in the hip-hop generation (between 1964 and 1985). Believing that hip hop leads students astray, Monica associated the audacious, sometimes bawdy, and frequently rough hip-hop personae with drug culture and the seemingly crass materialism that rappers appear to glamorize in their music and videos. Equating her brother's interactional styles and cultural tastes with "stupidity," she echoes the sentiments of those who consider hip-hop culture one of the detriments to Black and Latino youths' academic existence (Ferguson 2001; McWhorter 2001; Gates 2004). Although it remains an empirical question as to whether embracing hip-hop culture leads to downward mobility, Monica charged Black and Spanish youths to "do something with their [lives]" and not just listen to rap.

Moreover, aware of the negative portrayals of Blacks in larger society, Monica preferred that her brother identify primarily with his Dominican heritage, while Toni urged her to see how Alex preferred not to fracture his racial and ethnic identity, but rather to view himself as both ("they just think that Spanish and Black are the same thing"). Toni's was a plausible response, given that sociologists make distinctions between phenotypic and cultural groupings. Still, Monica, like many of her peers, conflated race, ethnicity, and class, ascribing certain behaviors to "blackness" and not recognizing that, in theory, her brother could maintain both identities.

Monica and Toni's passionate exchange also highlights how identities can break down across gender lines. Half of the Latino adolescents identified with a racial group, and more boys than girls chose a racial identity. Nine of the Latinos in the study described themselves as "Black Hispanic," two as "White Hispanic." All of the males who chose a racial and ethnic self-description identified as "Black Hispanic." Five of these seven boys' racial and ethnic identities reflected their mothers', while two had different identities than their mothers, who described themselves as White (see table 4.5).[6]

In several cases, brothers chose black racial identities, while their sisters preferred another identity. For instance, in another family, thirteen-year-old Felicia Escobar identified as White Hispanic on the survey I gave her, while her fifteen-year-old brother Federico identified as Black; both were fair complexioned. Meanwhile, their mother described herself as Black in her survey. Earlier, I mentioned Alma and Alberto Martinez. Alma, who proudly identified herself as Dominican, shared her concerns

TABLE 4.5 Racial, Ethnic Self-Identification of the Latina/o Adolescents by Gender

Percentage Identified as:	Hispanic Only	Black Hispanic	White Hispanic	Total
Female	8	2	2	12
Male	5	7	0	12
Total N	13	9	2	24

with me about Alberto whom she sensed was plagued by mistreatment from policemen because of his hip-hop appearance. The police had stopped Alberto in his car several times and according to Alma, the official complaint was that his music was too loud, although she believed that the police were harassing Alberto and his friends because of the stereotypes associated with hip-hop and urban minority boys.

> *Alma:* Yeah, like, when we see that [Alberto's] not following our footsteps and going his own way, hanging out with his friends, we always tell him . . . like, we know that it's harder because you're a guy . . . like, his friends are different types of friends. He has the types of friends who always like to hang out more than do schoolwork. For us, me and my sister, academics came first and everything else came second.

> *Prudence:* Why do you believe that the boys around this neighborhood tend to have a harder time?

> *Alma:* I think definitely they have a harder time, and the cops have the same attitude that the neighbors around here had when they first built these complexes. They thought that this was like the projects and that it was going to bring their property value down. . . . [Also] I just think that they're [boys are] so immature. I tell [Alberto] he's always a follower. Be a leader. They're [boys are] always so concerned with dress and what to wear.

Intent on raising themselves and their family out of semi-reliance on social services and of supplementing the meager income of their widowed mother (who spoke little English and worked as a caretaker for the elderly), Alma and her older sister Elena (who had already graduated from college) aspired to high socioeconomic levels. Alberto was no different in his desires. When I interviewed him, he was in the process of applying to Syracuse University, and his goal was to own a chain of auto body shops.

In contrast to their male counterparts, Alma and the other Latinas identified themselves by their particular ethnic groups or simply as "Hispanic." None embraced an unhyphenated "American" identity, however—evidence of the rupture in the assimilation process predicted by sociologist Milton Gordon (1964). "American" has yet to fully acquire the connotation suggested by the multicultural, pluralistic "melting-pot" metaphor used decades ago to describe a nation with myriad immigrant groups. In Alma's mind, for example, "American" belonged to a selective group and not to all of the inhabitants of the United States, whether citizens or not. She continued telling me:

> *Alma:* I'm proud. I'm very proud to be Dominican. The way that I look at it, I'm here and I was born in New York; but to the White majority, I'm always going to be a Hispanic, so, like, I'm proud to say that I'm Hispanic. So, like, saying that I'm American is ridiculous. It's like saying that I'm a part of a group that doesn't accept me.

> *Prudence:* So, who's American then? You say that you can't be part of a group that doesn't accept you. So does "American" connote "White" to you?

> *Alma:* That's the way I always see it.

For Alma, the term "American" has a racial subtext, and it connotes more than one's nationality. She also views "American" as tainted by its history of racial exclusion and discrimination. A high achiever and cultural straddler, Alma was aware of her political minority status in the United States. For her, though, doing well in school and asserting a strong ethnic identity were not mutually exclusive.

There were other Latinas, like Vincenzia Molina, a nineteen-year-old who refused to identify with a racial category and strongly claimed that she was just Puerto Rican (or Hispanic), but still invoked a pan-ethnic identity with Blacks when she referred to Whites

> *Vincenzia:* Well, everybody dresses the same. Certain people, they dress real crazy . . . but most of the Puerto Ricans, they dress like Blacks. Most of the Whites, they dress regular.

> *Prudence:* Regular? What does that mean?

> *Vincenzia:* With all them colors on, different kinds of color.

> *Prudence:* Do Puerto Ricans and Blacks act the same way?

> *Vincenzia:* Most of them, yeah. Some Puerto Ricans just dedicated to they jobs and everything, you know, and some of them are quiet. They like to dress real nice. Some of them, they like to be wild, get a job, leave it, get another job. They like to hang out a lot. So, I consider Black and Puerto Rican mostly the same.

For Vincenzia, Whites were "regular," while Blacks and Latinos were the "same," implicitly the "other." Still, she and other Latino youths used certain cultural markers to distinguish themselves from not only non-Hispanic Whites but also African Americans. The set of distinguishing cultural practices included colorful fashions with a Caribbean influence, a taste for music such as salsa and merengue, and most noted the Spanish language, as twenty-year-old Fernanda Morales says: [7]

> *Fernanda:* Like in school sometimes, like, if you have your Spanish friends, they'll be like, "Well, you're Spanish. Why don't you talk to me in Spanish?'" Or some Puerto Ricans will be more into the English culture, and just be here, more into America and stuff. They'll be, like, we're citizens. And I'm, like, that doesn't make any difference; we're not Americans, not full Americans anyway. I don't know. Like, my friends used to be fighting all the time. [And I] got into a fight once because some girl said that I wasn't Puerto Rican enough.

> *Prudence:* What does that mean?

Fernanda: That means that I don't speak Spanish enough . . . that I didn't dress in Spanish.

Prudence: What's "dressing in Spanish"?

Fernanda: Not wearing baggy pants down to your butt and stuff . . . 'cause my friends usually saw me in tight-fitting stuff. You know how Spanish people are portrayed like tropical. They like short stuff, tight stuff, so I tried to get out of it. You know you get out of certain things for a while, then you go back to it. Like, I'm always in tight stuff now. . . . Yeah, I got out of Spanish style for a while, and they were like, "Well, what happened? Are you trying to be black . . . trying to be white . . . trying to be this or that?'" I was trying to be who I was. I wasn't trying to be something else.

Fernanda and Vincenzia shared similar sentiments about "Spanish"—specifically Puerto Rican—cultural distinction. They made it known that black and Spanish cultural styles are not equivalent. Being Spanish meant knowing how to be Puerto Rican, Dominican, or Cuban for the Latino youth in this study. And the authenticity of the Spanish person came from her ability to speak the Spanish language, which primarily shaped the boundaries between the pan-ethnic identities of Latinos from the identities of the African American youths. Language difference is powerful marker between groups, and as Bailey (2000) has argued, the Latino or Spanish ethnolinguistic identity is in part a form of resistance among second-generation Latino youth to phenotype-racial classifications such as Black or White.

Yet despite their ethnic and cultural delineations, the sharing of an economic and social position provides more grounds for the sharing of political attitudes among Latinos and African Americans. Shared social statuses can facilitate a pan-minority identity of "non-White," or given the Latinos' immigrant history, an identity of "non-American." "We're not Americans, not full Americans anyway," Fernanda claims, alluding to the racial and ethnic exclusionary practices in U.S. society. Both Latino and African American students perceived the racial and ethnic climate of Yonkers and the nation similarly. Seventy-one percent of the Latinos and 81 percent of the African Americans believed that at least some racial and job discrimination existed and that this would hurt their chances of getting well-paying jobs. A much smaller percentage, only about one-third or less of each group, felt that Whites, in general, wanted to keep African Americans and Latinos at the bottom of the socioeconomic ladder (see table 4.6). Still, only 16 percent of the African Americans and 28 percent of Latinos felt that Whites wanted to give their respective groups "a better break" in the various sectors of society. A majority of each group felt that Whites did not care one way or the other how their social groups fared. On average, though, the African American youths felt significantly more pessimistic about the social, political, and economic prospects of Blacks than did their Latino peers, while more than twice as many Latinos were likely to believe that Whites wanted to give African Americans a "better break" (table 4.6).

Certainly, social factors such as race and class play significant roles in this pan-minority identity. These African American and Latino adolescents share a common reality—they are poor youth living in a racially

TABLE 4. 6 Beliefs and Perceptions of Job Opportunity and Race Relations by Ethnicity

Percentage who believe:	African Americans	Latinos
Racial/ethnic discrimination hurts the chances to get good paying jobs (some to a lot).	81%	71%
Whites in society want to give Blacks a better break.	16%	37%**
Whites in society want to keep Blacks down.	33%	33%
Whites in society do not care one way or the other what happens to Blacks.	51%	30%**
Whites in society want to give Hispanics a better break.	21%	28%
Whites in society want to keep Hispanics down.	23%	28%
Whites in society do not care one way or the other what happens to Hispanics.	53%	44%
Total N	44	24

**$p < .05$ (two-sided chi square)

stratified and class-stratified urban America. Opinions vary on whether the salience of ethno-specific Latino identities will remain high (Gans 1992), though some suggest that pan-ethnicity and pan-minority identity (a shared identity between both African Americans and Latinos) may well supplant both assimilation and ethnic particularism for racial/ethnic minorities (Espiritu 1992; Lee 1996).

Current research on the "new second generation" predicts a healthier socioeconomic forecast for immigrant youth, provided that the cultural patterns and styles that they encounter in poor and native minority communities do not derail them (Portes and Rumbaut 2001; Portes 1995). In this study, neither Latino nor African American youths in poor urban neighborhoods reject normative achievement ideology. In fact, they subscribe to it unequivocally, toeing the line of messages about how an education will lead to a good job. The findings support the notion that black cultural styles remain dominant in these communities, which African American males and Latinos share. In addition, the Latino youths at times shared a pan-minority identity with African Americans when the reference was to Whites; but at other times, these youths, especially Latinas, demonstrated a strong recognition of their position and African Americans' position in the social hierarchy. In the next section, I discuss how family and gender socialization tempered the degree to which Latinas shared the cultural styles of their African American peers, in comparison to Latinos.

THE ROLES OF FAMILY AND GENDER CONTROL

Families maintain and reproduce the patriarchal control of girls' and women's places in society by diligently monitoring their daughters' whereabouts. A brother and sister in the same household can have very different experiences of social engagement outside the home even at the same age. For adolescent girls, strict curfews are common, and often they are not allowed to move freely about the community without trusted supervision. Adolescent boys spend more time outside of the home on the basketball courts and hanging out with their friends. The Latinas in this study had different levels of interactions with African Americans in their neighborhoods than did the Latinos. I heard this from thirteen-year-old

Carlos Jimenez who admitted that at his twelve-year-old sister Carmen's age, he could do many things that she could not do at twelve, such as hang out with friends at late hours. When I asked him why, he exclaimed, "Because she's a girl!" Carlos's perspective, no doubt, came from his observations of parents' monitoring practices. Among the twenty Latino parents from whom I had gathered parental reports—ten males and ten females—eight of the ten parents of Latinas responded that they *often* knew their daughters' whereabouts, compared to only four of the parents of Latinos' parents.

For the African Americans, these differences by gender were not as stark; 83 percent and 80 percent of the males' and females' parents, respectively (out of forty-one reporting, twenty-four females, seventeen males), reported often knowing where their children were. Meanwhile, 40 percent of the Latinos' parents believed that their children's neighborhood peers were a bad influence, compared with 20 percent of the Latinas' parents.[8] Sociologists and psychologists alike argue that child rearing practices within Latino families tend to endorse and encourage clearly defined sex-role differentiation for boys and girls. Socialized to adopt group- and family-oriented identity, Latinas are often taught to be dependent, obedient, responsible, and submissive; disagreement and conflict with parents and elders are not tolerated (DeLeón 1996). Parents and other responsible adults watch, protect, and monitor girls' social relationships very closely, allowing their sons more personal and social autonomy.

Despite reported similarities in the parental monitoring of daughters across ethnicity and race, as represented in this study, I had informal conversations with Latina mothers who told me that they would not allow their daughters to socialize with African American girls in the community because the girls were considered "too womanish." One youth, Toni, who self-identified as Black and "Spanish" believed that some Latino parents often disparaged black culture, considering it less desirable, less controlled, and more morally questionable than Latino cultures:

> Like, one of my friends was Puerto Rican and Cuban, and one
> summer her mother wouldn't let her go to the movies by herself.
> I was, like, thirteen, and my mother let me go to the movies by
> myself, as long as I was with my friends. Her mother was like,
> "[Toni's] mother lets her do that because she's Black." And my

friend was like, "No, Mommy, Toni's Spanish, too." They were saying that in Spanish, assuming that I didn't understand what they were saying. But basically, she was saying that because she thought I was Black, I always did whatever I wanted. I could go out. All I had to do was tell my mother where I was going.

Although the Latinas in my study were, on average, two years older than the other study participants (average age: Latina, 17.58; Latino, 15.25; Black male, 15.61; and Black female, 15.73), their mothers kept a more vigilant watch over their peers, as Toni's comments suggest. In a prior study of immigrant youth in an urban school, Olsen (1997) also found evidence of strict parental monitoring of females' behavior. And perhaps this parental vigilance paid off. Olsen also found that schools became liberating places where girls could exercise their individuality and independence. Socialized to perform many different social roles, including that of the good student, the Latinas in my study were more apt to perform well in school, reporting a mean grade point average of eighty-six, eleven points higher than the Latinos' mean reported grade point average. Does tighter parental monitoring influence Latinas' educational performance? Sociologist Nancy Lopez (2003), in a study of Spanish Caribbean students, suggests that it does. Lopez finds not only that Latinas perform better than Latinos but also that because parents control their daughters' social movements more than those of their sons, they enable girls to make social connections leading to part-time jobs. In the long run, these jobs can put these young women on the path office jobs as administrative assistants, secretaries, clerks, and other professional jobs.

GENDER, WORK, AND IMMIGRANT MINORITY YOUTH

If we consider outward appearances and shared musical and clothing tastes—then the cultural behaviors of the Latino males in my study seems to support argument that the behaviors of immigrant youths in impoverished urban communities resemble those of their Black peers (1993; Portes and Stepick 1993). But again, the analytical focus should move beyond observing similarities in cultural tastes and styles in explaining possible downward mobility among second-generation Latino youths. Although the cultural styles of the Latinos resembled those of their African American male peers, their attitudes about work and their potential for job attainment were different.

I reported earlier that the Latinos aspired to service and blue-collar jobs. Their modal career or job preference was auto mechanic, while for the African American males the modal choice was either businessman or professional athlete. In addition, Latinos held significantly different attitudes and beliefs toward employment and gender roles. Seventy-seven percent of the Latino males, compared to 47 percent of the African American males, believed that their self-respect was linked to having a good job. More than three times as many Latino males as African American males believed that men should be the breadwinners outside of the home, while women should take care of the home and family (table 4.7). In short, for the Latino males in my study, work outside home defined "man" to a stronger degree than it did for African American males and both groups of females.

In an economy with different ceilings service-oriented work versus

TABLE 4.7 Beliefs about Gender Roles by Ethnicity and Gender

Percentage who agree:	African American Males	Latino Males	African American Females	Latino Females
Better for everyone if the man is the achiever outside the home and the woman takes care of the home	18%	62%***a	12%	17%
More important for a woman to be intelligent than attractive	65%	92%*b	92%	83%
The way for a man to get respect is to have a good job	47%	77%*b	62%	50%
Total N	17	13	26	12

*p< .10; ***p < .01 (two-sided chi square).

aSignificance between Latino males and all other groups.

bSignificance found between Latino males and African American males.

professional, managerial work and with different ceilings for those of different gender, race, and ethnicity, we might expect that the Latinos' job aspirations are more likely to be fulfilled. Statistics from the 1999 Current Population Survey (CPS) offer a national forecast for job possibilities. Service-oriented jobs make up some of the thirty fastest growing occupations projected for the decade from 1998 to 2008, the period in which these students will enter adulthood. I found that the majority of Black and Hispanic men working in the fastest growing occupations were in service-related areas; they were truck drivers, janitors and cleaners, marketing and sales or retail workers. According to responses to the 1999 CPS, 30 percent of employed Black, non-Hispanic men and 23 percent of Hispanic men held one of these jobs.

The African American males in my study, who mostly aspired to enter the professional classes, have a longer way to go and higher hurdles to overcome. Only 6 percent and 5 percent of all Black and Hispanic men from the 1999 CPS, respectively, held jobs as general managers and executives—two occupations projected to grow over the decade. In contrast, more than twice as many White males held these positions. I also found that Latino and White men with no college degree but with some college experience were more likely to obtain managerial and executive positions than were non-Latino Black men. In the CPS, managerial and executive positions were the modal occupational categories for Latino and White men with only "some college" experience. In contrast, Black men with some college experience were more likely to be truck drivers; general manager and executive became the modal occupational categories only after the completion of a bachelor's degree. And even among Black men with college degrees, only slightly more than half, 52 percent, held professional or specialty jobs, compared to 63 percent of Latino men.

The occupational patterns for Black and Latina women differ from that of Black and Latino men. In the 1999 CPS, Black and Latina women with college degrees were less likely to hold one of the fast-growing managerial and executive positions. Controlling for education and examining the women's distribution among the top-thirty occupations, I learned that Black women and Latinas with graduate and professional degrees were more likely to be working as elementary-school teachers. Furthermore, secretary, nursing aides, and housekeeper or janitor—the type of low-skilled jobs held by their mothers—were three of the jobs that Black and Latina women with less than an associate's degree were likely to hold. However, for all available occupations, 68 percent and 72 percent, respectively, of college-educated Black and Latina women in the CPS sample held professional, specialty occupations, including lawyer and doctor, the occupations of choice for my female students. This latter statistic among the college-educated Black and Latina women, which is higher than that of Black and Latino men with the same educational background, supports an earlier claim about an emergent gender gap in achievement between females and males (see chapter 3).

Finally, research shows that racial and ethnic hierarchies play an important role in the service sector of the economy. Discrimination in hiring tends to affect Black men more than Latinos who are beneficiaries of job markets or niches where employers tend to prefer immigrant minorities to native minorities (Holzer 1998). Some Latino males might be able to avoid the adverse effects of labor-market discrimination, especially if employers render some as "Black" and others as "not Black," and thus, be more likely to find jobs in markets where they have strong networks (Jencks 1992; Smith 1997; Waldinger 1996). What remains to be seen is whether Latinos like the boys whom I interviewed will have to disassociate their "male" presentations of selves from the influence of the cultural styles of their Black peers. Or will their more attainable aspirations and a segmented economy responsive to the immigrant minority afford Latino males more economic mobility than their native minority peers? As I argued in the previous chapter, the pressure to be "the man" among the males in this study encouraged more risky behaviors and less attention to school achievement. Consequently, they were assertive, independent, and bold in their expression of themselves. As members of the hip-hop generation, these Latino and African American students share various urban youth cultural codes. Yet with the effects of a host of social and economic factors, the consequences of this cross-cultural sharing might be different.

The social profiles of the youth in my study are telling. Given their modest school performances and limited forms of social and economic capital, the youths whom I have observed are at-risk. Hurdles appear as these boys and young men are evaluated by institutional gatekeepers as either worthy of opportunity or not. In the meantime, those who exhibit the "hard" stance, which I discussed in chapter 3, are likely to find themselves at a greater disadvantage than those who do not present this cul-

tural stance. Contrary to what the oppositional culture and poverty literature seem to suggest, these students are not culturally predisposed to failure in this society. They, too, are in search of respect at school and hope to
attain good jobs later in their lives. Another matter lies in how to help
these youths to achieve the success they desire in a society that parcels out
access to opportunity in culturally inequitable ways.

NEW "HEADS" AND MULTICULTURAL
NAVIGATORS

Race, Ethnicity, Poverty, and Social Capital

Increasing the school attachment and achievement of low-income African American and Latino students requires both improved academic skills and resources—economic, cultural, and social. Most will have some difficulty making their way out of poverty if they lack resourceful social connections— or social capital. "Capital"—there is that metaphor again, but in this instance it refers to the resources that come with personal connections and social networks (Bourdieu 1986; Coleman 1988; Loury 1976; Portes 1998). Contemporary wisdom has it that "it is who you know" that matters in our society. Personal and social networks—whether of peers, family members, teachers, or others—are seen by many researchers as important determinants of youth behaviors and of educational and socioeconomic outcomes; and effective social networks are critical to various forms of social attainment in U.S. society (Fischer 1977; MacLeod 1987; Granovetter 1973; Wilson 1987; Stanton-Salazar 2001; Sullivan 1989). Personal networks not only represent potential access to material resources but also provide socio-psychological benefits to individuals thirsting for inclusion in a collectivity, a family, a peer group, a church, or social organization (Coleman 1988).

At times sheepishly and at times boldly, the Yonkers students divulged that they did not have any proximate adult role models. For many of the adults whom they saw daily, they wanted to be "nowhere near [nothing] like them!" as fifteen-year-old Samurai Kitchens exclaimed. Continuing, he said, "I just want to get passed, just want to get higher up." He and others wanted mentors and role models who were on the move with stable jobs that paid good wages. Who might these role models or mentors be?

For one thing, "they're not 'sellouts,'" Samurai proclaimed as he described the people whom he viewed as role models. "They don't forget where they came from. They're proud of where they came from. [And] even if they struggled, it don't matter. They made it." Those who exemplified Samurai's idea of a role model were several native sons and a daughter who had achieved fame, from the rappers DMX and the LOXX to R & B singer Mary J. Blige. Hugely popular, wealthy, and from the poor and working-class neighborhoods of Yonkers, these celebrities had become the shining examples of success. They were the "new heads" to emulate. Most important, they had made it and achieved success without the appearance of denying their cultural, racial, ethnic, and socioeconomic origins. Further, as Samurai put it by invoking a sense of "fictive kinship," these famous people remembered to give back to their communities, something that he feared many middle- and upper-class Blacks had neglected to do while on the path of mobility.

Though she did not feel that it was a requirement, Loretta Lincoln concurred with Samurai and believed that the African American middle class should help to maintain economic support structures in communities believed to have aided them at some point. "Like when people do get high [up] or whatever, I don't think they have to give back to the community, but they should because they never know when they going to fall and probably be right back where they started," she said. The sense for communal obligation ran strong among this bunch of youth, and when mobile Blacks subscribed to individualistic—as opposed to communitarian—ideals, they, too, ran the risk of being perceived as "acting white." "Most Black people, once they get rich they don't associate with Blacks, they want to be with the White ones," claimed Teresa Anton. Like Samurai and Loretta, Teresa clung to beliefs in "fictive kinship," which as anthropologist Signithia Fordham argues (1988) are woven throughout the fabric of African American culture and identity.

Together, these three youths' comments crystallize running sentiments about the type of social capital they felt would benefit their communities and their lives. Some researchers report that most people with whom association would constitute social capital, including those whom Elijah Anderson refers to as "old heads," have left America's inner cities, leaving a concentration of poverty behind in their migration's wake (Wilson 1987). Old heads, who according to Anderson were the paragons of respectability and social modeling in many urban African American communities throughout the mid- to late-twentieth century, were the traditional, assimilative, paternalistic, moral authority figures who sometimes served as surrogate parents when parents or legal guardians were not home. They were the ones who regaled youth with tales of the past, elders sharing wisdom and knowledge with young minds, passing on the social history of African Americans, for example, and setting examples of getting a job, owning a home, and having family stability. They even disciplined mischievous youth and "whipped some behind" when parents were away and children were disobedient (Anderson 1990).

Anderson argued further that social and economic changes in the late-twentieth century left the doors open for "new heads" to replace old heads in urban communities of color. But some new heads are questionable role models. Now, according to Anderson, many new heads are involved in illicit activities, such as drugs and crime; some lead gangs and parade around neighborhoods with the fruits of their misdoings—the "bling bling" of ostentatious jewelry and cars—and thus, defy the ethics and codes of mainstream society. New heads also, in Anderson's analysis, do not uphold messages about the critical relevance of school and achievement.

Street gangs provide a form of nontraditional capital. Social success in the community can be earned by joining a gang and building a reputation as one not to "mess with." "Gangs also offer an alternative way to achieve in school, especially among youths who are offered little or no opportunity to achieve recognition in ways sanctioned by school," writes Nilda Flores-González (2002), who interviewed Puerto Rican students who had joined gangs. They sought to gain respect and a high standing in their communities, and joining gangs was one of the most immediate ways to build a reputation in school (for those who remained), Flores-González found. Thus, gang leaders—or the new heads—modeled for these youth how to enter and excel in a social field that offered mobility, namely, social prestige or notoriety.

While Anderson's concept of the new heads concentrates mainly on drug lords and street-gang leaders, I focus here on another type of new head. Though I observed drug dealers on street corners and even spoke with a few, including two I included in this study, most of these students expressed little or no respect for unemployed and drug-influenced family members and neighbors. Yet youth like Samurai, Loretta, Teresa, and many of their peers lived with the uncomfortable reality that many of the adults in their lives had not achieved the American dream of material success. So they looked for economic role models elsewhere. As conversations unfolded, I learned that people whom they did not know personally but whom they saw on television and heard on the radio became their role models. In describing these people the youths revealed the traits they would desire and appreciate in any social capital that they obtained. This social capital, like their cultural capital, had ethno-specific dimensions. It included persons who were not only mobile and socioeconomically successful but who also could negotiate between the wider society and their respective communities.

With the meteoric rise of hip-hop culture and rap music in the 1980s, new heads have emerged for the MTV and BET hard-rap generation, and their personal orientations have implications for the cultural traits required of role models. But first, let me say that role models are not the equivalent of social capital. To serve as capital for these students, such role models would have to be accessible and have relationships with them. Social capital "makes possible the achievement of certain ends that in its absence would not be possible," and "it exists in the *relations* among persons" (Coleman 1988, 98-101). So, pop stars are not social capital to these students. However, the fact that these youths respect hip-hop celebrities tells us much about what kinds of influences might be helpful in their lives. On the one hand, as I listened to them, I was tempted to dismiss their admiration for these top-selling artists to the fantasies that come with adolescence. Yet the reasons for *why* they respected these stars compelled me to examine these issues more carefully. Their explanations were about more than the musical genius of hip-hop stars and the adoration of popular youth cultural icons. They also perceived that these pop stars did not forsake their social origins in the process of achieving success—these celebrities were "keepin' it real."

Though hip-hop stars have maintained a following because of their musical, linguistic, and dress styles, they have prospered and achieved great financial success from the marketing and popularizing of cultural styles that do not signify conformity to perceived "white" middle-class cultural styles. And yet they are model economic success stories. They embrace a strong work ethic to produce albums, spreading ideas about money, power, and material success to which our contemporary, capitalist society assents. At the same time, they maintain the appearance of cultural nonconformity and cling to racial, ethnic and cultural distinction. These celebrities show that they do not have to culturally transform themselves to succeed or to disassociate themselves from their cultural heritage. That's one of the reasons why Samurai liked DMX. He believed that the hard-core rapper DMX, a fellow Yonkers native, had not only "made it" but had also not forgotten "where he came from."

These multimillionaires, with their ostentatious displays of wealth and politically insensitive lyrics, nonetheless, are charged with being problematic role models, accused of sending the wrong messages about the value of education (Ferguson 2001). Many low-income, urban youth imitate their styles and unfortunately get perceived as being unserious about school, and as lacking the skills to interact "properly" with customers if they seek jobs in mainstream retail stores. The paradox is that new heads, such as celebrity role models, exemplify upward mobility though their mobility is not based on the acquisition of school credentials, but rather on the development of musical talent and cultural skills and sometimes critical and politically conscious raps or rhymes.

I am not suggesting that most of these youth aspired to become famous entertainers. In fact, only ten of the sixty-eight aspired to be an actor, singer, or professional athlete. Moreover, I cannot say that their admiration for popular culture icons significantly differs from any of their contemporaries from other racial, ethnic, or socioeconomic groups. Teens of all races and ethnicities idolize pop stars. Yet these new heads have added an interesting twist to the idea of how social ties influence youths' subscription to dominant social norms about education, work, and family. They have proved that success can be attained without having to conform to the conventional office black, navy, or brown dress for work. Though many celebrities have not attended college or worked in other professional settings, hip-hop stars appeal because many come from poor communities, because some of them have spent time in the penitentiary and gangs, and because others spend time commenting on conditions such as poverty, unemployment, racial profiling, and discrimination.

Celebrity is not a realistic option for most youth. The majority will have to pursue the conventional routes to socioeconomic success through education and skill attainment. Thus, youths require more typical and proximate models—like next-door neighbors, teachers, family, friends or mentors in an after-school program—of social and economic self-sufficiency. And given their poverty, limited parental education, and family resources, most of these students require other social resources, other mentors to show them how to navigate school, the workplace, and society more effectively.

POVERTY, YOUTH, AND SOCIAL CAPITAL

What social contacts who could serve as social capital did these students already have? The survey I administered to them asked questions about up to twenty-six people in their lives, including their best friends, five close friends, five adult neighbors, five neighborhood kids about the students' own age, up to five persons in their household who were older, and five adult kin. Information gathered about these contacts included (1) their relationship to the student, (2) educational attainment, (3) employment status, (4) whether they worked in a professional setting, (5) whether they were perceived as an important source of job information for the student, and (6) whether the student could comfortably discuss with them their future plans and options. This particular information allowed me to construe a rough indicator of the students' social capital. Collectively, their responses produced portraits of these students' social networks and included information on more than fourteen hundred persons.

Snapshots of the students' social networks (see table 5.1),[1] as well as many of their assertions, reveal that these students felt they had few role models in their daily lives. When I examined responses to the questions of a contact's being in important source of job information, having some college experience, and working in a white-collar job, I found that slightly less than one-third of the students possessed some form of what social

TABLE 5.1 Mean Adult Demographic Traits of the Students' Social Networks

	Percent of Social Network
Adults mentioned who live in youth's neighborhood	61%
Black	72%
White, non-Hispanic	2%
Latino (any race)	28%
Age > 21	47%
High school graduate or GED	57%
High school graduate or GED, Adults over 21*	48%
Some college experience*	10%
Has a steady job, adults over age 21*	59%
Work in white-collar job*	15%
Respondent thinks is a good source for job information*	31%
Respondent talks to about future	31%

Note: All percentages, except where noted, are based on a total number of individuals reported in the respondents' social network (ranging from a low of 10 to a high of 25).

*Base: # of adults > age 21 in social network.

scientists would dub social capital. Seventeen-year-old Rayisha initially declined to say why none of the adults in her immediate surroundings were good resources for mobility, very likely because of her awareness of the moral and legal implications of the drug use in her family. She "did not want to put all of [her family's] business in the street," meaning that she did not want to make it public. As we talked more and she became more comfortable, Rayisha told me the reason she did not consider any of her family members to be role models was because of their frequent visits to the "street pharmacy." And Rayisha was not alone; only one of the thirteen girls who participated in one of my female-group interviews, which included Rayisha's sister Jelissa, could identify a positive role model in her family or immediate social circle. In a few cases, like those of two neighbors, John Jamison and Sean Anderson, a family member who had done relatively well in terms of his job served as someone to emulate. Though both lived apart from their biological fathers, John and Sean were comparatively better off in terms of social capital than the majority of their peers in the study. John's father was a commercial artist who worked for a national department store; Sean's father held a management position with the transit authority. Both boys had high hopes that they would be as financially successful as their fathers.

For other youths in the study, few adults in their social networks fit the profile of upward mobility, and less than one-third of their social contacts were people with whom these students felt comfortable discussing their futures (refer to table 5.1). Almost half of the adults age twenty-one or older were either high-school graduates or GED holders, but only 10 percent had any college experience. Perhaps, that is why the students considered slightly less than one-third of these adults to be "good sources of job information." That is not to say that these adults did not work. They did; almost 60 percent held steady jobs, though these were low-wage and low-skilled jobs. Only about 15 percent of the adults in their networks worked in professional settings, and perhaps this fact can be attributed to these adults' lack of higher education. A college diploma is more likely to enable adults to hold white-collar jobs than a high school diploma; and an analysis of national data from a December 1999 CPS survey shows that four to five times as many college-educated versus noncollege-educated, employed African Americans and Hispanics worked daily in professional, white-collar settings (U.S. Census Bureau 1999). More critically, more than a quarter of these youth could *not* think of any adult outside their household who could serve as a good source of information about jobs. These are the key indicators of the inverse relationship between poverty and social capital (Wilson 1987).

While there is a significant correlation between socioeconomic status and access to resourceful social connections, not all low-income African American and Latino youths lack such resources, as research on the success of low-income students of color recruited to elite U.S. high schools shows (Zweigenhaft and Domhoff 1991). Some low-income families manage to pool significant social resources from either an economically heterogeneous family network, from connections made through employers, fellow worshipers at church, or ties established in some other social context. These resources often place youths in an advantageous position for social attainment.

As table 5.2 shows, some differences were found among this group of students with modest means and little social capital. As indicators of social capital, I used the percentage of relatives and adult neighbors reported in their social networks who had (1) a high school diploma or GED, (2) some college experience, (3) a steady job, and (4) worked in a white-collar or professional setting.[2] Significantly, the cultural mainstreamers and the cultural straddlers could name more adult relatives working in professional and managerial (or white-collar) settings than could the noncompliant believers. Moreover, the cultural mainstreamers were more likely to be familiar with adult neighbors who had either a college education or and white-collar work experience or both than were either the cultural straddlers or the noncompliant believers.

Little racial, ethnic, and class variation existed in the social networks of

Table 5.2 Comparison of Family and Neighbor Social Ties by Group

	Cultural Straddlers	Cultural Mainstreamers	Noncompliant Believers
Mother (household head) works	72%	100%	66%
Relatives with high school diploma/GED	53%	43%	46%
Relatives with college experience	14%	17%	11%
Relatives with steady job	60%	60%	54%
Relatives in white-collar work	19%	23%	7%**
Adult neighbors with high school diploma/GED	49%	60%	36%
Adult neighbors with college experience	6%	20%*	4%
Adult neighbors with steady sob	62%	70%	52%
Adult neighbors in white-collar work	9%	30%**	6%
Total N	25	5	38

*p <. 10;**p <. 05

most of the students in the study. In a city where African Americans and Latinos make up 14 percent and 17 percent of the total population, respectively, both groups constituted more than 62 percent of the population of the southwest quadrant of the city, where half of these youths lived. The other half of the youth resided in a census tract where 88 percent of the residents were non-Hispanic White, yet they interacted with few of their White neighbors. And no matter the census tract, all of the youths lived in government-subsidized housing complexes where at least 96 percent were African American and Latino, and they interacted mainly with those who lived in their complexes. More of the noncompliant believers' social contacts lived near them than those contacts of the cultural mainstreamers and cultural straddlers (table 5.3). The cultural mainstreamers, in contrast, listed more Whites in their social networks, though overall they mentioned fewer people who they felt were good sources of job information. Both the cultural straddlers and the cultural mainstreamers mentioned having more adults to talk to about their future plans (table 5.3).

TABLE 5.3 Mean Demographic Traits of the Respondents' Social Networks by Group

	Cultural Straddlers	Cultural Mainstreamers	Noncompliant Believers
Live in respondent's neighborhood	56%	48%	65%**
Black	69%	61%	75%
White, non-Hispanic	2%	7%*	2%
Latino (any race)	29%	30%	27%
Respondent thinks is a good source for job information[a]	21%	9%***	21%
Respondent talks to about future[a]	43%**	33%	24%

Note: All percentages, except where noted, are based on a total number of individuals reported in the respondents' social network (ranging from a low of 10 to a high of 21).

[a] Base: # of Adults > age 21 in social network.

*p <. 10; **p <. 05; ***p <. 01 (two-sided chi square; a significant difference among the cultural mainstreamers, the cultural straddlers, and the noncompliant groups.

Relatives and neighbors, shifting back and forth between their work environments and their communities, serve as potential sharers of information and cultural know-how, especially of dominant culture. Researchers translating the abstract concept of social capital into concrete indicators about those types of individuals who possess particular skills and resources find that the percentage of "high-status workers" (i.e., managers and professionals) in a neighborhood is a significant predictor of educational and social outcomes for children and youth (Crane 1991; Wilson 1987; Carter and Wilson 1997; Brooks-Gunn et al. 1993). Such social ties expose students to specific messages about mobility and attainment. Deemed as "social leverage," these workers help one to solve problems or get ahead. They affect life chances by including job information, for example, or by providing a recommendation for a job, scholarship, or loan (Wacquant and Wilson 1993; Hannerz 1969; Briggs 1998).

Teresa Anton, a twenty-year-old mother, high-school dropout, and noncompliant believer with low social capital, appeared to be speaking from experience when she described the influence of those around her. "Like, people who don't do nothing all day…they don't go to school and you be around them and that's your best friend and she don't go to school, then you ain't gonna go to school 'cause she ain't going," says Teresa. Otherwise, "if she ain't around you then that'll motivate you more better. Or if you see her getting up and going to work every day or getting up and going to school every day, that'd motivate you more to want to do it," Teresa continued. Her mother did not work, and on more than one occasion Teresa implied that her mother's actions had influenced her own actions. When I asked Teresa how she intended her life to be different from her mother's, she replied, "Well, I'll be different from my mother because I'll be working; I'll be with my kids. My mother don't ever spend time on kids. She don't be at home." At the time of our discussion, Teresa, who had obtained her GED, remained at home daily with her two small children, supplementing her public assistance with off-the-book income earned from babysitting a more fully employed mother's children.

In contrast, one cultural mainstreamer, Adrienne, divulged that she had "so much pressure from [her] grandmother to go to college." Perhaps Adrienne's grandmother desired for her the dream that had been deferred for her own daughter (Adrienne's mother was a college dropout). Adrienne's family expected that she would do well in school, and she does. In addition, Adrienne had obtained a part-time job in the same optical shop where her mother worked as a technician.

The experiences of both Teresa and Adrienne support already documented findings that there is a strong link between family and other social influences and school performance. Further, those with limited family incomes yet strong social networks often overcome the odds of reproducing their family's class status. In communities where the family's economic situation is tenuous, "the social capital that has value for a young person's development does not reside solely within the family," James Coleman wrote (1988). Yet, nonfamilial contacts, particularly teachers and counselors, become critical, and Adrienne's profile illuminated the value of both familial and nonfamilial social capital. Possessing all of the signs of a bright student, Adrienne found her way to the school's honors program, not through her mother but through a teacher who had not even taught her. This teacher was someone to whom Adrienne felt close and who apparently saw her academic promise; and she encouraged Adrienne to apply to the honors program. Telling me about how she ultimately got into the program, Adrienne said, "It was my teacher and my mom—really my teacher. I missed the test at first, and then later my teacher drove me there, picked me up, and brought me home."

In this case, a teacher shared with Adrienne the rules of an academic game that has confounded many low-income, minority families: how to get into the upper academic tracks. After her mentor had encouraged Adrienne (and no doubt her mother, too, whose permission was needed), Adrienne did the rest; she passed the exam to get into the program. She had already told me that none of her own teachers had encouraged her to move into this program whose students were predominantly White. Hearing Adrienne's story, I wondered how many of her peers were overlooked for similar opportunities. We know that race, ethnicity, socioeconomic background, and the heavily examined test-score gap put students like Adrienne at a disadvantage because they tend to score lower and consequently, get passed over for selective educational tracks or courses (Jencks and Phillips 1998; Lareau and Horvat 1999). In this case, Adrienne's nonfamilial social capital increased her chances of fulfilling her aspirations to attend college and, ultimately, law school.

Adrienne's story contrasts strikingly with that of another young person who lived not far away and who required extrafamilial support but was either not as fortunate or did not know how to reach out for help and advice. Victoria Jalisco, a twenty-year-old mother, pregnant with her second child and a self-proclaimed "bad" student who was disruptive in school—a noncompliant believer—had managed to obtain her high-school diploma the year before I interviewed her. She aspired to be a gym teacher, but she had never had a conversation about her goal with the one person whom she considered a mentor: her gym teacher. Victoria, a single mother who lived with her own mother—a woman with no high-school degree who struggled to earn decent wages—possessed neither the social nor financial connections that could facilitate her passage out of poverty. Victoria fell into the lowest range of the social capital scale. None of her family members had attended college or held white-collar jobs, and only 13 percent of her relatives (the ones on which she reported) had completed high school. There were many others like Victoria. At least one out of five of the students possessed little to no social capital, and that is hardly a condition that would allow poor youths to achieve and thrive.

CALLING FOR MULTICULTURAL NAVIGATORS

In *The Truly Disadvantaged,* William Julius Wilson argues that the presence of "social buffers" provides models "that help keep alive the perception that education is meaningful, that steady employment is a viable alternative to welfare, and that family stability is the norm, not the exception" (1987, 56). Here is where I want to push the idea of social capital even further, since the assumptions about its value rarely explore the interplay among effective social ties, culture, and identity. Given what we know about the resources of diverse social ties, we can assume that students' exposure to persons possessing dominant cultural capital helps them climb the proverbial social ladder. Still, in a land of opportunity that is fraught with racial, ethnic, class, and sociocultural dynamics, many low-income African American and Latino youth desire exposure to those who understand their own social realities, and many, especially the non-compliant believers, value nondominant cultural capital. To increase these students' investments in their education, teachers, parents, and other concerned adults should consider the value of another type of social contact, the "multicultural navigator." Multicultural navigators demonstrate how to possess *both* dominant and nondominant cultural capital and how to be adept at movement through various sociocultural settings, where cultural codes and rules differ. Multicultural navigators possess some of the appeal of hip-hop stars, not because of fame, but because they can keep youths invested in the dream of upward mobility *and* show them how to retain their social and cultural origins.

Those students who most closely resemble the multicultural navigator are the cultural straddlers. Recall Moesha, a student who understood the power of language and proudly asserted her multilingual skills by moving between different speech codes at home and at school. Moesha was on the move, having already enrolled in college, though her family's limited means posed a challenge. Moesha spoke openly about the necessity for her to speak both Standard English and the black vernacular of her home and community, a tongue that she associated not with ignorance but rather with vibrancy and community cohesion. Moesha was particularly concerned about educators who denigrated her classmates for their use of vernacular. On the one hand, she had little power to confront these teachers about their lack of respect; on the other hand, she committed to becoming multilingual and developing the ability to play numerous cultural games, whether at school, at home, or at work. Multicultural navigators possess several cultural repertoires. They are skilled at tapping into the cultural codes of the environments through which they move in order to thrive and to communicate.

For students to become multicultural navigators, they require adult models. The teacher who comprehends and perhaps has even lived the experience of poverty, who can respect the multifaceted nature of culture, and who possesses enough insight to convey to students how to use different cultural know-hows, can serve as the model multicultural navigator. A teacher who inspires and excites students to grasp multiple kinds of knowledge, including reading, writing, and using analytical skills, and who respects the integrity of her or his own culture and other cultures fits the image of the multicultural navigator. Other adult multicultural navigators—from astronauts to book editors, cosmetologists to foreign diplomats, urologists to zoologists—might straddle multiple cultural spheres. These navigators' goals are not only socioeconomic attainment but also an appreciation of the mosaic that produces all of American culture. They are the creators of a "minority culture of mobility," a concept that captures how upwardly mobile racial and ethnic minorities negotiate in discernible ways their predominantly white spheres of work and their predominantly co-ethnic neighborhoods (Neckerman, Carter, and Lee 1999).

In a rich ethnographic portrait of Harlem, the so-called Mecca of Black America, John Jackson (2001) provides a vivid portrait of a potential multicultural navigator. Specifically, he describes "Paul," a handsomely paid architect who admittedly kept his two class-worlds apart, to the point of throwing two separate parties to celebrate his birthday, claiming, "it can just be easier to let my two parts stay apart." Paul did not want "people feeling uncomfortable around other people because they don't talk the same language, or do the same things" (89). Personifying someone who has pulled himself up by his bootstraps, Paul faced a common social dilemma: moving on up and strategically negotiating how his two worlds would avoid a head-on collision.

One could categorize Jackson's "Paul" as a rags-to-riches success story. I use Paul's story here for two reasons: (1) to illustrate exactly the type of personal conflict that the youths whom I interviewed might someday face; and (2) to provide an example of someone who attains a higher socioeconomic status and partakes of multiple social and cultural worlds. Paul divulged that he really had "two [social] lives," one with his peers from his professional environment and another with his "peops" [hanging buddies or peers] from his neighborhood. Though Paul had not figured out how to effectively bridge his two worlds, he has the potential to become a multicultural navigator because he refuses to simply acculturate—to appropriate "white" and middle-class cultural ways and ignore his community of origin. As "cultural brokers" (Lee 2002), multicultural navigators can effectively bridge the socioeconomic gap, often because their familial or kin network is class heterogeneous (Pattillo-McCoy 1999) and because they alternate between spaces of different races and classes.

Being middle-class, educated, and/or Black or Latino, or all of these is not sufficient to qualify as a multicultural navigator, however, particularly since research shows that the social distance between less-privileged Blacks and Latinos and their middle-class counterparts is great enough to threaten any form of cohesion or shared identity (Landry 1987; Benjamin 1991). Rather, multicultural navigators work to narrow the social divide between the privileged and the disadvantaged by acknowledging and communicating the values of both dominant and nondominant cultural capital. One might retort that we should all learn to negotiate the rules and norms of different social spaces. However, what I describe here is something that goes beyond the tacit understanding that we all engage in some form of cultural codeswitching. As sources of social capital, multicultural navigators become critical to the lives of low-income African American and Latino youths because they are successful at negotiating the different dynamics that ethnic and class minorities encounter when they enter white-dominant, middle-class social organizations (Feagin and Sikes 1994). Because so many of the ideals of work and responsibility are already coded as "white," Christian (echoing Protestantism and its ethics), and middle-class, multicultural navigators, as sources of social capital, facilitate relationships of trust and reciprocity between the cultural gatekeepers and these youths. They demonstrate how these kids might negotiate the not so easily penetrable boundaries of the opportunity structure without forsaking their origins as "raced," "ethnicized," and "classed" beings in a stratified society. Multicultural navigators broker communications between school officials and low-income minority families such that both sides begin to hear each other, to comprehend how inequality works through both material means and culture, and begin to work toward fuller incorporation of poor and minority youths in education and employment.

Furthermore, multicultural navigators need not defuse students' political consciousness about their social groups' standing in society, especially when structures of inequality remain rigid. Although socioeconomic mobility can bring increased contact with middle-class White America, as Jennifer Hochschild (1995) found in her study of the burgeoning African American middle class, this contact does not necessarily render racial identity and experience as less pertinent. According to Hochschild, middle-class African Americans now have more access to the American dream than ever before, yet they maintain a less than idealistic view of race relations. Similarly, in my analysis, comparing the views of the cultural mainstreamers' and the cultural straddlers' low-income parents—whose children seemingly have the greatest potential to enter the middle class—with those of the noncompliant believers' parents, I found no discernible differences (tables 5.4 and 5.5). For example, the parents of the cultural mainstreamers and cultural straddlers were as likely to perceive injustice and discrimination in society as were the noncompliant

TABLE 5.4 Parents' Perceptions of and Experiences with Race Relations by Group Type

Parents' Perceptions:	Cultural Straddlers	Cultural Mainstreamers	Noncompliant Believers
Believe that job discrimination exists (lots to some)	90%	100%	92%
Believe that housing discrimination exists (lots to some)	91%	100%	97%
Reported experiencing housing discrimination	26%*a	40%	44%
Reported being comfortable around Whites	69%*	60%*	35%
Believe that Whites either don't care about the progress of their racial/ethnic group or want to keep them down	79%*ab	60%*	97%
Total N	25	5	38

aSignificant difference between the cultural straddlers and the noncompliant believers
bSignificant difference between the cultural straddlers and the cultural mainstreamers
*p <.10.

TABLE 5.5 Students' Perceptions of Race Relations by Group Type

	Cultural Straddlers	Cultural Mainstreamers	Noncompliant Believers
Believe that job discrimination exists (lots to some)	76%	80%	78%
Believe that Whites either don't care about the progress of members of their racial/ethnic group or want to keep them down	76%	60%	87%
Total N	25	5	38

believers' parents. All of the cultural mainstreamers' parents perceived that racial discrimination occurs in housing and the workplace; and more than 90 percent of both the cultural straddlers' and the noncompliant believers' parents expressed the same sentiments.

Their actual experiences with housing discrimination differed from their attitudes, however. A federal court ruling to remedy segregated housing patterns in Yonkers, New York followed a long and costly court battle, which had directly affected most of these parents' current housing selections. These families were participants in a housing experiment that moved poor families from housing projects in low-income, predominantly black and Latino neighborhoods, to new town homes in middle-class, white sections of the city. White residents expressed much opposition to this court-supported policy, and the city of Yonkers resisted compliance with the court's order (Staples 2002). This political resistance exposed quite a bit of racial, ethnic, and class prejudice and amounted to highly discriminatory practice. Despite the situation in Yonkers, less than half of the parents in my survey reported an actual experience with housing discrimination.

Although parents perceived, and in some instances experienced discrimination and prejudice, their levels of comfort with white society did not necessarily correspond to these negative experiences. However, the levels of parents' comfort with Whites did vary by the students' cultural and ideological group type. That is, the cultural straddlers' and cultural mainstreamers' parents were significantly more likely to report being comfortable with Whites, compared to the noncompliant parents. These analyses cannot determine whether it is the association with Whites that shapes students' (and their parents') racial and ethnic ideologies, or the converse, whether their racial and ethnic ideologies determine their inclination to interact with Whites. The suggestion here is that the more contact with Whites these students have, the more familiar with dominant cultural capital they will become and the greater will be their comfort and ability to manage interracial relations.[3] Also, this increased contact is likely to provide upwardly mobile African American and Latino adults with a more heightened (as opposed to diminished) racial and ethnic consciousness precisely because they interact more with Whites in the workplace, in school, and in public settings (Feagin 1991). Thus, as opposed to what Samurai and Teresa intimated at the start of this chapter, this increased contact need not lessen one's commitment to one's own social groups' interests. It might even provide new opportunities to influence interracial and ethnic dynamics. Overall, the mobile multicultural navigators whom I envision possess not only a critical political consciousness that can be used to serve the interests of these communities but also the facility to help students like Samurai and Teresa interact more easily with many people as they move through various social and cultural contexts.

In terms of immediate social supports, these students require mentors and role models whose own lives serve as examples of how to make it without compromising one's culture. In this chapter, I have tried to extend the discussion about the role of social capital in the lives of low-income students. Older adults, including those of the Civil Rights era, and even some born of the hip-hop era who do not consider themselves hip-hoppers, wonder why DMX, Notorious B.I.G., Fifty Cent, Lil' Kim, and other celebrities have made such an impression on this generation. I have suggested that it is because they have "made it" without appearing to have acculturated or given in to the establishment. Why is this so important? These youth, though aspiring to social and economic success, want to make it in another way, not in the perceived "white" way, and not in a way that requires them to denigrate the dynamic linguistic, interactional, musical, or clothing styles. They aspire to be like those who appear to have maintained a critical perspective on how opportunities are parceled out in an undivided society. I have met many young people on the street who tell me, "You have to listen to him; that brotha is deep and he is telling it like it is," referring to the now almost legendary rapper Tupac Shakur. Scholar, writer, activist, and philosopher Michael Eric Dyson (2001) has made the same point about Shakur, a legendary rapper who was raised in poverty and on welfare and was the son of a cultural nationalist. According to Dyson, Shakur had a brilliant mind and read critical pieces on economics, politics, and philosophy, and Dyson argues that Shakur had the capability of being a bridge, a multicultural navigator; yet, tragically, his life was cut short by a bullet and internecine warfare. We can glean from this generation's love affair with hip-hop culture some insight into the kinds of social contacts that might help these youths become more invested in their schools. They require multicultural navigators who can demonstrate to them how to overcome poverty with critical, self-loving, and other-respecting perspectives, who do not make them ashamed of who they are but rather proud of how far they will go. They need teachers who have not only pedagogic skill and cultural sensitivity but also deeper social understanding and some capability to handle the many ways that students will differ from one another. As long as educators refuse to acknowledge the hierarchy of cultural meanings in schools, they help to reproduce a class of noncompliant students, students at risk for limited educational attainment and economic dependence.

SCHOOL SUCCESS HAS NO COLOR

6

Too often we adults take it for granted that we know what is best for children, and with the development and experience that come with age, we do. However, many of America's schoolchildren are sending us a loud and clear message about some breakdowns in the mechanisms of schooling, especially when it comes to how culture is infused into the classroom and how culture influences social actions. The empirical analyses provided here probed the multiple connections between culture and identity among a specific group of low-income Black and Latino students and their particular responses to a structural phenomenon—a hierarchy of cultural meanings that they believed inheres in schools.

What more empirical evidence do we need to understand that students like the Yonkers' youth embrace the normative values of academic achievement and success, but yet are looking to the gatekeepers of public education for signs that the boundaries of the culture of mobility are not as thick and rigid as they appear? To bring some clarity to the debate about how the process of resistance to "acting white" influences student achievement, I distinguished conceptually between students' values, intentions, and desires—that is, their achievement ideology, their claims that they want to be academically engaged, and their aspirations; their cultural and social practices; and their substantive critiques of education as an institution. Throughout I have argued that the students in this study did not equate high achievement in school and upward mobility with "acting white." Instead many students were critical of the representations of what is knowledge, the association of intelligence and competence with select styles, and the call for acculturation toward "white," middle class ways as a route to academic and socioeconomic success. For them, the resistance-to-"acting white" issue is less about the intrinsic value of educational achievement and more about the roles of culture and identity in schools. As the survey data have shown, the majority of the students in this study upheld the normative values about the roles of work and success. Pervasive social norms, notions of individualism, and the results of hard work and effort greatly influenced their thinking. Loretta Lincoln's view of success and achievement typifies the kinds of responses given to me when I asked about opportunity and success:

> *Prudence:* Can anybody make it in this society? Can anyone succeed?
>
> *Loretta:* If you put your mind to it and work at it, then you can, yes. I think you can. Yeah, I do think you can. It's just that . . . being a Black person, maybe we have to try a little bit harder, but I still think you can achieve, you know. Yeah, I think you can.
>
> *Prudence:* Why is it that we have to try harder?
>
> *Loretta:* Because of the stereotypes and the things . . . I don't know. Some White people just think that we're nothing; we can't never be nothing. We can't make it on our own or whatever.
>
> *Prudence:* Does that ever discourage you?
>
> *Loretta:* Yeah, sometimes. But it don't really even bother me, you know. Because I know what I have to do, and what I have to do is get myself together and that's what I'm going to do. I'm not going to sit around and wait for someone to tell me that I can't do it when I know I can.

Prudence: Are there jobs in this society that African Americans
will just never have?

Loretta: Yes.

Prudence: Like what?

Loretta: Presidency. I don't think there could ever be a Black
president. What else? Because we have Black lawyers, Black
doctors, scientists, astronauts. We have everything else
that's Black.

Loretta and her peers tried to reconcile several things in their minds.
First, they maintained a reasonable disrespect for the America-as-the-
land-of-opportunity tale. Constraints to opportunity and success marked
by racial disadvantage, in this case, limited what access they would have.
Yet, to avoid a fatalistic viewpoint that would undermine their desires to
achieve and be economically mobile, they often invoked explanations
about individual will and effort to explain how they would overcome
these structural obstacles. Students juggled several messages transmitted
through personal ties, experiences, or the media. On one hand, they acknowledged the existence of racism and discrimination and their impact
on their lives. On the other hand, they often emphatically exclaimed that
either their potential successes or failures were contingent on what "I do
for myself"—personal effort and will.

When I examined more thoroughly the cases of those students who
expressed disbelief in the ideals of education, I discovered that about thirteen students gave mixed responses to questions about their attitudes toward education, economic mobility, and success. They sometimes agreed
and sometimes disagreed with statements such as "Achievement and effort in school lead to job success later on" and "Getting a good education
is a practical road to success for a young person like me" (Mickelson
1990). In analyzing their beliefs about education's role and value, we may
expect to observe that these are students who might be inclined to resist
school because they perceive the idea of education as the great equalizer
as a myth. But even these more pessimistic students did not fully dismiss
the value of schooling. While half were noncompliant believers, the other
half were cultural straddlers who intended to use education as a vehicle
for mobility. Three of the thirteen had enrolled in college and aspired to

professional careers. Another three had dropped out of school, and one had enrolled in a community college after earning a GED. Thus, the majority of those who questioned dominant achievement ideology pressed on and continued to attend school; eleven aspired to college, and nine of these eleven expected to actually go. Given their social and economic experiences, did these students understand that more than mere excellence in school determined social mobility? Did their mixed views about education's worth reflect an issue of social and political consciousness, or an issue of understanding that a hurdle exists for certain groups when it comes to economic opportunities? Educational dilemmas often arise when underprivileged African American and Latino students' social practices and critiques of their academic environments do not mesh well with the expectations of mainstream society. These youths do not believe that they have to "act white" to succeed. Yet if they want to achieve in the conventional sense, then they must possess certain forms of dominant cultural capital. If they ignore dominant cultural capital in favor of their own, their means to success is disrupted as they inevitably battle with school officials and teachers. Grades suffer, absences increase, and the potential to drop out looms large (Fine 1991). Then, if they try to find either low-skilled or semi-skilled jobs, without a college diploma, they are likely to find employers who critically judge racial and ethnic minorities who lack "soft skills" (Kirschenman and Neckerman 1991; Moss and Tilly 1996).

Cultural styles associated with "acting white" are not the same as dominant cultural capital, however. That is, a low-income Black or Latino high-school senior might speak Standard English, maintain friendships with White youths, and play in the school orchestra, and yet still not possess cultural know-how about how to best fill out a college application that will impress the admissions committee of a competitive college. On the other hand, some practices of "acting white" can translate into dominant cultural capital. For instance, a student who befriends mostly White students and emulates their cultural practices might get recognized by a teacher or counselor, and if he or she does well, be recommended for advanced placement or other college-preparatory classes. Enrollment in such classes could expose the student to educational resources that could help land him or her in a top-notch college. Indirectly, "acting white" brought the student some benefit in the long run.

Surprisingly, the possession of dominant cultural capital, high socioeconomic status, or economic well-being does not guarantee increased social interactions among African Americans, Latino, and Whites. Reports from the Lewis Mumford Center for Comparative Urban and Regional Research at the State University of New York at Albany show that according to the 2000 Census, African Americans and Latinos earning sixty thousand dollars or more—the middle and upper classes—are more likely to live in economically disadvantaged neighborhoods than Whites earning thirty thousand dollars annually. Further, these upwardly mobile African Americans and Latinos are more likely to socialize with individuals from their own racial or ethnic backgrounds (Benjamin 1991). Such residential and social patterns make the benefits of embracing and maintaining their own cultural codes and styles apparent.

While dominant cultural capital can play a critical role in socioeconomic attainment, the possession of nondominant cultural capital is critical to the status of individuals from socially marginalized groups—to their sense of belonging, connection, and identity. The fact remains that African Americans, Latinos, and Whites share many cultural practices, beliefs, and norms. All have contributed to American culture. Still, many African Americans and Latinos, whether poor or nonpoor, confront the competing expectations of their ethnic communities and society. Although they may share common cultural practices with Whites, to only embrace practices perceived to be the cultural territory of Whites lends itself to in-group conflict. Meanwhile, to reject all of these practices and embrace only prescribed racial or ethnic cultural practices sets them up for negative judgments by cultural gatekeepers in schools, the workplace, and in public discourse that can have some profound consequences.

For low-income African American and Latino students, mobility often comes with acculturation to middle-class cultural patterns that have become co-terminus with whiteness; and social and psychological benefits arise from the sharing of cultural codes marked as "black" or "Spanish." The cultural straddlers best represented this perspective. They bridged the cultural gaps among peers, school, and wider society in a different way; they used strategies that would enable them to "act white" and succeed in the conventional sense but that would also immunize them from accusations of "acting white" by their co-ethnics. Fourteen-year-old

Jeremy James, heavily enrolled in honors classes, comes to mind. Not only did Jeremy do well in school but he was also a high-profile, popular student who wore the faddish clothing, had a command of black slang, and "hung black." Jeremy indicated that he easily got along with White, Black, and Latino peers, which undoubtedly further bolstered his popularity.

For noncompliant believers, the predicament is that dominant social, economic, and cultural authorities make it appear that these youth are being self-destructive in their refusal to adhere to the social and cultural mandates of the school and later, in the workplace. Indeed, it is a problem that they refuse to adhere to cultural rules that translate ultimately into academic success, and indeed, it is self-defeating if "success" is *only* achieved by following the social and cultural dictates of dominant powers. Conceivably, a cultural nationalist—a more politically and ideologically evolved representative of those whom I describe here as the noncompliant believers—would disagree with any assessment that states that African Americans and Latinos must subscribe to dominant culture, in addition to their own culture, to succeed collectively socioeconomically and politically. "Many nationalists argue that by nature white and black interests are opposed to each other," writes political scientist Michael Dawson. "Not only is race seen as *the* (author's emphasis) fundamental category for analyzing society, but America is seen as fundamentally racist," he continues (2001, 87). Hence, not only do nationalists support the full autonomy and self-determination of these groups but they also advocate various degrees of cultural, social, economic, and political separation from White America.

Two responses to these positions come to mind. First, fixed meanings and controlled identities for any racial or ethnic group—generated from both within and outside of the communities—disregard the multiplicity of identities held by members of any group. While African Americans and different ethnic Latino groups share collective histories of social and economic subordination, there are myriad voices within each of these communities. Even some of the meanings that African American and Latino youth (and even adults) use to define the contours of "blackness," "Spanishness," and "whiteness" can be so restrictive that they threaten an individual student's agency. The challenge lies in the development of meanings allowing for collective and individual practices that do not interfere with the individual's liberty. Otherwise, students like fifteen-year-old cultural mainstreamer Adrienne will be compelled continually to assert: "How am I talking 'white'? There's no law saying that you're Black, you have to speak this way, and if you're White you have to speak this way." Adrienne, like others who vocalized this sort of opposition, resisted the markers of black identity that were prescribed impermissibly.

Second, Black and Latino students should not view all the practices that they peg as "white" a threat to their worldview; nor should Whites see black and Latino cultural styles as antithetical to mobility and success. Multiple cultural repertoires do and should exist, and the common cultural repertoire that we share should be continually checked and balanced, revisited, revamped, and revitalized to ensure that it is representative of the entire society. At the same time, the students in this study and others like them require some help negotiating, expanding their ideas and presentations of self, and ultimately balancing different social "acts." They require guidance in how to maintain several cultural competencies. It is a matter of choice whether they to listen to soft rock or opera, or speak Standard English or black English. Role models and mentors, those whom I call multicultural navigators, can help and encourage them to ascertain what is appropriate in various social contexts.

If we simply listen carefully to students as they describe their school experiences, we might come closer to actually figuring out how to mend the cracks in our elementary and secondary school systems, and how to get at-risk students more fully engaged in school. The students whose stories, beliefs, and ideas are documented in this book provide much direction for thought. Students reveal that they experience schools as organized ineffectually and blind to their social, cultural, and material realities. Perhaps most important, students direct educators, social scientists, and society's attention to areas that must be addressed in order for them to have academic success. Moreover, students point to other conditions that are necessary to improve schools—in addition to their being well-financed schools and having highly qualified teachers—that they need in order for low-income Black and Latino students to be more competitive with their middle-class and White and Asian classmates.

Too often, the generational divide among teachers, parents, and students inhibit the elders from listening to the children. Instead the older generations say that youths are not what they used to be. No, they are not, and when these adults were kids, it is very likely that adults said the same things about them. We live in a new social and cultural era where children are exposed to different material resources, live in a more highly developed technological society, and are more outspoken. They also acquire much of their knowledge and information from the media, especially television and music. The federal, state, and local departments of education, foundations, and other nonprofit organizations can appeal to media giants to use these forums by enlisting their support for free public-service campaigns and motivational speeches from the popular athletes and entertainers to whom they look for messages about achievement and success. These public-service messages would not only raise societal consciousness about academic and cultural issues confronting our youth but would also encourage more individuals to lend a hand in their communities and assist educators with teaching and training the nation's youths.

Educators and other adults must also provide a context in which students can apply their own insights to facilitate positive and potentially transformative educational change. One potentially effective program for schools is to hold "town meetings" where students voice their concerns and suggestions for improving school practices and their engagement with school. Meetings are not enough, however, and should move beyond symbolic gestures. Educators and students can work together to figure out effective ways for students to engage as "teachers," too. Finally, education's proponents cannot simply ask students and their parents to cooperate and adapt; they must also demand participation from all the key actors. If these youth are to embrace multiple forms of cultural capital, then it will require educators to embrace multiple cultural capitals, too. If not, educators and students will find themselves perpetuating the status quo; and the noncompliant believers might continue to disengage because they lost the battle to the dominant cultural authorities in their quest for *both* cultural distinction and mobility.

SEEKING CULTURAL CAPITALS IN THE CLASSROOM: COMMENTARY ON KNOWLEDGE AND POWER

Noncompliant believers expose a critical social problem about our measurements of success and achievement. Implicitly, they pose the question "Why can't success be multicultural?" and "Why are schools inscribed with the select cultural practices of elite groups, which in itself automatically renders others as deviant if they do not conform?" Although many of our mainstream institutions are often perceived to be culturally neutral, we, nonetheless, find the primary influence of middle-class and Anglo Whites throughout them. The standard of neutrality institutionalized in social organizations, according to sociologist Mark Gould, presumes the life-world or the tacit commonsense culture of Whites (1999). Though Gould was not writing specifically about schools, he assessed the cultural milieu of contemporary society in which schools constitute one particular domain.

The multicultural debate spans decades, and it is still unsettled. Consequently, educational policymakers and practitioners become embroiled in debates about the roles and worthiness of certain social groups' histories, languages, literature, and cultures. James Banks, a major voice in the multicultural education movement in the United States, explains, "To implement multicultural education in a school, we must reform its power relationships, the verbal interaction between teachers and students, the culture of the school, the curriculum, extracurricular activities, attitudes toward minority languages, the testing program, and grouping practices. The institutional norms, social structures, cause-belief statements, values, and goals of the school must be transformed and reconstructed" (2001, 23). Political challenges emerge when we push teachers to value different learning and pedagogic styles and knowledge bases. The traditional perspective sees curriculum as neutral and apolitical, merely imparting the skills of literacy, numeracy, and critical thinking. Many, like former Secretary of Education William Bennett, view the curriculum as a means to pass on the history, art, and knowledge produced by Western thinkers and artists and as a means to enforce a common culture that reinforces an American identity (Schlesinger 1998; Hirsch 1996; Bennett 1988). Critical education theorists and multiculturalists, in contrast, argue that education is intimately and ideologically linked to power, politics, history, and culture, unfairly privileging the descendants of Euro-Americans. "Schools have always functioned in ways that rationalize the knowledge industry into class-divided tiers; that reproduce inequality, racism and sexism; and that fragment democratic social relations through an emphasis on competitiveness and ethnocentrism," writes Peter McLaren (1988).

But the debate continues, and some social scientists (Ogbu 1987;

Ogbu and Simons 1998) argue that if cultural differences and conflicts affect African American and Latino students' achievement, then why doesn't the cultural disadvantage work similarly for other minority groups who are on the social margins, namely various Asian American groups? "Just because having a different culture doesn't appear to function as a barrier to the school performance for some racial minorities (such as Asian Americans) doesn't mean that it is not a barrier for others," scholar Theresa Perry (2003) retorts. "If racial minorities occupy different sociopolitical positions in the larger society, it would stand to reason that their respective cultural formations do not carry the same social, ideological, or political salience," she continues. Moreover, some Asian students may benefit from the dominant "model minority" myth embraced by many, including teachers, as opposed to the "cultural pathology myth" generated about African Americans or Puerto Ricans (Wong, Lai, and Nagasawa 1998; Lee 1996). Thus, the variable degrees to which schools support different cultural narratives can influence academic outcomes. As Perry states, "The cultures of Chinese Americans and Korean Americans do not have the same meaning, politically or ideologically, as the culture of African Americans," which is continually perceived to be inferior and inherently political (2003, 64).

While adults in the political arena duke it out about what students should and should not be reading or writing, students who continually find their ancestors' cultural, economic, historical, and political experiences less honored or even ignored in the classroom find themselves teetering on the brink of disengagement. The question of what is knowledge, as well as the practices through which knowledge is communicated, must be the result of a dialogue over what counts as legitimate culture. Students like the ones with whom I spent months talking struggle to understand just how relevant their schooling is to their social realities because their social, cultural, and economic realities do not garner adequate attention. What gets counted as legitimate and empowering was especially evident for some noncompliant believers. Teresa Anton, a high-school dropout, said:

> They don't teach us interesting stuff. You know they don't have
> no black history classes. Like, if you in junior high and you can't
> just say, "Oh I don't want to go to social studies . . . I want to
> go to Black history." [In social studies] where they teach you all

about the White people all day long, how they took over the
United States and all of this mess, the United States, the universe
. . . maybe [that's why] Blacks don't pay attention.

Teresa raised a critical issue, illuminating an age-old epistemological
debate. European American historical and cultural perspectives dominate
school curricula and pedagogy (Hale 1991; Hilliard 1978; Spencer, Swanson, and Cunningham 1991). Educators and policymakers have often categorized other groups' histories and literature as "other," relegating them to
a lesser status. As a result, many U.S. schools fail to provide racial and ethnic minorities with multiple perspectives through which to view themselves. Teresa knew that history entailed more than what her teachers
shared with her. She yearned for more information on the cultural, material, and political realities of her ancestors.

The central philosophical issue in this debate is about the need to
value and expand the requisite knowledge base in U.S. society. This value
should be fused through every facet of teacher education programs, in
theory and in practice, and not simply placed under the rubric of "diversity" or "multiculturalism." Classrooms around the nation, from elementary school to graduate school, can be filled with teachers who are trained
and socialized to understand that history, language, math, and science can
be taught in myriad ways. Future educators learn this best by also being
taught this way. Many professional schools and universities set aside
courses for "diversity" credit instead of demanding that their faculty find
ways to broaden their syllabi and structure their courses so that they do
not center Western or European American knowledge as all knowledge.
Well-meaning teachers and faculty usually add a few works by scholars of
color or about marginalized communities or both to signal their appreciation for diversity and their awareness of other social groups' realities.
Yet that intention alone illuminates the gaps in their own worldviews
about what constitutes the teachable and what conveys expertise and
competences in their subject areas.

Most teachers will continue to ignore the veracity of Teresa's comments unless they are taught how to recognize their own participation in
perpetuating inequality. And the responsibility lies not just with their
professional training but also with their early socialization. When individuals either lead lives steeped in privilege or have no comprehension of

what inequality does to other groups, it can be difficult for them to understand the impact of their actions. While no particular race, gender, class, or other social factor precludes any of us from becoming multicultural navigators, there is reason to believe that many teachers do not themselves possess the requisite cultural competences to help students become multiculturally fluent. Deep familiarity with and comprehension of a "minority" standpoint in any social context encourage a richer type of cross-cultural enlightenment about how dominant groups affect subordinate groups.

Teachers must also be aware of the impact that low expectations can have. Sensitive and astute, these students read the cues and signals that adults send to them. Often we do not realize how a slight interaction can undermine the student's academic commitment. Consider the frustrations of thirteen-year-old Tiffany Michaels. Once, during an in-class discussion, several students, all White, mentioned that they would be attending Gramson High School, one of the most academically rigorous schools in the city, after they left middle school. Tiffany perceived that the teacher approved of their school choice since she responded to them affirmatively. But when Tiffany mentioned Gramson as her high school of choice, the teacher gave her "an evil look" and remained silent. Tiffany surmised that this teacher disapproved of her choice because she was a Black kid from the housing projects who did not seem to have what it takes to make it at Gramson. Tiffany's experience reflects the findings of some research, which has shown that teachers expect more from White students than from African American students and more from middle-class students than from working- and lower-class students (Alexander, Entwisle, and Thompson 1987; Ferguson 1998). If students like Tiffany are to be motivated to achieve, it will be because of the belief that any child can excel with the proper supports.

The teaching profession has too few members who come from backgrounds that reflect the general student population. One might attribute this lack to several social and economic factors. First, the teaching profession has been feminized, rendering it a "woman's job." Women, who make up half of the society's population, constitute more than 84 percent of the teaching force (Strober and Lanford 1986). Second, teachers colleges and universities have attracted fewer racial and ethnic minority men in particular. As a result, fewer males, especially Black and Latino, work in classrooms across the United States; and according to the National Center of Education Statistics (2002), the overwhelming majority of our nation's public school teachers are White and female. This latter group constitutes roughly 70 percent of the teaching population. As chapter 3 discussed, Black and Latino boys search for male role models and exemplars of black and Latino masculinity. One potential place to find these models is among teachers. Therefore, recruitment efforts need to be improved to attract Black and Latino men into the teaching profession where they can serve as cultural brokers and multicultural navigators.

Finally, fewer young professionals of any group aspire to teaching because of its poor financial incentives. Although, as a group, teachers have about as much influence over the direction of our lives as our parents, guardians, relatives, or other intimates, they are poorly compensated and their profession is not highly regarded. In the 1990s, an era of a bullish and robust economy that made millionaires out of many, the real average teacher salaries increased by less than $10,000, from $33,084 to $41,574. Basically, this increase accounts for slight per annum cost-of-living increases, roughly 2.5 percent a year. Meanwhile, in the 1990s the ratio of teachers' salaries to other full-time jobs decreased by nearly 10 percent (National Center for Education Statistics 2002). How might our educational system transform itself if we increased the stature of teaching and made it as competitive as other demanding fields such as law, medicine, or business? Schools may fail to lure many pedagogic, creative, and culturally informed teachers because they do not compensate as well as other professional job sectors. As a result, the profession of elementary- and secondary-school teacher is poorly regarded. The combination of low wages and low regard for the profession by the general public lead, in turn, to teacher shortages.

One way for teacher training programs to assist those apprentices who have already chosen to work in education to gain insight and become vigilant about how inequality works is to require them to participate extensively in simulation exercises where their positions as the privileged and nonprivileged shift. Social psychologists have begun to develop practices for students to experience how in-group/out-group dynamics develop and to observe the social dynamics that emerge in these contexts. Such activities are used to sensitize and familiarize "insiders" and "outsiders" in communicating with each other. Practically speaking, society requires a body of cultural practices to facilitate interracial, interethnic, and interclass relations, and as students and teacher trainees debrief and share their experiences, they can work together to develop wider repertoires of knowledge and communication while also building mutual respect for their cultural differences.

In sum, teachers' and other school officials' acknowledgment of multiple forms of cultural capital signifies a willingness to expand the body of knowledge and concede cultural equality in schools. It also helps to realize the potential of Horace Kallen's vision of an ethnic pluralist society that runs somewhat like an orchestra in which each instrument—or culture—plays a significant role in producing the music—or the national culture and body of knowledge. [Kallen's *Culture and Democracy* (1924) was considered to be the defining work of the cultural-pluralist view in the early twentieth century.] Though Kallen and other early twentieth-century cultural pluralists are criticized for their disregard of the possibility that pluralism might actually extend to non-White ethnic minorities, such as African Americans, Asian Americans, Latinos, and Native Americans (Hollinger 1995), the principle of cultural equality endures. From an educational standpoint and in its most ideal sense, cultural equality promotes parity among groups by enlarging the intellectual territory we call "knowledge." It decenters Anglo and Eurocentric experiences and brings the histories, contributions, and cultural productions of peoples of African, Asian, Caribbean, Central America, and Latin American descent into the fold, not merely as ethnocentric bases of knowledge but rather as universal and fundamental aspects of knowledge. A move toward cultural equality would challenge our conventional notions of the "educated" person who has simply absorbed the codes of success and intelligence created by dominant social groups.

ENLISTING MULTICULTURAL NAVIGATORS

Over dinner one evening, I participated in a highly charged debate with three educators from Mississippi whom I respect greatly. Together they had more than seventy-five years of experience in the public education system, all serving as teachers and one serving as a principal. As soldiers working in the public-education trenches, they encountered noncompliant believers daily. They described many students as belligerent, threatening, disrespectful, and utterly noncompliant. They lamented that some students are plainly "bad" boys and girls, lost and perhaps even hopeless cases, for whom expert counseling is needed. How, they asked, could I expect teachers to follow the mandates of the "No Child Left Behind" policy of the Bush administration, a policy of testing and accountability that holds teachers and principals responsible for the academic progress of each student? How could teachers educate and discipline and at the same time serve as mentors, surrogate parents, counselors, and child psychologists for so many "troubled students?" Did I expect teachers to accept inordinate responsibility for a job that pays poorly compared to other professions?

These poor and disadvantaged students had limited access to social ties that could confirm the veracity of the phrase "it's who you know that counts." Many of their parents had only a high-school diploma. Most parents, trying to make ends meet by working long hours in low-wage jobs, gave teachers and principals the major responsibilities for educating their children and opening the doors for more opportunities. Certainly, parents have a serious responsibility to contribute to their children's academic growth and development. However, parents with little to no dominant cultural and social capital are limited in the extent to which they can help their children navigate the educational systems. Yet schools cannot function properly without parents fulfilling their responsibilities for cultivating their children's interests and investments in their academic careers. Therefore, I responded that parents with limited dominant cultural capital need access to multicultural navigators serving these parents' communities through churches, volunteer organizations, community centers, and after-school programs. Working together, teachers, parents, and multicultural navigators could significantly impact the school engagement and attachment of these youths.

In turn, educators have a responsibility to welcome and engage many parents with limited capital into the schooling process. If students are dealt the hand of poverty, then how do we ensure that they get access to the social resources that will improve their opportunities for academic success? Sometimes we idealize schools as the great equalizer. But this and other studies inform us that schools tend to enforce or mirror students' social standings more than anything (Bourdieu 1977; MacLeod 1995;

Willis 1981). Thus, if educators desire to equalize opportunities, then schools will require teachers to be multicultural navigators, at ease with various perspectives and in possession of myriad cultural competences. If teachers, principals, and those of us committed to reducing the population of the undereducated could develop ourselves as multicultural navigators, then fundamental changes could ensue.

The need and demand for more multicultural navigators should also compel us to reexamine our assumptions about tracking in diversely populated schools. Multicultural navigators develop their competence and fluency in multiple cultural repertoires through varied cross-cultural and interracial and interethnic exchanges. Therefore, residential and school integration, and not a regression to segregated schools, the results of social preferences and increasing economic disparity as wealthier families self-segregate, are needed (Lee 2004; Bobo, Kluegel, and Smith 1997). Meanwhile, federal and state governments have lessened the demand for desegregated schools as busing laws have been repealed, and voluntary choice to remain in neighborhood schools segregated by race and income has sustained itself. Even within mixed-race and mixed-class schools, ability grouping and tracking are the new forms of segregation and, consequently, undermine social interactions across various racial, ethnic, class, and cultural boundaries (Mickelson 2001; Lucas 1999; Oakes 1985; Gamoran 1987). Such in-school stratification would limit the number of opportunities students would have to develop as multicultural navigators.

Not everyone agrees that we can achieve Kallen's vision of ethnic pluralism in a democracy where economic inequality thrives. In *The Ethnic Myth*, Stephen Steinberg (1989) argues that a cultural democracy can work against the interests of subordinate racial, ethnic, and socioeconomic groups in a society without economic parity. For him, a cultural democracy would support groups' rights to cultural self-determination and, consequently, would preclude the full integration of less-privileged groups into the powerful spheres of society. In other words, a cultural democracy could perpetuate academic, residential, occupational, social, political, and economic boundaries. Essentially, it is an "American dilemma" (Hochschild 1984) where liberal democracy, coupled with groups' self-interests, fuel separation, distinction, and the exclusion of the less fortunate from opportunities for mobility. Such dilemmas arise in a democracy where people follow their preferences and disregard the ills of social and economic segregation. The principles of integration must endure, however, and civil rights advocates should continue working to convey the critical need for altruism and sharing our resources so that a nation highly touted to be so great does not continue to contradict its self-image and widen the social and economic divide.

Finally, parents and communities have placed teachers and administrators in charge of their children's minds and lives for a substantial portion of each day. But they must work collectively to train and to prepare children to become socially conscious and productive adults and citizens. With the assistance of multicultural navigators, these children can learn to effectively move through the worlds of school, work, and community. Multicultural navigators exist both inside and outside schools, and they work in the various professional sectors, from academia to creative writing to law to software development to veterinary medicine. What we need also are formal partnerships between schools and social, economic, and political organizations that can link students like the ones in this study to conscientious multicultural navigators. These programs can build on already established mentorship programs, though they would also include workshops and trainings to convey to students how to successfully negotiate different cultural and social terrains.

How do we identify multicultural navigators? To recap the description in chapter five, multicultural navigators stand out because of their abilities to draw on skills and knowledge from the repertoire of the culture of power, which is linked to mobility in mainstream society and to draw on one or more nondominant cultural repertoires, which are linked to status and position within marginalized or subordinate cultural communities. Multicultural navigators know how and why members of nondominant ethno-racial groups might want to "keep it real" and maintain a commitment to their group and self-identities. They also fully grasp how things work in dominant and mainstream social institutions, organizations, places and cultural spheres. With a keen awareness of the enormous effects that dominant institutions have on individuals' economic, social, and political well-being and with a critical consciousness of how social and cultural inequality can inhibit their well-beings, multicultural navigators seek to raise consciousness and bring about equality and equity through actions and deeds. They dedicate themselves to both *personal* achievement and the *collective* achievement of groups with limited access to the opportunity structure, and they effectively demonstrate how the attainment of personal success helps to realize the goals of group success through the creation of more highly trained and skilled members of that social group.

Here, I have made recommendations that require contributions from us all: students, parents, educators, community leaders, and neighbors. Indeed, there's room for the village to increase African American and Latino students' engagement in school and to ultimately close the achievement gap. I am convinced that the educational problems I have discussed would benefit from multidisciplinary solutions. A dialogue among educational anthropologists helped to jump-start my analyses, and I have added a sociological component to the discussion. How students dealt with academic and cultural problems personally and collectively varied over time. Identities such as race, ethnicity, class, and gender dictate much of how students categorize and approach these problems. The challenge remains to acknowledge the relevance and depth of students' attitudes and beliefs and the critical insight they provide about schooling without trivializing and merely reducing their actions to the outcomes of youthfulness and misplaced values. By examining the hierarchy of cultural meanings in schools and paying attention to culture and how it influences many students' attachment to school, educators, parents, and students can work together to break the cycle of low-income African American and Latino youths ending up at the bottom rungs of the academic and socioeconomic ladders. Employing effective practices that move toward these goals would ensure that both in theory and in practice, school success has no color.

APPENDIX

The study's findings are based on surveys and interviews with sixty-eight Yonkers students that I conducted in 1997–1998 and from surveys with their parents I obtained in 1996 that were conducted under the auspices of the Yonkers Family and Community Project (YF&CP), directed by Robert Crain, Joseph Darden, Angela Aidala, and Joyce Moon Howard (Crain et al. 1997).

METHODOLOGY

The Sample

My study spun from a larger project and drew extensively on the sample and first-wave data collected by researchers of the YF&CP, a quasi-experimental longitudinal study of 317 African American and Latino families in various neighborhoods of Yonkers, New York. Funded primarily by the Ford Foundation, the YF&CP began as an evaluation of scattered-site public housing (SSPH) as a government intervention to reduce social and geographic isolation of minority poor. The study's original purpose was to compare families who entered public housing in white, middle-class neighborhoods to a control group of comparable families living in segregated private and public housing in a high-minority, high-poverty area of the same city. [1] The families who moved into these new housing units—as well as the control sample of families, who desired to move to these new units but could not because of limited availability—were interviewed within a thirteen-month pe-riod, from August 1994 to September 1995. Under the auspices of the YF&CP research, the female heads of household, their adolescent children, and their younger children were interviewed. Separate surveys were used for each group. One hundred thirty-nine African American and Latino adolescents (ages thirteen to seventeen) and 177 children (ages eight to twelve) responded to questions from a semistructured survey instrument.

For the purposes of this research, I chose to interview sixty-eight males and females, ages thirteen to twenty, who lived in two housing complexes with the largest populations of adolescents and youths (table A.1). One site was located in a high-poverty, high-minority neighborhood in southwest Yonkers; the other in a low-poverty, predominantly white neighborhood in east Yonkers. Previously, I worked on the YF&CP as a graduate research associate and had assisted in the survey design for the adolescent component of the study. Having personally interviewed many of the adolescents for the YF&CP, I had gained some entry into their peer

TABLE A.1 Gender, Ethnic, and Age Breakdown of Students in the Study

	African American	Latino	Total N	Ages 13–15	Ages 16–20
Female	25 (60%)	13 (50%)	38 (56%)	17 (50%)	21 (62%)
Male	17 (40%)	13 (50%)	30 (44%)	17 (50%)	13 (38%)
Total N	42 (100%)	26 (100%)	68 (100%)	34 (100%)	34 (100%)

communities. These youths and their families had previously agreed to be continual participants in the YF&CP study and thus agreed to be recontacted. For this follow-up research, interviews were conducted from November 1997 to June 1998.

Though the study from which I selected my research participants focused on neighborhood effects, this was not my intent for this project. Still, it is important to note that the research respondents are socially matched on key socioeconomic traits. Until 1994, all of these youths were growing up in the same high-poverty, predominantly minority neighborhoods. From baseline survey data, we found no significant differences on key demographic and family characteristics by neighborhood type (table A.2).

As table A.3 indicates, I attempted to contact all of the ninety-six youths who were residents in the two neighborhood sites I visited. After our first contact with them under the YF&CP, several youths had either moved to other neighborhoods or away from the city. I decided to limit the sample to only those youths who currently lived in the two chosen neighborhood sites. Therefore, the final number of eligible respondents was eighty-five; and eighty percent of the eligible respondents agreed to participate in the study.

TABLE A.2 Students' Family Context by Neighborhood Type

	Southwest (High poverty, predominantly minority)	East (Low poverty, predominantly White)
Total sample N	31	37
Household income below $10,000	57%	54%
Wage earner in the household	52%	70%
Single-parent household	74%	68%
Parent has less than high school diploma	55%	52%
Ever received AFDC	87%	92%

TABLE A.3 Eligibility and Response Rate of Sample

Number contacted (A)	96
Number ineligible because they moved (B)	11
Total Eligible (C = A-B)	85
Number of refusals by race/ethnicity:	
African American	13
Latino	4
Number who "refused" to participate (%)	17 (20%)
Number of refusals by gender	
Female	8
Male	9
Total number who agreed to participate	68 (80%)

Data Collection

To increase the understanding of the students' cultural, social, economic, and educational realities, I weave together both quantitative and qualitative information—survey and interview data. Using a phenomenological inquiry that allows people to "tell" their own personal perspectives—revealing how they "make sense" of the world, given present and past social experiences (McCracken 1988; Patton 1990)—I decided early in the research to take an inductive approach and to allow meanings to emerge from the context, from the students themselves—after all they are the best experts in telling us why they do what they do. All of the students participated in at least two ways: through semi-structured surveys and in one-on-one face-to-face interviews held either in their homes or in a local neighborhood center. At least half of these students also participated in small-group interviews of eight, which a research assistant and I facilitated. Originally, I had planned to facilitate all of the group interviews myself, but after I began to suspect that my male respondents did not divulge information with me about gender that might make them appear too "soft" or more vulnerable (see chapter 3), I hired a male facilitator. Some of the data on gender that I obtained from my male respondents comes from this male-only group interview. Nonetheless, I am confident that my insider status as an African American; my being relatively close to their age (ranging from eight to fifteen years' difference at the time of the interviews), my familiarity with minority youth cultural and language styles, and my prior association with these youths in another research study greatly facilitated the data collection process.

Through surveys and interviews, I explored students' beliefs, attitudes, and practices about racial and ethnic identity, as well as the students' experiences in school and with their teachers, and their beliefs about economic opportunity, race relations, culture and styles, and the means to success and achievement in this society. Individually, they shared with me their beliefs about educational and career aspirations, gender roles, "appropriate" ethnic or cultural behavior among their peers and family (e.g., speech, dress, codeswitching), and social and job mobility. I also made inquiries of their racial, ethnic, and gender identities and asked such questions as, "In your family, are there expectations related to your [racial or ethnic and gender] background, for how you should act? What about among your friends? How do you feel about these rules? What are your feelings about the ways you're 'supposed' to behave as a [member of racial or ethnic group and gender]?" For more sensitive questions about academic performance, delinquency, school truancy, self-esteem, and peer and family associations, I relied on the self-administered survey. Finally, I gathered information on students' friends, peers, families, neighbors, and other social contacts to assess how their social networks might be associated with different behaviors and attitudes.

In addition, I gathered information from students in a group context, specifically from three single-sex group interviews, which averaged about two and a half hours. Youths who participated in these groups lived in the same housing complexes. I deliberately chose youths who knew one another so that I could observe and hear about their peer-group interactions. The representation of African American and Latino youth in the groups reflected their numbers in the overall study where African Americans outnumbered Latinos almost two to one. I used this information to complement and triangulate the data gathered from the individual interviews and surveys. Moreover, I used the group setting to listen and observe how students operate around peers. Group interviewing allowed me to elaborate upon statements and locate the bases of shared and collective meanings (Frey and Fontana 1991; Lofland and Lofland 1984). How do youth discuss issues of culture, race, identity, and achievement among one another? What are the most salient social factors for them as a group? Similarly, these semi-structured group interviews explored the meaning behind beliefs, attitudes, and actions that deal with racial, ethnic, and gender identity, culture and identity, as well as the students' beliefs about the opportunity structure, race relations, and the means to success and achievement in this society. This approach allowed opinions and beliefs to "volley" back and forth through the group.

Initially, I avoided asking explicit questions about "acting white," being desirous to observe and hear how it manifests spontaneously. Sometimes it did, but more often it did not, even though study participants hinted at it. Sometimes, they hesitated to invoke language about race unless I mentioned it first. They did not want to appear to be too "racial" (a misnomer for their concern about appearing too racially conscious or even racist). After a handful of interviews, I decided to ask directly about blackness, "Spanishness," or "acting white" at any moment I believed the respondent was hinting at ideas that were pertinent to these notions. Doing this often resulted in visible signs of relief on the students' part. By describing explicit and symbolic acts and meanings, including beliefs, art forms, language, gossip, dress, stories, and rituals of daily life, the study participants cataloged behaviors associated with "blackness," "Spanishness," and "whiteness."

DATA ANALYSIS

The analyses laid out here are mainly descriptive and primarily based on the sixty-eight in-depth face-to-face individual interviews and three group interviews. All of these interviews were fully transcribed and coded. I categorized students' responses by themes and topic areas, using a coding program developed by a graduate-school colleague, Chauncy Lennon. This program allowed me to assign multiple thematic codes to each question and the responses to it. At first, I used umbrella themes (such as ones that denoted "race in school" or "gender in school") and then moved to more specific dimensional codes (such as one that denoted "beliefs about girls [or boys] and their academic ability"). Overall, I generated forty thematic codes. Lennon's program also allowed me to systematically search for patterns and collate these responses by gender, ethnicity, and various other groupings, such as age or neighborhood settings.

Furthermore, in several instances, I relied on survey analyses based on data input into an SPSS data file. In these analyses, I utilized categorical analyses, means comparisons, or ANOVA procedures; and depending upon its appropriateness, chi-square, t- or F-tests were used to test for statistical significance. I caution the reader to interpret the survey findings in the context of this study, since they are not generalizable to the entire population of low-income African American and Latino students in either Yonkers or the United States. Nevertheless, the patterns found here are illustrative of social and cultural phenomena that may occur in the wider population.

NOTES

Preface

1. Race terms like "black" and "white" are capitalized throughout the text when they refer to individuals or groups (e.g., "Black students" or "Whites"). When I refer to concepts, ideas, or things as either "black" or "white," the terms will be lowercase.
2. Sociologists tend to be particular sticklers for differentiating between race and ethnicity. Many ethnic, national, and cultural groups comprise any one race, which forces a careful researcher to qualify the uses of these concepts. Thus, when I write "Black," I am referring to African American youth. Those of Hispanic heritage compose the other half of the students in this study, and while several of them identify as "Black," "White," or prefer not to identify with any race, I use "Latino" to refer to that group of students whose parents immigrated to the United States from places in Central and Latin America and the Spanish Caribbean. These youths' immigrant backgrounds place another slant on the explanations for how culture, identity, and education interrelate (see chapter 4).
3. TANF is a block grant program designed to make dramatic reforms to the

nation's welfare system by moving recipients into work and turning welfare into a program of temporary assistance. TANF replaced the national welfare program known as Aid to Families with Dependent Children (AFDC) and the related programs known as the Job Opportunities and Basic Skills Training (JOBS) program and the Emergency Assistance (EA) program.

4. These data were obtained directly from the Yonkers Public School District.

Introduction

1. In his last published book before his untimely death, Ogbu appeared to have retreated somewhat from the proclamation that he and Fordham made in 1986 that Black students consider making good grades in schools as "acting white." Still, he felt that the attitudes that they perceived or interpreted as White were conducive to earning good grades and asserted that these behaviors had little to do with collective identity: "The behaviors and attitudes that some Shaker Heights Black students rejected included speaking standard English, enrollment in honors and AP classes, being smart during lessons, and hanging around too many White students. Before high school, most Shaker students did not equate making good grades with acting White, although they criticized other Blacks with White attitudes and behaviors conducive to making good grades. The reasons given for the labeling had little to do with collective identity" (2003, 198).

2. Though a few of these youth were no longer in school, and some of them had already entered into adulthood, I refer to them as "students" for the sake of simplicity and brevity when I write about them as a group. The term "student" is appropriate because most of their stories in this book inform us about the interrelationships between their identities and their schooling practices.

3. Using the National Longitudinal Study of Adolescent Health (ADDHEALTH), Johnson and colleagues measured engagement as the minimal level of participation in schools—specifically, how may times the student had skipped school, had trouble getting homework done, and had trouble paying attention in school. Their measure of engagement can be thought of as the absence of disengagement, which is indicated by not paying attention, cutting school, and not completing homework. Their study does not differentiate students at higher levels of engagement. Thus, their findings should be interpreted as the idea that African American students may more likely to be minimally engaged in school, though they may or may not be the most engaged in school (2001, 334).

4. Ann Swidler's notion of the cultural "tool kit" characterizes how culture influences action where "[c]ulture in this sense is more like a style or a set of skills and habits than a set of preferences or wants" (1986, 275).
5. For a critical review of the application of cultural capital theory in U.S. social science research, see Lamont and Lareau (1988) and Kingston (2001).
6. I use the phrase "dominant" culture to refer to the system of mainstream and widely acceptable social practices and ideas, often based on the ways of life of social groups with the most power in our society. Throughout, I will refer to "dominant" culture and "nondominant" culture. The former refers to the both institutionalized and informal practices of the social groups who hold the power to either permit or deny access to opportunities, whether academic, economic, political, social, cultural, or otherwise. Nondominant, in contrast, refers to the practices of those groups who historically have had limited access and means to control the major institutions and organizations. The privileged status of many of European ancestry, especially British and Western European heritage in earlier eras, is now one of the most widely recognized themes in the study of United States social history (Hollinger 1995). Thus, White Americans are perceived as the dominant racial group in American society. Moreover, since class shapes and determines much of an individual's life outcomes, the privileged status and dominance of the upper and middle classes in U.S. history is also tacitly understood in American society (Sennett and Cobb 1993; Bowles and Gintis 1976). When race and class are the referents, those of either European or nonpoor status comprise the dominant social groups, since they maintain the greatest advantages, access, and power in U.S. society, and possess the highest cultural standings, as well. Let me be clear, not all dominant group members enjoy higher cultural, social, economic political power, and conversely, not all nondominant group members are without power. Rather, these terms are used to denote how collectively dominant group members are overrepresented and nondominant group members are underrepresented at higher levels of advantage in intergroup resource competition (Doane 1999).

Chapter 1: Beyond Belief

1. To protect their identities, I use pseudonyms for the students and their high schools throughout the book.
2. Mercer Sullivan (1989) provides extensive ethnographic detail on the notion of "getting paid."

3. The other two components of Sellers and colleagues' multidimensional racial identity model include racial *salience* and *regard*. *Salience* refers to the extent to which one's race is a relevant part of one's self-concept. Usually, salience is concerned with a particular event or situation and the degree to which one is inclined to define oneself in terms of race in that social situation. *Regard* refers to a person's evaluative judgment of his or her race, the extent to which he or she feels positively about it (Sellers et al. 1998).

4. Sellers et. al's work was developed primarily around the racial identity of Blacks. Still, I extrapolate from their conceptual model and add "ethnic" here because of the centrality of ethnic identity discovered among the Latino students of different ethnic heritages in the study. Since race generally refers to phenotype or physical features, the Latino students could define themselves in both racial and ethnic terms, just as the African American students might define themselves in ethnic terms. As Bailey (2000) argues, however, language is central to second-generation Latino students' inclination to avoid phenotype-racial classifications and to focus on their ethnic and linguistic identities.

5. The specific questions I asked were: (1) How do you talk about being (racial/ethnic identity) with your family? Your friends? (2) What are your feelings about your heritage? What kinds of things do you do with your family that reflects your background? With your friends? (3) In your family, are there expectations related to your background, about how you should act? What about among your friends? How do you feel about these expectations? (4) What are your feelings about how you're "supposed" to behave as a (racial/ethnic identity)? (5) How much say or power do you think Black (Spanish or Latino) people have in American life and politics? Why do you say that? (6) For you personally, do you think that your chances in life depend more on what happens to Black (Spanish or Latino) people as a group, or does it depend more on what you yourself do?

6. Moreover, as Nathan Glazer (1993) has documented, early views of assimilation developed by social scientists often eclipsed any discussion of those who were not White. Consequently, assimilation became a politically volatile and disreputable concept that many do not accept as an intended goal for all, especially as racial and ethnic differentiation and inequality persist. "The concept of assimilation looked toward Europe," Glazer wrote. "It referred to the expected experience and fate of the stream of [white ethnic] immigrants who were a permanent part of American life and consciousness from the time of the first settlements on the Atlantic seaboard to the 1920s, when it was thought—incorrectly—that we were now done with mass immigration of varied backgrounds to the United States" (1993, 124).

7. Scholars of assimilation have moved beyond the Anglo-conformity model and have broadened the concept of assimilation, particularly given the social and economic patterns of groups immigrating to the United States from Africa, Asia, and the Caribbean after the repeal of restrictive immigration quotas in 1965. Now social scientists consider assimilation toward other nondominant groups who are concentrated in areas where immigrants or other social groups may reside. In Chapter four, I discuss the "segmented assimilation" theory of sociologists Alejandro Portes and Min Zhou (1992) who refer to "downward mobility" or assimilation towards native, poor minority cultural practices.

8. Other ideas about oppositional culture go beyond the notion that nondominant group members collude in their personal and collective failure through their resistance to the power of dominant social groups. Oppositional cultures have arisen in many forms: for example, in class revolutions (Marx 1978); slave rebellions (Genovese 1974); protest movements among the poor for improved economic conditions and opportunity (Piven and Cloward 1979); or youth dress and slang subcultures (Hall and Jefferson 1993; Kelly 1994).

9. Even in wider society, attitudinal-behavioral paradoxes abound. Many of us are inconsistent in our ideals and our behaviors. For example, survey research on the general adult White population's viewpoints about racial integration in schools shows divergences in beliefs and practices. Schuman et al. (1998) document how White Americans generally profess belief in ideals of racial and ethnic integration, yet they continue to live in de facto segregated neighborhoods and send their children to segregated schools (see Massey and Denton 1993; Orfield 2001).

10. Although Mickelson (1990) is right to argue for a differentiation between abstract and concrete attitudes and beliefs about the value of education, arguably some of her concrete measures could be categorized as abstract, and conversely some of her abstract indicators seem concrete. For exaple, many respondents could have interpreted one particular question, "Studying in school rarely pays off with good jobs" (labeled as a "concrete" item by Mickelson), as a more "abstract" connection between education and jobs, and not have interpreted it with regard to their own personal situations.

11. Other scholars also have argued about the importance of distinguishing between normative and cognitive expectations within an ideological system. See also Gould (1999) and Merton (1968).

12. The last item included in Mickelson's concrete attitude about school is, "When our teachers give us homework, my friends never think of doing it." While this item contributes to the validity of the scale, I do not mention it

here since it taps into another social dimension of students' academic realities that, on the surface, has less to do with their concrete attitudes about race and education.

13. W. E. B. Du Bois' notion of double consciousness is one of the earliest references to some form of dual or separate socialization processes among African Americans in his 1903 publication of *The Souls of Black Folks*. Darder (1991) discusses a number of frameworks that have used various constructs to explore dual or separate socialization processes among peoples of color. For a review of studies examining the psychological impact if biculturalism, see LaFromboise, Coleman, and Gerton (1993).

14. Some researchers have challenged the idea of an attitude-achievement paradox among Black students. "The myth that Black students' reported attitudes have no relationship to their behaviors has persisted in the social sciences for too long," write James Ainsworth-Darnell and Douglas Downey (1998). They found that the attitude and behavior correlations for Blacks are in the same direction and similar to Asian Americans, who, as a group, have performed quite well academically, even outperforming Whites. Furthermore, in their national study, Downey and Ainsworth-Darnell found that the correlation between attitudes and actual school behaviors is only slightly less for Asians, Blacks, and Latinos than they are for Whites.

Chapter 2: "Black" Cultural Capital and the Conflicts of Schooling

1. Portions of this chapter were published previously in an article entitled, "'Black' Cultural Capital, Status Positioning and Schooling Conflicts for Low-Income African-American Youth." 2003. *Social Problems*, vol. 50 (1): 136–55.

2. Let me say that I use this dominant-nondominant binary for heuristic purposes, not to deny that many nondominant social groups have contributed greatly to the cultural fabric of our society regarded as American culture. Nor is it used to deny that across many races, ethnicities, classes, religions, other social groups, and both genders those in U.S. society share a plethora of norms, beliefs, and cultural practices that have emerged out of the "melting pot."

3. Given their varied ethnic backgrounds, cultural contexts, and family immigrant status, I exclude my Latino respondents from this discussion and return to a discussion of their multiple identities in chapter 4. Nevertheless, I would suggest that the arguments that I posit here are not limited to the social and cultural lives of low-income, urban Black students.

4. For the sake of brevity, I use "African American" and "Black" interchangeably throughout this book, though I recognize that the latter group covers a much broader group of peoples. Although various cultural standpoints may exist among African Americans, particularly in terms of class and region, they share many cultural tastes and preferences across these lines, and, consequently, some points of agreement about "black" culture.

5. Many of the cultural styles that characterize "blackness" emerged from the urban ghetto, today promulgated by the popularity of hip-hop culture and rap music, an oft-used mechanism of social commentary on poor, Black life (Kelley 1994). Several thinkers have documented how since the 1980s, hip-hop culture has come to be an integral aspect of contemporary black culture and identity (Rose 1994; George 1998).

6. See Morgan (2002) for a recent discussion on this issue between language, intelligence, and power.

7. There exist crossover artists such as Elizabeth Catlett, Romare Bearden, and Jacob Lawrence, whose extraordinary works should augment the cache of dominant cultural capital for individuals in U.S. society. Nevertheless, African American art forms often tend not to be perceived as forms of dominant cultural capital, but indeed for the African American middle class, an awareness of these forms gives one "black" cultural capital. Paul DiMaggio and Francie Ostrower found that controlling for educational background, Black Americans participate at somewhat lower rates than White Americans in viewing European American art. However, they participate substantially more than Whites in historically African American art forms (DiMaggio and Ostrower 1980).

8. For a linguistic anthropologist's insight on this communicative style, see Goodwin (1991).

9. In 1998, Latino and Black students were less likely than Asian/Pacific Islander and White students to complete advanced mathematics, some advanced science, and some advanced English classes. For example, about one-quarter of Latino and Black students (26 and 30 percent, respectively) completed advanced mathematics courses, whereas about one-half of Asian/Pacific Islander and White students (56 and 45 percent, respectively) did so (National Center for Education Statistics 2003a; 2003b).

10. See also Fordham (1993).

11. In the summer of 1987, the comprehensive Educational Improvement Plan II (EIP II), which was created and approved by the Yonkers Board of Education, included a component that restructured the curriculum and encouraged the development of a multicultural curriculum and services for language-minority students. However, the degree to which the curriculum

and pedagogy were fundamentally restructured is unknown and would require a more in-depth site-based study (Brenner 1998).

Chapter 3: Between a "Soft" and a "Hard" Place

1. The African American and Latino girls in the study also adhered to styles
   and tastes that are distinctive from those of their White counterparts. Not
   only did they speak "slang," which Samurai associated and conflated with
   "black talk," but these girls also embraced conspicuous differences in interactional and other styles, such as nail and hair care. Many argue that
   African American, Latino, and White females will experience different social and cultural responses because of the varied impact of gender, race,
   and class dynamics in their lives (Collins 1991; Anzaldua 1990; hooks 1984;
   King 1996; Rollins 1985). Parker et al. (1995) have found that African American adolescent females and White adolescent females differ significantly in
   their concepts of beauty, body image, and weight concerns. African American females were found to be more flexible than their White counterparts
   and spoke more about "making what you've got work for you." In contrast,
   many White females expressed dissatisfaction with their body shape and
   were found to be rigid in their concepts of beauty.
2. That many of my female respondents easily discussed gender issues illuminates one of this study's methodological dilemmas. During face-to-face interviews with me, the males did not tend to confront issues of masculinity
   and femininity as often as the females did. In fact, much of the data I have
   on gender from the male respondents comes from a group interview of
   African American and Latino males that was facilitated by an African
   American male whom I hired. This observation speaks to the relevance of
   the methodological debate about racial, ethnic, and gender matching for
   surveys and interviews during social science research.
3. Historian Jacqueline Jones (1985) documents how, historically, African
   American women have worked and toiled outside of the home, a social fact
   inculcated within the minds of many African American males and females.
   This historical fact might explain why relatively few African American males
   (18 percent v. 62 percent of the Latino males) would subscribe to these beliefs about a woman's place being inside of the home. The cultural and social
   status of Latino males differs from their African American counterparts,
   particularly given their parents' immigrant status in this country.
4. It is important to note the difference between the "soft" that my male respondents used to characterize femininity, and the "soft" that Moss and

Tilly (1996) use to describe noncognitive skills preferred by White employers. Although these two connotations of "soft" are quite interrelated, the former most often refers to the quality of perceived female traits and femininity, with male sex roles as the reference category. The latter connotation takes mainstream (white) cultural styles as the reference point and characterizes as "soft" those noncognitive tastes and skills that are preferable and more pervasive in certain workplaces.

5. Similarly, Holland and Eisenhart (1990) found that Black college women found it necessary to project a "together person" image, one who is not easily messed with, made fun of, and who could not be manipulated.

6. Professional, specialty occupations would require, at minimum, a college degree.

7. While there may exist higher percentages of women of color in white-collar jobs, research has shown that segmentation exists within the labor market for women of color. Despite their increased representation in the office setting and "white-collar" jobs, African American women and Latinas are usually overrepresented in clerical or administrative support jobs and drastically underrepresented in senior-level positions. Their male counterparts have a slightly greater representation, though relatively low compared with White men and women in the workforce (King 1993).

Chapter 4: Next-Door Neighbors

1. All of the youth categorized as "Cuban" had mixed parentage from both Cuba and Jamaica. And many of their mothers had emigrated here at young ages, having lived in the United States an average of twenty-four years.

2. A debate about whether either Blacks or Latinos have the largest representation ensues, and it speaks to measurement issues and the tricky nature of racial and ethnic ascription. When race is included in the consideration (that is, whether one is either Black or White Hispanic), the statistics shift, giving Blacks the advantage. However, in terms of raw numbers, more people identify as being of Hispanic heritage.

3. More specifically, segmented assimilation theory argues that immigrant minority students do not necessarily choose the straight-line assimilation paths that the progeny of White ethnic immigrants from the late-nineteenth and early-twentieth centuries have taken. Often, the immigrant youth's myriad interactions with the social context and individuals surrounding him or her shape the pattern of acculturation. First they have the option of acculturation into White, middle-class society. Another option is

for immigrant students and their families (especially poor ones) to acculturate into the so-called "black" oppositional cultures of the impoverished urban centers where they reside. Or finally, they can choose to fully incorporate themselves into immigrant ethnic enclaves where small businesses, economic capital, and beneficial social ties such as neighbors, kin, or compatriots from their native land provide both social and economic resources. The degree to which either native or immigrant youth become socially and economically mobile depends upon several factors, such as job access, the ability to afford higher schooling, family resources, social networks or social capital, and the size and structure of preexisting co-ethnic communities.

4. Milton Gordon (1964) explained, "There is no good reason to believe that white Protestant America has ever extended a firm and cordial invitation to its minorities to dance. Therefore, the attitudes of the minority-group members themselves on the matter have been divided and ambiguous."

5. These findings differ from those of Rumbaut (1995) who found that males were more likely to identify in unhyphenated terms as American or by national origin, whereas females were more likely to choose an additive binational (or hyphenated) identity label.

6. The mothers of five of the seven males who identified as Black Hispanic also described themselves as Black Hispanic, while the other two males' mothers identified as White. For the two Latinas who identified as White Hispanic, one mother identified as Black and the other as Puerto Rican or Hispanic only.

7. In addition, the celebration of certain Spanish or Latino holidays such as Three Kings Day formed another cultural boundary separating the African American and Latino youths. In surveys asking them questions about how they expressed their racial, ethnic, and cultural identities, the latter were twice as likely as the African Americans to mention celebrating ethnic holidays.

8. Parents of the youth in this study completed a survey on each of their children approximately one to one and one-half years earlier than when I interviewed their children.

Chapter 5: New "Heads" and Multicultural Navigators

1. Using a survey grid, I asked each respondent to report on a maximum of twenty-six persons in their lives: friends, individuals older than they who lived within their households, neighborhood peers, relatives who lived out-

side of their homes, and adults in their neighborhoods.

2. Percentages were calculated by dividing the total number of adult persons in their network who fell into each category by the total number of adults reported on in their social network.

3. Some have documented the use of conversational ploys and demeanors enlisted by upwardly mobile racial minorities to put White acquaintances or coworkers at ease (Zweigenhaft and Domhoff 1998; Cose 1993).

Appendix

1. The control group of families was matched according to the selection criteria used by the Yonkers Housing Authority (YHA) to fill low-income, scattered-site public-housing units. First, families selected for the control group had to meet the YHA's criteria for family size and income, rental payment history, and record of cleanliness. In addition to the basic eligibility measures, the control group was matched according to traits known to be associated with getting a job, educational attainment, and other forms of social attainment; demographic characteristics such as race/ethnicity; life stage; family composition; and human capital factors such as education, prior work history, and initial income level. In addition, we checked for interest in and concrete attempts to enter the SSPH program in order to address the "motivational problem."

BIBLIOGRAPHY

Adler, Patricia A., Steven J. Kless, and Peter Adler. 1992. "Socialization to Gender Roles: Popularity among Elementary School Boys and Girls." *Sociology of Education* 65 (3): 169–87.

Ainsworth-Darnell, James W., and Douglas B. Downey. 1998. "Assessing the Oppositional Culture Explanation for Racial/Ethnic Differences in School Performance." *American Sociological Review* 63 (4): 536–53.

Akom, A. A. 2003. "Reexamining Resistance as Oppositional Behavior: The Nation of Islam and the Creation of Black Achievement Ideology." *Sociology of Education* 76 (4): 305–25.

Alba, Richard, and Victor Nee. 1997. "Rethinking Assimilation Theory for a New Era of Immigration." *International Migration Review* 31 (4): 826–74.

Alexander, Karl L., Doris R. Entwisle, and Maxine S. Thompson. 1987. "School Performance, Status Relations, and the Structure of Sentiment: Bringing the Teacher Back." *American Sociological Review* 52 (5): 665–82.

Anderson, Elijah. 1980. "Some Observations on Black Youth Employment." In *Youth Employment and Public Policy,* edited by B. E. Anderson and I. V. Sawbell. Englewood Cliffs, N.J.: Prentice-Hall.

———. 1990. *Streetwise: Race, Class and Change in an Urban Community.* Chicago: University of Chicago Press.

————. 1999. *Code of the Street: Decency, Violence and the Moral Life of the Inner City*. New York: Norton.

Anzaldua, Gloria, ed. 1990. *Making Face, Making Soul: Haciendo Caras*. San Francisco: Aunt Lute Foundation Books.

Bailey, Benjamin. 2000. "Language and Negotiation of Ethnic/Racial Identity among Dominican Americans." *Language in Society* 29 (4) 555–82.

Banks, James A. 2001. "Multicultural Education: Characteristics and Goals." In *Multicultural Education: Issues and Perspectives*, edited by J. Banks and C. McGee. New York: John Wiley & Sons.

Beale, Frances. [1979] 1995. "Double Jeopardy: To Be Black and Female." In *Words of Fire: An Anthology of African-American Feminist Thought*, edited by B. Guy-Sheftall. New York: New Press.

Bean, Frank D., and Marta Tienda. 1999. "The Structuring of Hispanic Ethnicity: Theoretical and Historical Considerations." In *Majority and Minority: The Dynamics of Race and Ethnicity in American Life*, edited by N. Yetman. Boston: Allyn & Bacon.

Belluck, Pam. 1999. "Reason Is Sought for Lag by Blacks in School Effect." *New York Times*, July 4, 1999.

Benjamin, Lois. 1991. *The Black Elite*. Chicago: Nelson-Hall.

Bennett, William J. 1988. *Our Children and Our Country: Improving America's Schools and Affirming the Common Culture*. New York: Simon & Schuster.

Bluestone Barry, and Bennett Harrison. 1982. *The Deindustrialization of America: Plant Closings, Community Abandonment, and the Dismantling of Basic Industry*. New York: Basic Books.

Bobo, Larry, James Kluegel, and Ryan Smith. 1997. *Laissez-Faire Racism: The Crystallization of Kinder, Gentler, Anti-Black Ideology*. New York: Russell Sage Foundation.

Bourdieu, Pierre. 1977a. "Cultural Reproduction and Social Reproduction." In *Power and Ideology in Education*, edited by J. Karabel and A. H. Halsey. New York: Oxford University Press.

————. 1977b. *Outline to a Theory of Practice*. London: Cambridge University Press.

————. 1986. "The Forms of Capital." In *Handbook of Theory and Research for the Sociology of Education*, edited by J. G. Richardson. New York: Greenwood Press.

Bourgois, Philippe. 1995. *In Search of Respect: Selling Crack in El Barrio*. New York: Cambridge University Press.

Bowles, Samuel, and Herbert Gintis. 1976. *Schooling in Capitalist America: Educational Reform and the Contradictions of Economic Life*. New York: Basic Books.

Bowman, Philip, and Cleopatra Howard. 1985. "Race-related Socialization, Motivation, and Academic Achievement: A Study of Black Youth in Three-Generation Families." *Journal of the American Academy of Child Psychiatry* 27: 134–41.

Brenner, Elsa. 1998. "Yonkers Teachers Study Diversity." *The New York Times,* July 26, 1998.

Briggs, Xavier de Souza. 1998. "Brown Kids in White Suburbs: Housing Mobility and the Many Faces of Capital." *Housing Policy Debate* 9 (1): 177–221.

Brooks-Gunn, Jeanne, Greg Duncan, Pamela Klebanov, and Naomi Sealand. 1993. "Do Neighborhoods Influence Child and Adolescent Development?" *American Journal of Sociology* 99 (2): 353–95.

Browne, Irene, ed. 1999. *Latinas and African American Women at Work: Race, Gender and Economic Inequality.* New York: Russell Sage Foundation.

Bucholtz, Mary. 2002. "Youth and Cultural Practice." *Annual Review of Anthropology* 31: 525–52.

Burke, Peter J. 1989. "Gender Identity, Sex, and School Performance." *Social Psychology Quarterly* 52 (2): 159–69.

Butler, Judith. 1993. *Bodies That Matter: On the Discursive Limits of "Sex."* New York: Routledge.

Carter, Deborah, and Reginald Wilson. 1997. "Minorities in Higher Education (1996–1997 Fifteenth Annual Status Report)." American Council on Education, Washington, D.C.

Carter, Prudence. Forthcoming. "Intersecting Identities: 'Acting White,' Gender, and Academic Achievement." In *Beyond Acting White: Reassessments and New Directions in Research on Black Students and School Success,* edited by C. O'Connor and E. Horvat. New York: Rowan & Littlefield.

Catsambis, Sophia. 1994. "The Path to Math: Gender and Racial-Ethnic Differences in Mathematics Participation from Middle School to High School." *Sociology of Education* 67 (3): 199–215.

Cauce, Ana M., Yumi Hirage, Diane Graves, Nancy Gonzales, Kimberly Ryan-Finn, and Kwai Grove. 1996. "African American Mothers and Their Adolescent Daughters: Closeness, Conflict, and Control." In *Urban Girls: Resisting Stereotypes, Creating Identities,* edited by B. J. R. Leadbeater and N. Way. New York: New York University Press.

Coleman, James S. 1988. "Social Capital in the Creation of Human Capital." *American Journal of Sociology.* Suppl. no. 94: S95–S120.

Collins, Patricia Hill. 1991. *Black Feminist Thought.* New York: Routledge.

———. 2004. *Black Sexual Politics: African Americans, Gender and the New Racism.* New York: Routledge.

Collins, Randall. 1979. *The Credential Society: An Historical Sociology of Education and Stratification.* New York: Academic Press.

Collins, Sharon M. 1989. "The Marginalization of Black Executives." *Social Problems* 36 (4): 317–31.

Community College Week. 2000. "ACE Study Explodes Widespread Gender 'Crisis' in College Enrollment." December 11, 2000, vol. 13 (9):3.

Connell, Robert W. 1995. *Masculinities.* Berkeley and Los Angeles: University of California Press.

Cook, Philip J., and Jens Ludwig. 1998. "The Burden of 'Acting White': Do Black Adolescents Disparage Academic Achievement?" In *The Black-White Test Score Gap,* edited by C. Jencks and M. Phillips. Washington, D.C.: The Brookings Institution.

Cose, Ellis. 1993. *The Rage of a Privileged Class.* New York: HarperCollins.

Cose, Ellis, and Allison Samuels. 2003. "The Black Gender Gap." *Newsweek,* March 3, 2003, 46.

Crain, Robert, Joseph Darden, Angela Aidala, David Abramson, Xavier Briggs, Prudence Carter, and Joyce Moon Howard. 1997. "Yonkers Revisited: The Early Impacts of Scattered Site Public Housing on Families and Neighborhoods." Unpublished report New York, N.Y.: Ford Foundation.

Crane, Jonathan. 1991. "Effects of Neighborhoods on Dropping Out of School and Teenage Childbearing." In *The Urban Underclass,* edited by C. Jencks and P. E. Peterson. Washington, D.C.: The Brookings Institution.

Crenshaw, Kimberlé. 1992. "Whose Story Is It Anyway? Feminist and Anti-Racist Appropriations of Anita Hill." In *Race-ing Justice, En-gendering Power,* edited by T. Morrison. New York: Pantheon.

Crocker, Jennifer, and Brenda Major. 1989. "Social Stigma and Self-Esteem: The Self-Protective Properties of Stigma." *Psychological Review* 96 (4): 608.

Dance, L. Janelle. 2002. *Tough Fronts: The Impact of Street Culture on Schooling.* New York: Routledge Falmer.

Danesi, Marcel. 1994. *Cool: The Signs and Meanings of Adolescence.* Toronto: University of Toronto Press.

Darder, Antonia. 1991. *Culture and Power in the Classroom: A Critical Foundation for Bicultural Education.* New York: Bergin and Garvey.

Davis, James E. 2001. "Transgressing the Masculine: African American Boys and the Failure of Schools." In *What about the Boys? Issues of Masculinity in Schools,* edited by W. Martino and B. Meyenn. Buckingham: Open University Press.

Dawson, Michael. 2001. *Black Visions: The Roots of Contemporary African-American Political Ideologies.* Chicago: University of Chicago Press.

de Beauvoir, Simone. 1989. *The Second Sex.* New York: Vintage.

DeLeón, Brunilda. 1996. "Career Development of Hispanic Adolescent Girls." *Urban Girls: Resisting Stereotypes, Creating Identities,* edited by B. J. R. Leadbeater and N. Way. New York: New York University Press.

Delpit, Lisa. 1995. *Other People's Children: Cultural Conflict in the Classroom.* New York: New Press: Distributed by Norton.

———. 1997. "The Silenced Dialogue: Power and Pedagogy in Educating Other People's Children." In *Education: Culture, Economy and Society,* edited by A. H. Halsey, H. Lauder, P. Brown and A. S. Wells. New York: Oxford University Press.

Deway, John. 1966. (1944). *Democracy and Education: An Introduction to the Philosophy of Education.* New York: Free Press.

Deyhle, Donna. 1995. "Navajo Youth and Anglo Racism: Cultural Integrity and Resistance." *Harvard Educational Review* 65 (3): 403–44.

DiMaggio, Paul. 1982. "Cultural Capital and School Success: The Impact of Status Culture Participation on the Grades of U.S. High School Students." *American Sociological Review* 47 (April): 180–201.

DiMaggio, Paul, and John Mohr. 1985. "Cultural Capital, Educational Attainment, and Marital Selection." *American Journal of Sociology* 90 (6): 1231–61.

DiMaggio, Paul, and Francie Ostrower. 1980. "Participation in the Arts by Black and White Americans." *Social Forces* 68 (3): 753–78.

Doane, Ashley, 1999. "Dominant Group Ethnic Identity in the United States: The Role of 'Hidden' Ethnicity in Intergroup Relations." In *Rethinking the Color Line: Readings in Race and Ethnicity,* edited by C. A. Gallagher, 6th ed. Mountain View, Ca.: Mayfield Publishing Company.

Du Bois, W. E. B. 1961. *The Souls of Black Folk: Essays and Sketches.* Greenwich, Conn.: Fawcett Publications.

Duncan, Greg J., and Jeanne Brooks-Gunn, eds. 1997. *Consequences of Growing Up Poor.* New York: Russell Sage Foundation.

Duranti, Alessandro. 1992. "Language and Bodies in Social Space: Samoan Ceremonial Greetings." *American Anthropologist* 94 (3): 657–91.

Dyson, Michael E. 2001. *Holler If You Hear Me: Searching for Tupac Shakur.* New York: Basic Civitas Books.

———. 1993. *Reflecting Black: African American Cultural Criticism.* Minneapolis: University of Minnesota Press.

Epstein, Debbie, V. Hey, and J. Maw, eds. 1998. *Failing Boys: Issues in Gender and Achievement.* Buckingham: Open University Press.

Erikson, Bonnie H. 1996. "Culture, Class and Connections." *American Journal of Sociology* 102 (1):217–51.

Espiritu, Yen. 1992. *Asian American Panethnicity: Bridging Institutions and Identities.* Philadelphia: Temple University Press.

Farkas, George, Robert P. Grobe, Daniel Sheehan, and Yuan Shuan. 1990. "Cultural Resources and School Success: Gender, Ethnicity, and Poverty Groups Within An Urban School District." *American Sociological Review* 55 (1): 127–42.

Feagin, Joe. 1991. "The Continuing Significance of Race." *American Sociological Review* 56: (1) 101–16.

Feagin, Joe R., and Melvin P. Sikes. 1994. *Living with Racism: The Black Middle Class Experience.* Boston: Beacon Press.

Fenstermaker, Sarah, and Candace West., eds. 2002. *Doing Gender, Doing Difference: Inequality, Power, and Institutional Change.* New York: Routledge.

Ferguson, Ann Arnett. 2000. *Bad Boys: Public Schools in the Making of Black Masculinity.* Ann Arbor: University of Michigan Press.

Ferguson, Ron. 2001. "Test-Score Trends along Racial Lines 1971 to 1996: Popular Culture and Community Academic Standards." In *America Becoming: Racial Trends and Their Consequences,* edited by N. Smelser, W. J. Wilson and F. Mitchell. Washington, D.C.: National Academy Press.

————. 1998. "Teachers' Perceptions and Expectations and the Black-White Test Score Gap." *The Black-White Test Score Gap,* edited by C. Jencks and M. Phillips. Washington, D.C.: The Brookings Institution.

Fernández Kelly, M. Patricia. 1995. "Social and Cultural Capital in the Urban Ghetto: Implications for the Economic Sociology of Immigration." In *The Economic Sociology of Immigration: Essays on Networks, Ethnicity and Entrepreneurship,* edited by A. Portes. New York: Russell Sage Foundation.

Fine, Michelle. 1991. *Framing Dropouts: Notes on the Politics of an Urban Public High School.* Albany: State University of New York Press.

Fischer, Claude. 1977. *Networks Places: Social Relations in the Urban Setting.* New York: Free Press.

Flores-González, Nilda. 2002. *School Kids/Street Kids: Identity Development in Latino Students.* New York: Teachers College Press.

Fordham, Signithia. 1988. "Racelessness as a Factor in Black Students' School Success: Pragmatic Strategy or Pyrrhic Victory?" *Harvard Educational Review* 58 (1): 54–84.

————. 1993. "Those Loud Black Girls: (Black) Women, Silence, and Gender Passing in the Academy." *Anthropology and Education Quarterly* 24 (1): 3–32.

————. 1996. *Blacked Out: Dilemmas of Race, Identity, and Success at Capital High.* Chicago: University of Chicago Press.

Fordham, Signithia, and John Ogbu. 1986. "Black Students' School Success: Coping with the 'Burden of Acting White.'" *Urban Review* 18:176–206.

Frankenberg, Ruth. 1993. *White Women, Race Matters: The Social Construction of Whiteness.* Minneapolis: University of Minnesota Press.

Frazier, E. Franklin. 1957. *The Black Bourgeoisie: The Rise of a New Middle Class in the United States.* Glencoe, Ill.: Free Press.

Freeman, Donald J., Susan M. Brookhart, and William E. Loadman. 1999. "Realities of Teaching in Racially/Ethnically Diverse Schools: Feedback from Entry-Level Teachers." *Urban Education* 34 (1): 89–114.

Frey, James, and Andrea Fontana. 1991. "The Group Interview in Social Science Research." *Social Science Journal* 28 (2): 175–87.

Fuller, Mary. 1980. "Black Girls in a London Comprehensive School." In *Schooling for Women's Work,* edited by R. Deem. London: Routledge and Kegan Paul.

Furstenburg, Frank, Theodore Herschberg, and John Modell. 1975. "The Origins of the Black Female-Headed Family: The Impact of Urban Experience." *Journal of Interdisciplinary History* 7 (2): 211–33.

Gallas, Karen. 1998. *Sometimes I Can Be Anything: Power, Gender, and Identity in a Primary Classroom.* New York: Teachers College Press.

Gamoran, Adam. 1987. "The Stratification of High School Learning Opportunities." *Sociology of Education* 60 (3): 135–55.

Gans, Herbert J. 1999. "The Possibility of a New Racial Hierarchy in the Twenty-First Century United States." In *The Cultural Territories of Race: Black and White Boundaries,* edited by M. Lamont. Chicago: University of Chicago Press.

———. 1992. "Second Generation Decline: Scenarios for the Economic and Ethnic Futures of the Post–1965 American Immigrants." *Ethnic and Racial Studies* 15: 173–92.

———. 1967. "The Negro Family: Reflections on the Moynihan Report." In *The Moynihan Report and the Politics of Controversy,* edited by L. Rainwater and W. L. Yancey. Cambridge, Mass.: MIT Press.

Gates, Henry L. 2004. "Breaking the Silence." *The New York Times.* August 1, 2004, p. 11, section 4.

———. 1988. *The Signifying Monkey.* New York: Oxford University Press.

Genovese, Eugene. 1974. *Roll, Jordan, Roll: The World the Slaves Made.* New York: Pantheon.

George, Nelson. 1998. *Hip Hop America.* New York: Viking.

Gibson, Margaret. 1988. *Accommodation without Assimilation: Sikh Immigrants in an American High School.* Ithaca, N.Y.: Cornell University Press.

———. 1991. "Ethnicity, Gender and Social Class: The School Adaptation Patterns of West Indian Youths." In *Minority Status and Schooling: A Comparative Study of Immigrant and Involuntary Minorities,* edited by M. A. Gibson and J. U. Ogbu. New York: Garland.

Gilligan, Carol. 1982. *In a Different Voice: Psychological Theory and Women's Development.* Cambridge, Mass.: Harvard University Press.

Glazer, Nathan. 1993. "Is Assimilation Dead?" *The Annals of the American Academy of Social and Political Sciences.* 530 (November): 122–36.

Goodwin, Marjorie. 1991. *He-Said-She-Said: Talk as Social Organization among Black Children.* Bloomington: Indiana University Press.

Gorard, Stephen, Gareth Rees, and Jane Salisbury. 1999. "Reappraising the Apparent Underachievement of Boys at School." *Gender and Education* 11 (4): 441–54.

Gordon, Milton Myron. 1964. *Assimilation in American Life: The Role of Race, Religion, and National Origins.* New York: Oxford University Press.

Gould, Mark. 1999. "Race and Theory: Culture, Poverty and Adaptation to Discrimination in Wilson and Ogbu." *Sociological Theory* 17 (2): 171–200.

Gramsci, Antonio. 1994. *Letters from Prison.* Edited by F. Rosengarten. New York: Columbia University Press.

Granovetter, Mark. 1973. "The Strength of Weak Ties." *American Journal of Sociology* 78 (6): 1360–80.

Gurin, Patricia, and Edgar Epps. 1975. *Black Consciouness, Identity, and Achievement.* New York: John Wiley and Sons.

Guy-Sheftall, Beverly, ed. 1996. *Words of Fire: An Anthology of African-American Feminist Thought.* New York: New Press.

Hale, Janice. 1991. "The Transmission of Cultural Values to Young African American Children." *Young Children* 46: 7–14.

Hall, John R. 1992. "The Capital(s) of Culture: A Nonholistic Approach to Status Situations, Class, Gender, and Ethnicity." In *Cultivating Differences: Symbolic Boundaries and the Making of Inequality*, edited by M. Lamont and M. Fournier. Chicago: University of Chicago Press.

Hall, Stuart, and Tony Jefferson, eds. 1993. *Resistance through Rituals: Youth Subcultures in Post-war Britain.* London: HarperCollins Academic Press.

Hallinan, Maureen T. 1988. "Equality of Educational Opportunity." *Annual Review of Sociology* 14: 249–68.

Hallinan, Maureen T., and Aage B. Sorensen. 1983. "The Formation and Stability of Instructional Groups." *American Sociological Review* 48 (6): 838–51.

Hannerz, Ulf. 1969. *Soulside: Inquiries into Ghetto Culture and Community.* New York: Columbia University Press.

Harrington, Richard. 1996. "Guilty: Free Speech In the First Degree; Bennett's Targets Can Be as Nasty as They Wanna Be." *The Washington Post,* Sunday Arts, pg. G04.

Hays, Sharon. 1994. "Structure and Agency and the Sticky Problem of Culture." *Sociological Theory* 12 (1): 57–71.

Hemmings, Annette. 1996. "Conflicting Images? Being Black and a Model High School Student." *Anthropology and Education Quarterly* 27: 20–50.

Henry, Tamara. 2000. "Closure Sought for Hispanic Education Gap." *USA Today*. September 26, 2000.

Hilliard, Asa. 1978. "Equal Educational Opportunity and Quality Education." *Anthropology and Education Quarterly* 9: 110–26.

Hirsch, Eric Donald. 1996. *The Schools We Need, and Why We Don't Have Them*. New York: Doubleday.

Hoberman, John. 1997. *Darwin's Athletes: How Sports Has Damaged Black America and Preserved the Myth of Race*. New York: Houghton Mifflin.

Hochschild, Arlie Russell. 1973. "A Review of Sex Role Research." *The American Journal of Sociology* 78 (4): 1011–29.

Hochschild, Jennifer L. 1984. *The New American Dilemma: Liberal Democracy and School Desegregation*. New Haven, Conn.: Yale University Press.

———. 1995. *Facing Up to the American Dream: Race, Class, and the Soul of the Nation*. Princeton, N.J.: Princeton University Press.

Holland, Dorothy C., and Margaret A. Eisenhart. 1990. *Educated in Romance: Women, Achievement and College Culture*. Chicago: University of Chicago Press.

Hollinger, David A. 1995. *Postethnic America: Beyond Multiculturalism*. New York: Basic.

Holzer, Harry J. 1998. "Customer Discrimination and Employment Outcomes for Minority Workers." *Quarterly Journal of Economics* 113: 835–67.

———. 1996. "Employer Skill Needs and Labor Market Outcomes by Race and Gender Institute for Research on Poverty." Discussion Paper # 1087–96. Institute for Research on Poverty: University of Wisconsin-Madison.

hooks, bell. 1984. *From Margin to Center*. Boston: South End Press.

Hunt, Matthew. 1996. "The Individual, Society, or Both? A Comparison of Black, Latino, and White Beliefs about the Causes of Poverty." *Social Forces* 75 (1): 293–322.

Jackson, John. 1999. "Doing Harlem: Practicing Race and Class in Post–Civil Rights America." Ph. D. diss., Columbia University.

———. 2001. *Harlemworld: Doing Race and Class in Contemporary Black America*. Chicago: University of Chicago Press.

Jacobs, Jerry A. 1996. "Gender Inequality and Higher Education." *Annual Review of Sociology* 22: 153–85.

Jaynes, Gerald, and R. M. Williams. 1989. *A Common Destiny: Blacks and American Society*. Washington, D.C.: National Academy Press.

Jencks, Christopher. 1992. *Rethinking Social Policy: Race, Poverty, and the Underclass*. Cambridge, Mass.: Harvard University Press.

Jencks, Christopher, and Meredith Phillips, eds. 1998. *The Black-White Test Score Gap*. Washington, D.C.: Brookings Institution.

Johnson, Monica K., Robert Crosnoe, and Glen H. Elder Jr. 2001. "Students' Attachment and Academic Engagement: The Role of Race and Ethnicity." *Sociology of Education* 74(4): 318–34.

Jones, Jacqueline. 1985. *Labor of Love, Labor of Sorrow: Black Women, Work and the Family from Slavery to Present.* New York: Basic.

Journal of Blacks in Higher Education. 1999. "Special Report: College Degree Awards: The Ominous Gender Gap in African American Higher Education." 23 (Spring): 6–9.

Kallen, Horace M. 1924. *Culture and Democracy in the United States.* New York: Boni Liveright.

Kao, Grace, and Jennifer S. Thompson. 2003. "Racial and Ethnic Stratification in Educational Achievement and Attainment." *Annual Review of Sociology* 29: 417–42.

Katz, Michael. 1990. *The Undeserving Poor: From the War on Poverty to the War on Welfare.* New York: Pantheon.

Kelley, Robin. 1994. *Race Rebels: Culture, Politics and the Black Working Class.* New York: Free Press.

King, Deborah K. 1996. "Multiple Jeopardy, Multiple Consciousness: The Context of Black Feminist Ideology." In *Words of Fire: An Anthology of African-American Feminist Thought,* edited by B. Guy-Sheftall. New York: New Press.

King, Mary C. 1993. "Black Women's Breakthrough into Clerical Work: An Occupational Tipping Model." *Journal of Economic Issues* 27 (4): 1097–1126.

Kingston, Paul W. 2001. "The Unfulfilled Promise of Cultural Capital Theory." *Sociology of Education* 74 (Extra Issue): 88–99.

Kirschenman, Joleen, and Kathryn M. Neckerman. 1991. " 'We'd Love to Hire Them But': The Meaning of Race for Employers." In *The Urban Underclass,* edited by C. Jencks and P. E. Peterson. Washington, D.C.: The Brookings Institution.

Kitwana, Bakari. 2002. *The Hip Hop Generation: Young Blacks and the Crisis in African American Culture.* New York: Basic Civitas.

Kleinfield, N. R. 2000. "Guarding the Borders of the Hip-Hop Nation." *The New York Times,* July 6, 2000.

Kochman, Thomas. 1981. *Black and White Styles in Conflict.* Chicago: University of Chicago Press.

Kozol, Jonathan. 1991. *Savage Inequalities: Children in America's Schools.* New York: Crown.

Ladsen-Billings, Gloria. 1994. *The Dreamkeepers: Successful Teachers of African-American Children.* San Francisco: Jossey-Bass.

LaFrombiose, Teresa L., Hardin L. K., and Jennifer Gerton. 1993. "Psychological

Impact of Biculturalism Evidence and Theory." *Psychological Bulletin* 114 (3): 395–412.

Lamont, Michèle. 1992. *Money, Morals and Manners: The Culture of the French and the American Upper-Middle Class.* Chicago: University of Chicago Press.

———. 2000. *The Dignity of Working Men: Morality and the Boundaries of Race, Class and Immigration.* Cambridge, Mass. and New York: Harvard University Press and the Russell Sage Foundation.

Lamont, Michèle, and Annette Lareau. 1988. "Cultural Capital: Allusions, Gaps and Glissandos in Recent Theoretical Developments." *Sociological Theory* 6: 153–68.

Lamont, Michèle, and Virág Molnár. 2002. "The Study of Boundaries in the Social Sciences." *Annual Review of Sociology* 28: 167–95.

Landry, Bart. 1987. *The New Black Middle Class.* Berkeley and Los Angeles: University of California Press.

Lareau, Annette and Erin McNarara Horvat. 1999. "Moments of Social Inclusion and Exclusion: Race, Class and Cultural Capital in Family-School Relationships." *Sociology of Education* 72 (1): 37–53.

LeDuff, Charles. 2000. "At a Slaughterhouse, Some Things Never Die: Who Kills, Who Cuts, Who Bosses Can Depend on Race." *The New York Times,* June 16, 2000, 1.

Lee, Chungmei. 2004. *Is Resegregation Real?* Cambridge, Mass.: Harvard University Civil Rights Project.

Lee, Jennifer. 2002. *Cities of Civility.* Cambridge, Mass.: Harvard University Press.

Lee, Jennifer, Prudence Carter, and Kathryn Neckerman. 1999. "Pan-Minority Identity: A Theoretical Framework." Paper presented at the annual meeting of the American Sociological Association, Chicago.

Lee, Stacey J. 1996. *Unraveling the "Model Minority" Stereotype: Listening to Asian American Youth.* New York: Teachers College Press.

Lewin, Tamar. 2000. "Growing Up, Growing Apart." *The New York Times,* June 25, section 1, p.1.

———. 2000. "How Boys Lost to Girl Power." *The New York Times,* December 13, WK 3.

Lewis, Amanda E. 2003. *Race in the Schoolyard: Reproducing the Color Line in School.* New Brunswick, N.J.: Rutgers University Press.

Liebow, Elliot. 1967. *Tally's Corner: A Study of Negro Streetcorner Men.* Boston: Little Brown.

Lofland, John, and Lyn H. Lofland. 1984. *Analyzing Social Settings.* 2nd ed. Belmont, Calif.: Wadsworth.

Lopez, David, and Yen Espiritu. 1990. "Panethnicity in the United States: A Theoretical Framework." *Ethnic and Racial Studies* 13 (2): 198–224.

Lopez, Nancy. 2003. *Hopeful Girls, Troubled Boys.* New York: Routledge.

Louie, Vivian. 2001. "Parents' Aspirations and Investment: The Role of Social
Class in the Educational Experiences of 1.5- and Second-Generation Chinese Americans." *Harvard Educational Review* 71 (3): 438–74.

Loury, Glenn. 1976. "Essays in the Theory of the Distribution of Income." Ph. D.
diss., Economics, Massachusetts Institute of Technology, Cambridge, Mass.

Lucas, Samuel. 1999. *Tracking Inequality: Stratification and Mobility in American
High Schools.* New York: Teachers College Press.

Mac An Ghaill, M. 1994. *The Making of Men: Masculinities, Sexualities and
Schooling.* Buckingham: Open University Press.

Maccoby, Eleanor E., and Carol N. Jacklin. 1974. *Psychology of Sex Differences.*
Stanford, Calif.: Stanford University Press.

MacLeod, Jay. 1995. *Ain't No Makin' It: Aspirations and Attainment in a Low-
income Neighborhood.* Boulder, Colo.: Westview.

Major, Clarence, ed. 1994. *Juba to Jive: A Dictionary of African-American Slang.*
New York: Penguin.

Marx, Karl. 1978. "Manifesto of the Communist Party." In *The Marx-Engels
Reader,* edited by Robert C. Tucker. New York: W. W. Norton and Company.

Massey, Douglas. 1993. "Latinos, Poverty, and the Underclass: A New Agenda for
Research." *Hispanic Journal of Behavioral Sciences* 15 (4): 449–75.

Massey, Douglas, Camille Charles, Garvey F. Lundy, and Mary Fischer. 2003. *The
Source of the River: The Social Origins of Freshmen at America's Selective
Colleges and Universities.* Princeton, N.J.: Princeton University Press.

Massey, Douglas, and Nancy Denton. 1993. *American Apartheid.* Cambridge,
Mass.: Harvard University Press.

McCracken, Grant. 1988. *The Long Interview.* Newbury Park, Calif.: Sage
Publications.

McLaren, Peter. 1988. *Life in Schools: An Introduction to Critical Pedagogy in the
Foundations of Education.* 3rd ed. New York: Longman.

McWhorter, John. 2001. *Losing the Race: Self-Sabotage in Black America.* New
York: Perennial.

Mehan, Hugh, Lea Hubbard, and Irene Villanueva. 1994. "Forming Academic
Identities: Accommodation without Assimilation among Involuntary
Minorities." *Anthropology and Education Quarterly* 25 (2): 91–117.

Merton, Robert. 1968. *Social Theory and Structure.* New York: Free Press.

Mickelson, Roslyn Arlin. 2001. "Subverting Swann: First and Second-generation
Segregation in Charlotte-Micklenberg Schools." *American Educational Research Journal* 38: 215–252.

————. 1990. "The Attitude-Achievement Paradox among Black Adolescents." *Sociology of Education.* 63 (1): 44-61.

————. 1989. "Why Does Jane Read and Write So Well? The Anomaly of Women's Achievement." *Sociology of Education* 62 (1): 47–63.

Mirande, Alfredo. 1997. *Hombres y Machos: Masculinity and Latino Culture.* Boulder, Colo.: Westview.

Morgan, Marcyliena. 2002. *Language, Discourse and Power in African American Culture.* Cambridge, Mass.: Cambridge University Press.

Moss, Philip, and Chris Tilly. 1996" 'Soft' Skills and Race: An Investigation of Black Men's Employment Problems." *Work and Occupations* 23: 252–76.

Murray, Charles, and Richard J. Herrnstein. 1994. *The Bell Curve: Intelligence and Class Structure in American Life.* New York: Free Press.

Nagel, Joanne. 1994. "Constructing Ethnicity: Creating and Recreating Ethnic Identity and Culture." *Social Problems* 41 (1): 152–76.

National Center for Education Statistics. 2003A. "Status and Trends in the Education of Blacks" (NCES 2003–034), by Kathryn Hoffman and Charmaine Llagas. Washington, D.C.: U.S. Department of Education.

————. 2003b. "Status and Trends in the Education of Hispanics (NCES 2003–008), by Charmaine Llagas. Washington, D.C.: U.S. Department of Education.

————. 2002. *Digest of Education Statistics,* 2001 (NCES 2002–130). Washington, D.C.: U.S. Department of Education.

Neckerman, Kathryn, Prudence Carter, and Jennifer Lee. 1999. "Segmented Assimilation and Minority Cultures of Mobility." *Ethnic and Racial Studies* 22 (6): 945–65.

Noguera, Pedro A. 1996. "Responding to the Crisis Confronting California's Black Male Youth: Providing Support without Furthering Marginalization." *Journal of Negro Education* 65 (2): 219–36.

————. 2003. "The Trouble with Black Boys: The Impact of Social and Cultural Forces on the Academic Achievement of African American Males." *Urban Education* 38 (4): 431–50.

Nowell, Amy, and Larry V. Hedges. 1998. "Trends in Gender Differences in Academic Achievement from 1960 to 1994: An Analysis of Differences in Mean Variance, and Extreme Scores." *Sex Roles* 39 (1/2): 21–43.

Oakes, Jeannie. 1985. *Keeping Track: How Schools Structure Inequality.* New Haven, Conn.: Yale University Press.

Oboler, Suzanne. 1995. *Ethnic Labels, Latino Lives: Identity and the Politics of (Re)Presentation in the United States.* Minneapolis: University of Minnesota Press.

Ogbu, John. 1974. *The Next Generation: An Ethnography of Education in an Urban Neighborhood.* New York: Academic Press.

———. 1978. *Minority Education and Caste.* New York: Academic Press.

———. 1987. "Variability in Minority School Performance: A Problem in Search of an Explanation." *Anthropology and Education Quarterly* 18 (4): 312–34.

———. 2003. *Black Male Students in a Affluent Suburb: A Study of Academic Disengagement.* Mahwah, N.J.: Erlbaum Associates.

Ogbu, John, and M. E. Matute-Bianchi. 1986. "Understanding Sociocultural Factors: Knowledge, Identity, and Adjustment in Schooling." *Beyond Language: Social and Cultural Factors in Schooling Language Minorities.* Sacrament, Calif.: California State Department of Education, Bilingual Education Office.

Ogbu, John U., and Herbert D. Simons. 1998. "Voluntary and Involuntary Minorities: A Cultural-Ecological Theory of School Performance with Some Implications for Education." *Anthropology and Education Quarterly* 29 (2): 155–88.

Olsen, Laurie. 1997. *Made in America: Immigrant Students in Our Public Schools.* New York: New Press.

Omi, Michael, and Howard Winant. 1994. *Racial Formations in the United States.* New York: Routledge.

Orfield, Gary. 2001. "Schools More Separate: Consequences of a Decade of Resegregation." Report published by The Harvard Civil Rights Project, Cambridge, Mass.

Oyserman, Daphna, Markus Kemmelmeir, Stephanie Frybero, Hezi Brosh, and Tamera Hart-Johnson. 2003. "Racial-Ethnic Self Schemas." *Social Psychology Quarterly* 66 (4): 333–48.

Park, Robert E. 1950. *Race and Culture.* Glencoe, Ill.: Free Press.

Parker, Sheila, Mimi Nichter, Mark Nichter, Nancy Vuckovic, Colette Sims, and Cheryl Ritenbaugh. 1995. "Body Image and Weight Concerns among African American and White Adolescent Females: Differences That Make a Difference." *Human Organization* 54 (2): 103–14.

Patterson, Orlando. 1998. *The Ordeal of Integration.* City: New York: Basic Civitas.

Pattillo-McCoy, Mary. 1999. *Black Picket Fences.* Chicago: University of Chicago Press.

Patton, Michael Q. 1990. *Qualitative Evaluation and Research Methods.* Newbury Park, Calif.: Sage Publications.

Perry, Pamela. 2002. *Shades of White: White Kids and Racial Identities in High Schools.* Durham, N.C.: Duke University Press.

Perry, Theresa. 2003. "Up from the Parched Earth: Toward a Theory of African-American Achievement." In *Young, Gifted and Black: Promoting High Achieve-*

ment among African American Students, edited by T. Perry, C. Steele, and A. G. Hilliard III. Boston: Beacon.

Perry, Theresa, and Lisa Delpit, eds. 1998. *The Real Ebonics Debate: Power, Language, and the Education of African-American Children*. Boston: Beacon.

Peterson, Richard A. 1997. *Creating Country Music: Fabricating Authenticity*. Chicago: University of Chicago Press.

Piven, Frances F. and Richard Cloward. 1979. *Poor People's Movement*. New York: Vintage Books.

Pollock, Mica. 2004. *Colormute: Race Talk Dilemmas in an American School*. Princeton, N.J.: Princeton University Press.

Portes, Alejandro, ed. 1995. *The Economic Sociology of Immigration: Essays on Networks, Ethnicity, and Entrepreneurship*. New York: Russell Sage Foundation.

———. 1998. "Social Capital: Its Origins and Applications in Modern Sociology." *Annual Review of Sociology* 24: 1–24.

Portes, Alejandro, and Ruben Rumbaut. 2001. *Legacies: The Story of the Immigrant Second Generation*. Berkeley and Los Angeles: University of California Press.

Portes, Alejandro, and Alex Stepick. 1993. *City on the Edge: The Transformation of Miami*. Berkeley: University of California Press.

Portes, Alejandro, and Min Zhou. 1992. "Gaining the Upper Hand: Economic Mobility among Immigrant and Domestic Minorities." *Ethnic and Racial Studies* 15 (4): 491–522.

———. 1993. "The New Second Generation: Segmented Assimilation and Its Variants." *Annals of the American Political and Social Sciences* 530 (November): 74–96.

Richey, Amanda, and Dante Petretti. 2002. "What Can I Do about Teacher Apathy?" *English Journal* 92 (2): 20–23.

Rollins, Judith. 1985. *Between Women: Domestics and Their Employers*. Philadelphia: Temple University Press.

Rose, Tricia. 1994. *Black Noise: Rap Music and Black Culture in Contemporary America*. Hanover, N.H.: Wesleyan University Press.

Rumbaut, Rubén. 1995. "The Crucible Within: Ethnic Identity, Self-Esteem, and Segmented Assimilation among Children of Immigrants." *International Migration Review* 28 (4): 748–94.

Schlesinger, Arthur Meier. 1998. *The Disuniting of America: Reflections on a Multicultural Society*. New York: Norton.

Schuman, Howard, Charlotte Steeh, Lawrence Bobo, and Maria Krysan. 1998. *Racial Attitudes in America: Trends and Interpretations*. Cambridge, Mass., Harvard University Press.

Scott, James. 1985. *Weapons of the Weak: Everyday Forms of Peasant Resistance.* New Haven, Conn.: Yale University Press.

Sellers, Robert M., Stephanie A. J. Rowley, Tabbye M. Chavous, and J. Nicole Shelton. 1997. "Multidimensional Inventory of Black Identity: A Preliminary Investigation of Reliability and Construct Validity." *Journal of Personality and Social Psychology* 73 (4): 805–15.

Sellers, Robert M., Mia A. Smith, J. Nicole Shelton, Stephanie A. J. Rowley, and Tabbye M. Chavous. 1998. "Multidimensional Model of Racial Identity: A Reconceptualization of African American Racial Identity." *Personality and Social Psychology Review* 2 (1): 18–39.

Sennett, Richard, and Jonathan Cobb. 1993. *The Hidden Injuries of Class.* New York: Norton.

Slavin, Robert E. 1979. "Integrating the Desegregated Classroom: Actions Speak Louder than Words." *Educational Leadership* 36 (5): 322–25.

Smith, Robert. 1997. "Racial and Ethnic Hierarchies and the Incorporation of Mexicans in New York City: Transnational Communities and Labor Market Niches." Paper presented at the annual meeting of the Eastern Sociological Society, Baltimore.

Solomon, R. Patrick. 1991. *Black Resistance in High School, Frontiers in Education Series.* Albany: State University of New York Press.

Solorzano, Daniel G. 1992. "An Exploratory Analysis of the Effects of Race, Class, and Gender on Student and Parent Mobility Aspirations." *The Journal of Negro Education* 61 (1): 30–44.

Spencer, Margaret Beale, Dena Phillips Swanson, and Michael Cunningham. 1991. "Ethnicity, Ethnic Identity, and Competence Formation: Adolescent Transition and Cultural Transformation." *Journal of Negro Education* 60 (3): 366–87.

Stanton-Salazar, Ricardo D. 2001. *Manufacturing Hope and Despair: The School and Kin Support Networks of U.S.-Mexican Youth.* New York: Teachers College Press.

Staples, Brent. 2002. "Yonkers Shows How Not to Desegregate a School District." *The New York Times*, January 18, 2002.

Staples, Robert. 1982. *Black Masculinity: The Black Male's Role in American Society.* San Francisco, Calif.: Black Scholar Press.

Steinberg, Stephen. 1989. *Ethnic Myth: Race, Ethnicity and Class in America.* 3rd ed. Boston: Beacon.

Stevens, Joyce W. 1997. "African American Female Adolescent Identity Development: A Three-Dimensional Perspective." *Child Welfare* 76 (1): 145–72.

Stevenson, Harold W., and Richard S. Newman. 1986. "Long-Term Prediction of Achievement and Attitudes in Mathematics and Reading." *Child Development* 57:646–59.

Streitmatter, Janice. 1993. "Gender Differences in Identity Development: An Examination of Longitudinal Data." *Adolescence* 28 (109): 55–66.

Strober, Myra H., and Audri Gordon Lanford. 1986. "The Feminization of Public School Teaching: Cross-Sectional Analysis, 1850–1880." *Signs* 11 (2): 212–35.

Sullivan, Mercer. 1989. *Getting Paid: Youth Crime and Work in the Inner City*. Ithaca, N.Y.: Cornell University Press.

Swartz, David. 1997. *Culture and Power: The Sociology of Pierre Bourdieu*. Chicago: University of Chicago Press.

Swidler, Ann. 1986. "Culture in Action: Symbols and Strategies." *American Sociological Review* 51 (2): 273–86.

Tajfel, Henri. 1974. "Social Identity and Intergroup Behaviour." *Social Science Information* 13 (2): 65–93.

———. 1982. *Social Identity and Intergroup Relations*. Cambridge, Mass.: Cambridge University Press.

Taylor, Jill McLean, Carol Gilligan, and Amy M. Sullivan, eds. 1995. *Between Voices and Silence: Women and Girls, Race and Relationship*. Cambridge, Mass.: Harvard University Press.

Tuan, Mia. 1999. "Neither Real Americans nor Real Asians? Multigeneration Asian Ethnics Navigating the Terrain of Authenticity." *Qualitative Sociology* 22 (2): 105–25.

Tyson, Karolyn. 1998. "Debunking a Persistent Myth: Academic Achievement and the 'Burden of Acting White' among Black Students." Paper presented at the annual meeting of the American Sociological Association, San Francisco.

Tyson, Karolyn, William Darity, and Domini Castellino. Forthcoming. "Breeding Animosity: The Significance of School Placement Patterns in the Development of a 'Burden of Acting White.'" *American Sociological Review*.

U.S. Census Bureau. 1991. "1990 Census of the Population, School Enrollment-Social and Economic Characteristics of Student." U.S. Department of Commerce, Economics, and Statistics Administration.

———. 1999. December 1999 Current Population Survey Data. Washington, D.C., Bureau of the Census.

Valenzuela, Angela. 1999. *Subtractive Schooling: Issues of Caring in Education of U.S.-Mexican Youth*. Albany: State University of New York Press.

Wacquant, Loic, and William Julius Wilson. 1993. "The Cost of Racial and Class Exclusion in the Inner City." In *The Ghetto Underclass: Social Science Perspectives*, edited by W. J. Wilson. Newbury Park, Calif.: Sage.

Waldinger, Roger. 1996. *Still the Promised City: African Americans and New Immigrants in Postindustrial New York*. Cambridge, Mass.: Harvard University Press.

Waters, Mary. 1990. *Ethnic Options: Choosing Identities in America.* Berkeley and Los Angeles: University of California Press.

———. 1996. "The Intersection of Gender, Race, and Ethnicity in Identity Development of Caribbean American Teens." *Urban Girls: Resisting Stereotypes, Creating Identities,* edited by B. J. R. Leadbeater and N. Way. New York: New York University Press.

Waters, Mary C. 1999. *Black Identities: West Indian Immigrant Dreams and American Realities.* New York: Russell Sage Foundation; Cambridge, Mass.: Harvard University Press.

Way, Niobe. 1996. "Between Experiences of Betrayal and Desire: Close Friendships among Urban Adolescents." In *Urban Girls: Resisting Stereotypes,* edited by B. J. Leadbeater and N. Way. New York: NYU Press.

Wells, Amy Stuart, and Irene Serna. 1996. "The Politics of Culture: Understanding Local Political Resistance to Detracking in Racially Mixed Schools." *Harvard Educational Review* 66 (1): 93–118.

White, Shane. 1989. "A Question of Style: Blacks in and around New York City in the Late Eighteenth Century." *The Journal of American Folklore* 102 (403): 23–44.

Willis, Paul. 1977. *Learning to Labor: How Working Class Kids Get Working Class Jobs.* New York: Columbia University Press.

Wilson, William J. 1987. *The Truly Disadvantaged: The Inner City, the Underclass, and Public Policy.* Chicago: University of Chicago Press.

———. 1996. *When Work Disappears: The World of the New Urban Poor.* New York: Knopf.

Wong, Paul, Chienping Faith Lai, and Richard Nagasawa. 1998. "Asian Americans as a Model Minority: Self-perceptions and Perceptions by Other Racial Groups." *Sociological Perspectives* 41 (1): 95–118.

Zhou, Min, and Carl L. Bankston. 1998. *Growing Up American: How Vietnamese Children Adapt to Life in the United States.* New York: Russell Sage Foundation.

Zweigenhaft, Richard L., and G. William Domhoff. 1991. *Blacks in the White Establishment? A Study of Race and Class in America.* New Haven, Conn.: Yale University Press.

———. 1998. *Diversity in the Power Elite: Have Women and Minorities Reached the Top?* New Haven, Conn.: Yale University Press.

INDEX

A student discussed in the text is indexed under her/his first name. Page numbers in italics refer to tables or figures in the text.

advanced placement classes, 50, 53, 69, 73, 160
affirmative action programs, 33–34
Aid to Families with Dependent Children (AFDC), ix, 183
Ainsworth-Darnell, James, 25, 188
Akom, A. A., 30–31
Alberto (student), 74, 92, 125–26
Alexander, Karl, 70
Alex (student), 121
Alma (student), 74, 92, 108, 114, 125–26
"American" identity, 126, 165
Anderson, Elijah, 36–37, 66, 91, 94, 139–40
Asian students, 25, 73, 166
aspirations: educational, 41, 43
  career, 23, 133–134
  gender and, 87–88, 133–135
assimilation, 15, 28–31, 63, 85, 110, 116–17, 187
  segmented, 17, 111, 117, 119, 191
  at-risk youth, 19–20, 112, 135
attachment. *See* engagement with school
attitude-achievement paradox, 11–12, 39–46
authenticity, 6, 50, 54–59, 61, 128

Bailey, Benjamin, 128
Banks, James, 165
Beale, Frances, 90
Bennett, William, 165
Bettina (student), 61–62
"black" cultural capital, 47–76, 161
  authenticity and, 50, 54–59, 61
  contexts and, 51, 60–64
  description of, 51–53
  dominant capital theory and, 47–51
  functions of, 54–60
  hierarchy of cultural meanings and, 64–72, 155
  positive self-image and, 57–58
  tracking and, 53, 69, 72–76
Black power movement, 91
Blige, Mary J., 138
Bourdieu, Pierre, 7, 10, 15, 49, 51
Bourgois, Philippe, 119

Bowles, Samuel, 68
Brown v. Board of Education, vi

Carlos (student), 131
Castañeda v. Pickard, vi
Castellino, Domini, 74
codeswitching, 150, 152, 179
Coleman, James, 148
college preparatory classes, 25, 53, 73–74, 160
colorism, 108
communal obligations, 138, 141
communicative styles: speech codes, 10, 50, 58–62, 83, 92, 128
  verbal play, 68, 96–97
Connell, R. W., 90
contexts, 51, 60–64
Crosnoe, Robert, 10, 184
Cubans, 108, 114, 191
cultural appropriators, 63
cultural capital, vi–vii, 5–6, 9–10, 15–16
  dominant, 10, 29, 47–51, 160–61
  multiculturalism and, 165–70
  multicultural navigators and, 149–55
  theory of, 7, 10, 15. *See also* "black" cultural capital
cultural-ecological theory, 7–8, 25–26, 111. *See also* oppositional culture theory
cultural gatekeepers, viii, 6, 46, 69, 119, 135, 152
cultural mainstreamers, 15, 19–46
  academic achievement of, 14, 33, 42
  "acting white" and, 33
  attitude-achievement paradox and, 40–43
  contexts and, 64
  description of, 12–13, 28–29, 161
  educational values of, 40
  ethnic distribution of, 112–13
  gender socialization and, 85–86
  hierarchies of cultural meanings and, 76
  profiles of, 31–34
  race relations perceptions of, 43, 152–54
  social networks of, 14, 145–46

cultural meanings, hierarchy of, vi, 6,
9, 51, 64–72, 155, 157–58, 165–70,
174
cultural nationalism, 162
cultural straddlers, 15, 19–46
academic achievement of, 14, 38, 42
"acting white" and, 30, 161
attitude-achievement paradox and,
40–43, 188
contexts and, 62–64
description of, 12–14, 30, 161–162
educational values of, 40, 159
ethnic distribution of, 113–114
gender socialization and, 85–86
hierarchies of cultural meanings and,
76
as multicultural navigators, 150
profiles of, 37–39
race relations perceptions of, 43,
152–54
social networks of, 14, 145–46
culture: 6–9
dominant vs. nondominant, 9–10,
185
"of power," 12, 47–48
curricular content, 14, 35, 165–67

Dance, J. Lori, 79
Daniel (student), 84–85
Darder, Antonia, 45
Darity, William, 74
Dawson, Michael, 162
DeAndre (student), 14–15, 34–37, 54, 92
Delpit, Lisa, 12, 47–48
desegregation. See schools, desegrega-
tion of
Dewey, John, 19
Deyhle, Donna, 45
DMX (rap star), 55, 138, 141, 155
dominant cultural capital, 10, 29, 47–51,
160–61
dominant achievement ideology, 12,
23–25, 43, 66, 113, 160
Dominicans, 108, 114
Downey, Douglas, 25, 188
downward mobility. See socioeconomic
mobility

dress styles, 35–37, 56, 65–66, 92–93, 128
Du Bois, W.E.B., 63, 188
Dyson, Michael Eric, 155

educational values, 8, 19–25, 157–60
and abstract attitudes, 39–41, 187
"acting white" and, v–vi, 5, 157–58
attitude-achievement paradox and,
11–12, 39–46
and concrete attitudes, 39–44, 187
of cultural mainstreamers, 40
of cultural straddlers, 40, 159
ethnic distribution of, 111–17
expectations and, 41, 43
hip-hop stars and, 141
of noncompliant believers, 30, 36,
159
educator attitudes, vi, viii, 9–10, 18,
46, 52, 168–69. See also teachers
Elder, Glen, 10, 184
engagement with school, viii, 6–8,
10–12, 66–68, 76, 87, 164, 166
enrollment rates, xi
Entwisle, Doris, 70
Epps, Edgar, 20, 30, 43
ethnic identity. See racial/ethnic
identity
eye contact, 48, 66

family relations, 7, 17, 97–98. See also
parents
Federico (student), 124
Felicia (student), 124
feminization of achievement. See gen-
der socialization
Ferguson, Ann, 85
Fernanda (student), 127–28
"fictive kinship," 138
Fine, Michelle, 115
Flores-González, Nilda, 139–40
Fordham, Signithia, 4–5, 84, 138

Gallas, Karen, 69
gangs. See street gangs
gender socialization, 7, 16–17, 77–105
description of, 77–85
femininity and, 94–105, 169

migration. *See* immigration.
mobility. *See* socioeconomic mobility
Moesha (student), 61–62, 67–69, 103–4,
  150
Monica (student), 115–18, 121–24
Monk, Sierre, 74
Moss, Philip, 92
multiculturalism, 165–70
multicultural navigators, viii, 17–18,
  149–55, 163, 171–74

Nagel, Joanne, 123
National Longitudinal Study of Adoles-
  cent Health (ADDHEALTH), 184
National Association for the Advanced
  of Colored People (NAACP), x
Nation of Islam students, 30–31
Native American students, 8, 29, 45, 73
Navajo students, 45
Neal (student), 118
Nelia (student), 92
"new heads," 138–41, 155
New York Times, 69, 74, 120
Ngozi (student), 20
Nina (student), 67, 69
"No Child Left Behind" policies, viii, 171
noncompliant believers, 15, 19–46
  academic achievement of, 36, 42
  attitude-achievement paradox and,
    39–43, 46
  contexts and, 64
  description of, 12, 29–30, 161–62
  educational values and, 30, 36, 159
  ethnic distribution of, 113
  gender socialization and, 16, 85–86
  hierarchies of cultural meanings and,
    65, 75–76, 155, 166
  peer relationships and, 14
  profiles of, 34–37
  race relations perceptions of, 43,
    152–54
  social networks of, 14, 145–46
nondominant cultural capital, 16, 49–52,
  152

occupational aspirations, 23, 82–83, 88–
  89, 90–94, 98–100, 132–36, 141, 169

Ogbu, John, 4–5, 7, 29, 111, 184
"old heads," 139, 155
Olsen, Laurie, 132
oppositional culture theory, vii, 4–10,
  16, 29, 111, 119
Oyserman, Daphna, 45

pan-minority identity, 107–12, 118–30
parents: cultural capital and, 50, 71–72,
  171–72
  educational levels of, 114
  gender socialization and, 16, 81–82,
    97–105, 130–32
  race relation perceptions of, 152–
    54
Park, Robert, 110
Pashan (student), 56–57
Patterson, Orlando, 63
Paul (architect), 151
Paula (teacher), 70
Perry, Theresa, 166
Personal Responsibility and Work
  Opportunity Reconciliation Act
  (PRWORA), ix
"playing the dozens," 97
Portes, Alejandro, 17, 111
power, 12, 47–48, 165
poverty and, 4, 17, 19–20, 25, 114–115,
  137–139, 142, 155
  academic achievement, 111
  assimilation, 111
  economic changes, 86–89
  study sample, ix, 176–178
  social capital, 137, 142, 144, 149–150,
    171
  urban schools, 35–36, 63, 71
  neighborhoods, 86
Puerto Ricans, 108, 114
Punjabi Indian students, 30–31

race relations, perceptions of, 43–45, 58,
  120–21, 128–29, 152–54
racial centrality, 12, 27
racial/ethnic identity, 12, 27, 43–46, 123,
  162–63
  "acting black/white/Spanish" and, vi,
    5, 9, 16, 18, 38, 54, 58, 121–23, 157–58

team sports, 88–89, 99–100, 141

Temporary Assistance for Needy Families (TANF), ix, 183

Teresa (student), 101–2, 138, 147, 166–167

test-score gaps. *See* academic achievement

Thompson, Maxine, 70

Tiara (student), 80–81

Tiffany (student), 168

Tilly, Chris, 92

Toni (student), 121–24, 131–32

tracking, 31–32, 53, 69, 72–76, 172

Tyson, Karolyn, 74

upward mobility. *See* socioeconomic mobility

Valenzuela, Angela, 119

Valerie (student), 37–39

verbal play, 68, 97

Victoria (student), 149

Vincenzia (student), 126–27

Waters, Mary, 84, 111

Way, Niobe, 96

welfare programs, 114–15. *See also* Aid to Families with Dependent Children Personal Responsibility and Work Opportunity Reconciliation Act and Temporary Assistance for Needy Families.

West Indian youth, 84

White students, xi, 10–11, 25, 73–74

Willis, Paul, 91–92

Wilson, William Julius, 149

Wilson (student), 59

Wyla (student), 21–22

Yonkers, N. Y., ix–xi, 69

Zhou, Min, 17, 111